LITES - Legal Issues in Transdisciplinary Environmental Studies

Volume 6

The 'Legal Issues in Transdisciplinary Environmental Studies' (LITES) Book Series is based on the assumption that the process of dialogue and cultural integration between law, life and earth sciences, and social and human sciences should be strengthened and updated, by relying on transdisciplinary research platforms such as agroecology, environmental studies, environmental science, and sustainability science. According to the new paradigm of social-ecological systems (SES), the concept of the environment is conceived as a complex system of relationships between ecological and social factors, including the cultural and economic ones. The primary purpose of law, in this conceptual framework, is to preside over the durability of the essential conditions for the survival of the social-ecological systems and the protection of life at all scales (of individuals, societies, ecosystems).

LITES Series aims to explore the relationships between legal and environmental sciences according to a transdisciplinary perspective. On the one hand, natural and social environmental sciences need to integrate the point of view of law: this entails to study the complexities of SES in the light of normative and institutional variables, with the lens of categories such as rights, duties, powers, responsibilities, and procedural safeguards. On the other hand, law is called upon to review its own internal geometries, confronting them with the holistic approach toward sustainability in the scientific debate. Accordingly, law should address the need of changing the approach that so far has led to both hypertrophy and disarticulation when regulating closely linked matters such as the environment, agriculture, forestry, landscape and cultural heritage, energy, and food.

LITES Series is addressed to a wide international and interdisciplinary readership, targeting academic researchers and scholars, experts and practitioner lawyers, public administrations, judges, and law-makers. Its volume editors and contributing authors have different backgrounds and come from all over the world in order to provide a forum for discussion and normative analysis about new legal frontiers of human-environment interactions across disciplinary barriers.

Felipe Jardim

Right to Food in Community Gardens

Springer

Felipe Jardim
Law (UERJ)
Friedrich-Schiller University Jena (FSU)
Jena, Germany

Sociology (FSU)
State University of Rio de Janeiro (UERJ)
Rio de Janeiro, Brazil

ISSN 2522-5049 ISSN 2522-5057 (electronic)
LITES - Legal Issues in Transdisciplinary Environmental Studies
ISBN 978-3-032-19611-8 ISBN 978-3-032-19612-5 (eBook)
https://doi.org/10.1007/978-3-032-19612-5

This Springer imprint is published by the registered company Springer Nature Switzerland AG
The registered company address is: Gewerbestrasse 11, 6330 Cham, Switzerland

Preface

From an inter-and transdisciplinary doctoral research focused on Law and Sociology, this book aims to tackle problems related to two urban resources: food and land. Firstly, regarding the violation of the human right to adequate food (food availability, accessibility, acceptability, and sustainability). Secondly, vacant land, a multifaceted problem, contributing to social-spatial segregation and socioeconomic disparities.

Given these issues, transformative actions are demanded to secure the rights of individuals and communities, reduce inequalities, and sustain life on our planet. In that sense, global studies highlight community gardens as a potential strategy for repurposing vacant land and advancing the realization of the right to food.

Nonetheless, a research gap exists regarding the relation between community gardens and urban food sharing, particularly in Berlin and Rio de Janeiro. Therefore, this empirical investigation contrasts urban food sharing practices in community gardens in these two global cities facing vacant land and right to food problems.

The central inquiry guiding this investigation is: How do the principles of the right to food relate to food sharing practices within community gardens in Berlin and Rio de Janeiro, and what factors explain the similarities and differences in these connections within and between these cities?

The hypothesis suggests that urban food sharing within community gardens can be linked to right to food. These connections may vary based on unique socioeconomic contexts and urban challenges in each city.

To empirically assess this hypothesis, the study formulated the theoretical proposition that the human right to food, the concept of urban commons, and the establishment of community gardens serve as mechanisms for addressing urban land and food crises. In-depth empirical investigations between 2019–2023 characterized community gardens' territorial and sociodemographic profiles and engaged with gardeners and experts. Interviews and questionnaires were administered to 40 participants (20 individuals from each city). The data had a thematic coding and analysis, a combined approach between case study and content analysis methods to produce information, insights, and arguments from the sources of evidence by deductive and inductive reasoning. Based on that, several similar and different urban food sharing activities were investigated within and between the same cities.

The results demonstrated that in Berlin, community gardeners and experts' motivations primarily focused on socialization and environmental concerns, while in Rio de Janeiro, food security was the primary focus, followed by ecological and economic topics. An unexpected finding was that in Berlin, employment opportunities in enhancing food accessibility and the economic dimension of food sustainability were important for gardeners. Conversely, in Rio de Janeiro, one community garden is used to promote gender empowerment (social sustainability).

Acknowledging certain limitations, especially due the COVID-19 pandemic, the book confirmed the hypothesis that food sharing practices contribute to different dimensions of the right to food, with variations based on specific socioeconomic contexts. However, agroecological food production emerged as a unifying factor across both cities, demonstrating a shared commitment to sustainable practices. This suggests a significant international step toward social-ecological transformation in urban food and land management.

The findings are interesting for academic and non-academic audience curious about the right to food, urban commons and community gardens. The study expanded the existing literature on the role of urban agriculture and commons. Another important contribution is the alert for the necessary promotion and protection of community gardens, followed by policy recommendations in that sense.

Jena, Germany
Rio de Janeiro, Brazil

Felipe Jardim, Dr. jur./Dr. phil

Felipe Jardim Postdoctoral researcher in Public Law and Governance at Law School, Tilburg University, the Netherlands. Post-doctoral fellow in Environmental Humanities at Rachel Carson Center, Ludwig-Maximilians University of Munich, Germany. Doctor in Law at State University of Rio de Janeiro, Brazil & in Sociology at Friedrich-Schiller University Jena, Germany. Master's degree in Urban Development at Federal University of Pernambuco, Brazil. Bachelor's degree in Law at Catholic University of Pernambuco, Brazil.

Acknowledgements I am grateful to the many individuals and groups who have contributed to this book, principally the interviewees, the supervisors and universities' staff. Moreover, I am thankful to my family and friends for the support during the study development. Furthermore, the following funding agencies were crucial throughout the years of research: CAPES, Brazil (Programa de Demanda Social 2019–2020), DAAD, Germany (Bi-nationally Supervised Doctoral Degrees/ Cotutelle Program 2020–2021, Code 57507869), Friedrich-Schiller University Jena, Germany (Promotionsabschlussstipendien 2022–2023), and Ludwig Maximilians University of Munich, Germany (Rachel Carson Center/Landhaus Fellowship 2024–2025).

Jena, Germany Felipe Jardim
Rio de Janeiro, Brazil

Competing Interests The author has no competing interests to declare that are relevant to the content of this manuscript.

Contents

Chapter 1
Introductory Guidelines to the Investigation of Community Gardens in Berlin and Rio de Janeiro

This Introduction is organized in eleven parts. They represent the initial and crucial elements to understand the developed research.

1.1 Main Concepts

Focused on Law and Sociology, this interdisciplinary research background is based on two current urban crises: food and land. The first is the infringement of the **human right to adequate food.** The Human Right to Adequate Food, enshrined in Article 25 of the United Nations Universal Declaration of Human Rights, is integral to ensuring health, well-being, and the fulfillment of other human rights. This is a guide for our **common** future. It extends beyond mere charity or the prevention of hunger, encompassing the notion that every individual, whether alone or within a community, should have continuous physical and economic access to food that is culturally acceptable, sustainably produced and consumed, and preserves resources for future generations.

This principle comprises four key components recognized by the United Nations (General Comment N°. 12/1999). Firstly, it emphasizes the physical *availability* of food to meet the dietary needs of individuals, allowing for freedom of choice in production and distribution, including self-provision and availability in markets and shops. Secondly, it underscores the importance of economic and physical *accessibility* over time, ensuring that access to food does not compromise human rights, basic needs, or the resources available for future generations, while also considering intangible qualities linked to food and its consumption. Thirdly, it highlights the *acceptability* of food, which should be free from adverse substances and align with cultural norms regarding consumption, catering to diverse needs based on factors, includings age, living conditions, health, occupation, and gender. Lastly, it

F. Jardim, *Right to Food in Community Gardens*, LITES - Legal Issues in Transdisciplinary Environmental Studies 6,
https://doi.org/10.1007/978-3-032-19612-5_1

emphasizes the economic, social, and environmental *sustainability* of food production and consumption, guided by principles such as improving resource efficiency, conserving and enhancing natural resources, protecting rural livelihoods and social well-being, enhancing resilience, and implementing responsible governance mechanisms. These principles collectively underscore the importance of sustainable agriculture in ensuring the right to adequate food for all individuals, both now and in the future.

The second urban issue is **vacant land**. This concept can be categorized into three types: *unused land*, which is not currently in full use and may be disused or in a state of disrepair; *underutilized land*, which still has potential for use but falls below parameters defined by laws such as the Master Plan or construction codes; and *unbuilt land*, which is completely unoccupied with no structures and can be classified as closed or abandoned based on its current status. They can be linked to many problems, including socio-spatial segregation and maintenance of socioeconomic inequalities.

Given these problems, there is a urgent demand for change. This means a **social-ecological transformation** of social values, norms, practices, and conflicts relating to nature. The aim is to provide more access to rights, reduce socioeconomic disparities, and sustain life in cities and on Earth. In this sense, the urban commons are one of the possible ways.

Urban commons are the collectively management *(governance)* by a social group *(commoners)* to promote social, economic, and environmental sustainability though social practices and relations *(commoning)*. The urban commons play a crucial role in facilitating the *social-ecological transition* by encouraging shared responsibility and benefits related to urban *resources*, from local to global level, such as parks, streets, but also knowledge. The **Human Rights** can also be understood as commons supporting the governance of a sustainable urban life. In addition, the **Right to the City** aligns with this view because it encapsulates the fair and inclusive access to urban spaces, guided by principles of sustainability, democracy, equity, and social justice. It is a communal entitlement for city dwellers, particularly those marginalized, granting them the authority to organize and act based on their customs and needs. The goal is to realize the full spectrum of rights, including **food,** self-determination, and decent quality of life within urban environments.

Following this path, when applied to the food system, urban commons offer an alternative to the agri-industrial production model. The reason is that commons prioritize the *use-value* of resources (such as land, food, seeds, knowledge, sunlight, water, tools, and human labor) over their exchange-value as commodities. This is largely noticed by the worldwide literature through the case of **community gardens.** In the last decades, they are a crescent strategy to occupy vacant land and they can be related to the right to food.

The community gardens' land *(resource)* ownership can be categorized into public or private areas, with urban vacant land often being underutilized and unbuilt. Community gardens are established in various locations such as streets' sidewalks, residential areas, school buildings, and public parks. These gardens sometimes thrive in economically and socially vulnerable areas, reclaiming spaces once overrun by illicit activities. While often temporary, these gardens play a crucial role in enhancing neighborhood safety and liveability. The transformation of abandoned lots into community gardens serves as a grassroots solution to blight, fostering cooperation among citizens to address local challenges.

The *commoners* have diverse demographics, including individuals, families, and migrants, with motivations ranging from environmental stewardship to social engagement. Community gardens are often initiated by self-organized groups comprising volunteers, including neighborhoods, schools, churches, and NGOs. While some gardens are managed solely by volunteers, others may hire professionals to handle administrative tasks or provide educational support. The gardeners have socioeconomic divides, involving individuals from diverse income levels, ages, education levels, and ethnicities. Motivations for participating in community gardening vary, including creating safe spaces, connecting with nature, engaging in physical activities, fostering community spirit, and promoting urban development and visibility.

While community gardens' *governance* is driven by non-profit interests, they may adopt various bottom-up financing methods such as plot rentals or contributions to courses and events. These gardens can operate independently of governmental support and may lack specific legal regulations. Despite this, they play a significant role in enhancing neighborhood liveability and promoting social cohesion. In addition, while food production (*commoning*) is a regular focus, some gardens prioritize medicinal or ornamental plants. Nevertheless, benefiting both participants and the wider community, the produced food *(resource)* play a relevant role in promoting the *right to food* and often engage with other urban food sharing initiatives (food banks, community kitchens etc.).

In the gardens happen the **urban food sharing activities**. This includes sharing food portions with others, giving food to those in need, and collectively using spaces for food-related activities including growing, cooking, and eating. It embodies a communal approach to food, emphasizing shared ownership and access rather than commodification. This concept aligns with the principles of the *commons*, advocating that food should be sustainably treated as a shared resource rather than a commodity. For example, gardening encompasses a range of tasks from planting trees and maintaining lawns to cultivating food crops using **agroecological principles,** a food production in the balance between plants, animals, people, and their environment. This also means that there is no use of artificial chemicals, fertilizers, and pesticides etc.).

1.2 Relevance

Investigating community gardens is relevant to **Law and Sociology** because public policies related to community gardens could address the state's legal duty to provide human rights, the right to the city and inclusive urban development. The state could promote social and environmental justice and equity by increasing access to fresh food and green space in marginalized areas. In addition, legal frameworks and social factors could contribute to or disturb the achievement of Sustainable Development Goals, such as hunger eradication (Goal #2), sustainable cities and communities (Goal #11), and responsible consumption and production (Goal #12). Furthermore, investigating the human right to food is a complex issue in inter- and transdisciplinary debates. For instance, the concept of human rights is not always understood, which triggers contestation between pro- and anti-human rights actors. Moreover, international relations are also affected by conflicts and humanitarian crises generated by the lack of food availability. Additionally, promoting the human right to food could involve individual and group actions to determine how food systems should be and address the root causes of their violation. This includes access to natural resources, such as clean water, native seeds, and healthy soil, through community-based initiatives in the natural sciences perspective or on the social and legal functions of urban property and land use in the city.

Specifically relevant to **Law**, studying how the *right to food*'s key components are improved or infringed is crucial for establishing adequate legal protection for individuals and vulnerable groups. This involves creation, adaptation, extinction, and application of laws from local to international level. When a violation happens, responsibility can be required in a legal system. However, a suit must guarantee access to justice, which could take a long time to produce concrete effects, but a person facing the consequences of infringement of the right to food, such as hunger, could have no opportunity to wait long periods. Then, this study also matters to Law as a practical issue of right assurance before the need for a legal jurisdiction. Furthermore, the right to food requires developing and implementing policies, monitoring systems, and laws. This includes topics on food production, distribution and access, land rights, agricultural subsidies, and trade agreements. If the implemented instruments are insufficient, discriminatory, non-participative, or fail to address cases of right to food violation, it could be considered a transgression of human rights. More than that, food is essential to health and well-being and is a means to fulfill other human rights, such as work and education.

The link of *community gardens* to **Law** can be observed, for example, in the occupation of vacant land. It provides food that lights up the discussion on urbanistic law, including Master Plan, construction licenses and regulations, land use and zoning law, real estate speculation, and land tenure and property. Indeed, property rights can stimulate or disturb land access and tenure. This could require judicial and extrajudicial (mediation and arbitration) demands involving different stakeholders, such as private and public landowners, gardeners, politicians, voluntary associations, district representatives, and researchers. Additionally, community gardens are aligned with environmental law. Food sustainability can promote education, nature regeneration, and conservation, support local ecosystems, and reduce carbon emissions with food long-distance' transport.

On the other hand, *food availability, accessibility, acceptability, and sustainability* matter to **Sociology.** To illustrate, there are issues regarding how the instruments mentioned above are created and who they impact for better clarity. Additionally, there are dissimilarities of ethnic-racial access to the right to food. For example, the lack of physical and economic access to healthy and fresh food for Black, Indigenous, and other communities of color within a reasonable distance represents a problem for equality, democracy, and justice. This can be understood as environmental racism. Income, gender, social class, and education are also related to food inequalities, such as lack of money to buy food, no stable access to piped water to clean and prepare the food, and exclusion of girls' right to education aiming to improve life conditions through a future qualified work. Another bond is that individual and collective norms and values shape a food system's use, offer, and demand. This represents consequences to access, preferences, and consumption patterns, such as food without meat or avoiding fast food. Government policies, such as tax benefits or restrictions on certain products, and social movements advocating for or against certain food companies can influence these patterns. The COVID-19 pandemic also brought insights into social priorities, collective mobilization for food access, and behavior change related to food safety.

Research on *community gardens* is also relevant to **Sociology**. For instance, the study of motivation for uses, target individuals and goals, benefits, and challenges across different social groups and through various community gardens from similar social groups. Moreover, community gardens can host social integration and the inclusion of people from different backgrounds. Also, they could create a sense of belonging for new residents, introduce education for children about food culture, or open space for memory preservation for immigrants. Community gardens have the potential to supply local markets, impact health, and raise the connection to nature. Other possible research interests are the collective form of land administration and the background of causes for moving or closing a community garden.

1.3 Literature Review and Research Gap

Much of the current literature on community gardens in *Berlin* has mentioned *food availability* on the topic of transformed vacant land as a space for small-scale food production, *food acceptability* through the promotion of food education, and food culture preservation, besides *social and environmental food sustainability* dimensions by community building and environmental education. In contrast, a significant portion of previous research on community gardens in *Rio de Janeiro* focuses on *food availability*, repurposing vacant land to alleviate food insecurity, including efforts to mitigate the effects of the COVID-19 pandemic; *food accessibility,* tackling segregation on food distribution; *food acceptability*, by preserving the culture of medicinal plants; and *social* (human interaction and social cohesion), *economic* (affordability and work opportunities), *and environmental* (remediating degraded space) *sustainability* dimensions.

What is essential from the publications is that several studies have begun to examine issues related to **food availability** provided by community gardens in *both cities*. What is similar is the use of vacant land to transform territories as a strategy that is not centered on food-related reasons but on changing or preventing wastelands and dump grounds,[1] as well as on social justice and environmental sustainability.[2] However, in *Rio de Janeiro,* there was also an effort to avoid drug sales and consumption and the construction of more houses. This study was focused on community gardens on public land without a cross-country analysis.[3] Additionally, efforts to address food insecurity[4] include mitigating the impacts of the COVID-19 pandemic.[5] The difference is that *food availability* in *Berlin* was also indirectly investigated by the integration of community gardens and private allotment gardens (two different categories of urban agriculture) in a cross-country study to Poland (Warsaw).[6]

According to the literature, **food accessibility** is part of *both cities.* In *Berlin,* there is an economy related to subsistence agriculture and physical access to organic food, representing symbolic economic savings.[7] The difference to *Rio de Janeiro* is that various studies explicitly assess the contribution of community gardens to physical food accessibility to mitigate—not solve—food insecurity, especially in low-income and Black communities without markets and street fairs (food apartheid).[8]

In addition, **food acceptability** in community gardens has been indirectly investigated in *both cities. In Berlin,* it was connected to information and education of food culture, especially knowledge on food manipulation and consumption for children[9] and on memory preservation, giving space for people to cultivate plants from their original country or city.[10] In *Rio de Janeiro,* the cultural link to ancestral knowledge regarding medicinal plants was prevailing.[11]

Thus far, previous studies have attempted **food sustainability** (long-term *food availability* and *accessibility*) in *both cities.* Even so, the focus in *Berlin* was on the *social*[12] and *environmental*[13] *sustainability* dimensions. The cross-country research involving these dimensions in *Berlin* included Italy, Hungary, and Spain[14]; Germany (Cologne), Switzerland, Austria, the United States of America, Canada, the United

[1] Magalhães (2021), Véron (2023).

[2] Rekow (2015).

[3] Magalhães, op. cit.

[4] Rekow, op. cit.

[5] Magalhães, op. cit.

[6] Ferrari et al. (2023).

[7] Halder (2017), Steuri and Vignola (2022).

[8] Beck (2018, pp. 9–383), Lima (2019), Siniscalchi (2020, p. 241 et seq.), and Zanotto (2016).

[9] Gobster et al. (2004, pp. 149–151).

[10] Karge (2015).

[11] Magalhães, op. cit. and Silva (2014).

[12] Colding et al. (2013, pp. 1039–1051).

[13] Gobster et al., op. cit.

[14] Ochoa et al. (2019).

Kingdom[15]; France[16]; and other German cities, as well as New Zealand.[17] In *Berlin*, the long-term maintenance of a garden is threatened when the state (as the landowner) develops new interests in land use, often for recreational purposes, leading to potential threats and forced relocations.[18] In *Rio de Janeiro*, the literature presents the importance of *social, economic, and environmental sustainability* dimensions of community gardens as a security (food and peace) strategy that is threatened by criminal agents.[19]

As a brief illustration of the investigation's relevance, research in other cities also reported, directly or indirectly, one or more elements of the right to food in community gardens. In São Paulo, the biggest Brazilian city, a study on the effects of the pandemic of COVID-19 on urban agriculture reported that *food availability* was affected and work on community gardens was reduced but did not stop. Without governmental support and ways to obtain materials, there were negative consequences to *accessibility*.[20] Also, simultaneous results indicate debates on *food acceptability* given the educational role of community gardens.[21] The challenges to *food accessibility* and *sustainability* in São Paulo were secondarily investigated in contrast to Melbourne.[22] Furthermore, a study focusing on urban activism in São Paulo and Paris provided insights into *food availability* in both cities.[23] In Vienna, community gardens are one of the elements for eco-political *economic sustainability*,[24] and *food availability* is connected to the desire for self-produced fresh food but not linked to poverty.[25]

Only a single study[26] has a similar theoretical approach to the common and methodological strategy of interviewing stakeholders to identify how community-based initiatives contribute key elements for food democracy (participation, the **right to food**, sustainability, and reorienting control). Thus, the right to food forms a subcategory in the analysis. This is in stark contrast with this doctoral investigation because, here, the right to food is a central category. Moreover, the above-mentioned study collected data on community gardens, food banks, and community kitchens in *Berlin*, London, and Dublin, while here, the empirical collection was only on community gardens from *Berlin* and *Rio de Janeiro*. The overall essential result regarding community gardens is that the study revealed a link from community gardens to *food availability* (providing space for local food production), *access* (opportunities for accessing healthy, locally grown food), *acceptability* (empowering individuals to

[15] Göttl and Penker (2020, pp. 30–43).

[16] Jackisch (2012).

[17] Fox-Kämper (2028, pp. 59–68).

[18] Davies et al. (2019, pp. 8–20).

[19] Rekow, op cit. and Rekow (2017).

[20] Biazoti et al. (2021).

[21] Nagib and Nakamura (2021).

[22] Amato-Lourenco et al. (2021, pp. 2785–2796).

[23] Visoni and Nagib (2019, pp. 88–91).

[24] Deflorian (2022).

[25] Mayrhofer (2018, pp. 1207–1224).

[26] Davies and Legg (2018, p. 18).

learn how to grow their food), and *sustainability* (urban green). Specifically on food *availability*, the study presented the challenges of the lack of legal land use guarantee and no zone law classification as parks or green areas in the three cities.[27] Following the citation track of the aforementioned researchers/research group, it was possible to observe a list of **urban food sharing activities**,[28] which proved to be extremely relevant for this investigation's method proceedings.

To obtain results, the above investigations shared common topics, such as the occupation of **vacant urban land**, benefits, and challenges to creating and maintaining a community garden. This is relevant to understand what is behind the urban transformation and land dispute. The results also included **urban commons** as the main instrument or accessory tool of the theoretical framework in *Rio de Janeiro*,[29] in *Berlin*,[30] and in cross-country studies.[31] Regarding methodology, the aforementioned studies have primarily employed qualitative approaches, consisting of empirical case studies based on semi-structured interviews conducted in both cities,[32] as well as international studies.[33]

The strengths of that research are that they are multidisciplinary, reinforcing the importance of community gardens for society, even those unrelated to food, and bringing contributions to different fields. Despite that, they have some weaknesses. Regarding the local case studies, there are just a few publications related to *Rio de Janeiro*,[34] and the literature review demonstrated that it is a city is not involved in any cross-country study. At the same time, *Berlin* has many cross-country investigations focused on European cities. A few cases in Berlin also mentioned community gardens that no longer exist or moved to new places, such as Himmelbeet and Peace of Land. Moreover, there are three other main relevant points. First, *food acceptability* and *food economic sustainability* are not as much investigated as the others. Secondly, the studies usually support the urban commons theory but not as a central theoretical framework. Third, some studies were not exclusive to community gardens. Consequently, the interviews analysed were combined with other research objects, such as allotment gardens and community kitchens.

This identified a **research gap** for a comprehensive cross-country study on the urban food sharing relationship of community gardens or the human right to adequate food, based on the theory of urban commons, particularly focusing on *Berlin* and *Rio de Janeiro*.

---

[27] Davies et al. (2018), op. cit.

[28] Davies et al. (2018), op. cit.

[29] Pernes et al. (2019, p. 131 et seq.) and Viriato (2020, p. 241 et seq.).

[30] Karge, op. cit.; Rosol (2012, pp. 239–257).

[31] Chen, op. cit.; Landman and Silverman (2019, pp. 275–290).

[32] Zanotto, op. cit.; Pernes et al., op. cit.; Karge, op. cit.; Halder, op. cit.

[33] Davies et al., op. cit.

[34] For instance. The search for "'community garden' AND 'Rio de Janeiro' on the Web of Science has no results while substituting the city for "Berlin," there are 12 studies. In ScienceDirect, following the same terms, there are 41 results regarding Rio de Janeiro, and 241 research regarding Berlin.

1.4 Methodological Strategies

This research[35] has a predominantly[36] qualitative approach[37] in developing an exploratory investigation[38] with a mixed inductive and deductive approach. Here, the case study is the empirical methodological strategy adopted. The reason for choosing the case study method is because case studies are indicated when the research question is related to "how" and "why" in investigating a contemporary real-life phenomenon.

Furthermore, community gardens are urban commons,[39] and a proper qualitative research method for investigating the collective action on commons is case study.[40] This methodological strategy is important to "direct attention to the complexity of relationships between social and ecological systems"[41] by "appreciating nonlinear and context-specific relationships between group characteristics and the prospects for collective action."[42]

In view of the above, "**the case**" means community gardens' urban food sharing activities connected to the human right to food.

---

[35] The following publication was essential for writing this study: Morley (2014).

[36] Given that "every qualitative phenomenon is also naturally endowed with quantitative faces and vice versa." Demo (2012, p. 8) apud Marconi and Lakatos (2022).

[37] "Qualitative research presupposes the establishment of one or more objectives, the selection of information, and the carrying out of field research. Then, if necessary, hypotheses are constructed that will explain the identified problem and the field and everything that will be needed to collect the data are defined. Once the data has been collected, we move on to the analysis phase. However, unlike quantitative research, in qualitative research the process is not sequential; the researcher advances to the next phases, but constantly goes back to previous phases, for reformulations, always looking for deep meanings. [...] The qualitative study develops in a natural situation, offering a wealth of descriptive data, as well as focusing on reality in a complex and contextualized way." Marconi, op. cit. p. 302.

[38] "Exploratory research's main purpose is to develop, clarify and modify concepts and ideas, with a view to formulating more precise problems or researchable hypotheses for subsequent studies. Of all types of research, these are the ones with the least rigidity in planning. They usually involve bibliographic and documentary research, non-standardized interviews and case studies. Sampling procedures and quantitative data collection techniques are not usually applied in these surveys. Exploratory research is developed with the aim of providing an approximate overview of a given fact. This type of research is carried out especially when the chosen topic is little explored and it becomes difficult to formulate precise and operational hypotheses about it." Gil (2008, p. 27).

[39] Guttmann (2023) and Rogge and Theesfeld (2018, p. 255).

[40] "The case study method refers to a research strategy of focusing intensively on individual cases to draw insights about causal relationships in a broader population of cases. Close examination of individual cases offers opportunities to develop concepts and theory, identify the limits of general relationships and disprove deterministic hypotheses, control for confounding effects through within-case comparisons, and disentangle causal processes. The case study method is especially appealing when trying to make sense of complex processes. It is the only option for empirical field-based research when cross-case data are not readily available. Key disadvantages relate to limited external validity, problems of indeterminancy, and the difficulty of replication." Poteete et al. (2009, p. 78).

[41] Poteete et al., op. cit, p. 86.

[42] Poteete et al., op. cit, p. 77.

Given that, the **research question** guiding this investigation is how do notions of the right to food connect to food sharing activities in Berlin and Rio de Janeiro community gardens, and, within and between cities, how to explain these connections' similarities and differences?

The **hypothesis** is that urban food sharing activities in community gardens can be connected to food availability, accessibility, acceptability, and sustainability. Still, the relations may differ based on specific socioeconomic contexts and unique urban challenges within and between cities.

To test it, the research **general objective** is to examine the food sharing activities of community gardens in Berlin and Rio de Janeiro, contrasting them based on the conceptual and territorial focus detailed above.

To answer the research question, an initial step was the **theoretical** investigation of the aforementioned urban crises by exploring their precedents and contemporary situations. This made it possible to understand that problems involving food and land have multiple causes and consequences, including social, environmental, and economic dimensions, and they are based on the same roots of resource commodification, the view that a resource must be explored as much as possible to provide profit to a limited group of beneficiaries. This path pointed out the importance of human rights, commons (alternative governance in opposition to commodity), and urban agriculture to guide the change (*specific objective "a"*). More precisely, the human right to food, urban commons, and community gardens were defined as three standards for mitigating urban land and food emergencies (*specific objective "b"*). The integration of these elements demonstrated that *community gardens are urban commons transforming vacant urban land. The new land use (resource) embraces people (commoners) doing food sharing activities (commoning) with social, economic, and environmental dimensions developed in connection to the human right to adequate food.*

After settling the theoretical ground, the next step was to define an empirical methodological strategy to investigate and test the hypothesis by characterizing the profile of territory, gardeners, and experts related to community gardens in Berlin and Rio de Janeiro, along with examining the urban food sharing activities connected to food availability, accessibility, acceptability, and sustainability in these gardens (*specific objective "c"*).

1.5 Data Collection

The selected qualitative techniques for data collection were the interview,[43] sociodemographic questionnaire,[44] and documentary research on archives.[45] The literature review supported this choice. After completing the specific objectives "a" and "b,"

---

[43] Gil, op. cit., p. 109 and Yin, op. cit., p. 112.

[44] Gil, op. cit, p. 121.

[45] Marconi, op. cit., p. 204.

these techniques were developed under the focus of the aforementioned theoretical framework to provide the extraction of empirical evidence to confirm or deny the hypothesis. To achieve this, given the nature of the hypothesis (related to socioeconomic and demographic differences among cities), it is necessary to identify the community gardeners' sociodemographic profile in *Berlin* and *Rio de Janeiro*, their urban food sharing activities related to food *availability, accessibility, acceptability, and sustainability*, along with their motivations for these activities (*specific objective "c"*).

This process required a research **protocol**[46] (identification of the project, responsible researcher, sponsoring entity, period of realization, and place of the research) that was part of the Consent Term. Additionally, other parts of the protocol (introduction specifying the theoretical and practical relevance of the study, identification of the beneficiaries of the research, definition of the people who will be the object of the study, as well as the strategies to be used to obtain information; questions necessary for data collection; data analysis procedure) are presented during this Introduction.

Considering each case, the selected **qualitative techniques for data collection** included semi-structured *interview* with thirty-one in-depth and open-ended questions, sociodemographic *questionnaire* with closed-ended questions, and archival document research. The targets were *gardeners* and *experts*, the commoners. The "*experts*" were the professionals related to agriculture with or without work paid by/income related to a community garden, public agents, and researchers on community gardens, food systems, and similar topics. The "*gardeners*" were the ones not included as *"experts"*; the *"gardeners"* were doing gardening or administrative activities in a community garden during the field visit, including volunteers and amateurs with financial support. There were forty eligible participants, twenty in person, in *Berlin*, and twenty online, in *Rio de Janeiro*.[47]

Initially, the interview is a traditional qualitative approach in the social sciences.[48] The interview was semi-structured with thirty-one in-depth and open-ended questions organized into categories: personal experience and relation with the locals, to study the history of the place, how the person related to it and community gardens, such as routine and interests; social relations to understand the group relations; global connections, to explore how the interviewee situates themself and their activities in the garden on worldwide perspectives, such as agri-industrial food system, and sustainability; in addition to local, and international legal issues, to comprehend the role of law and government. One extra methodological component was a photographic association exercise. Ten photos were to be described, aiming to understand the concept of urban community gardens. However, many participants in *Rio de*

[46] Yin, op. cit., p. 89.

[47] "In qualitative research, data collection typically occurs to the point of saturation. Essentially, this means that researchers continue interviews to the point where little new information is shared by participants. In other words, people continue reporting essentially the same ideas and the law of diminishing returns is at work in the information-gathering procedure. Collecting more data, at that point, does not produce novel results." Firmin (2008, p. 869).

[48] Yin, op. cit, p. 112; Marconi, op. cit., p. 320.

Janeiro had problems accessing the images in digital media. Consequently, this last part was not included in the results.

In addition to the interview, all participants responded to a sociodemographic questionnaire with closed-ended questions. The questionnaire comprised twenty-two personal questions related to their life and activities in the garden, such as age, gender, income, employment status, political affiliation, time living in the city, food habits, and products cultivated in the garden. This was important to provide a personal background of the interviewee, an important element in identifying the social aspects behind the practices and speeches. The questionnaire in *Berlin* did not include ethnic-racial identification to avoid ethical conflicts or triggers related to the Reich Citizenship Law (RBG)[49] on 15 September 1935.

The information was impossible to obtain from the interviews and questionnaires, and the information required to discuss the results with previous studies was obtained by the literature review[50] and documentary research on public and private archives, as well as on non-written sources (images, photographs, digital audiovisual media, and cartographic material).[51]

1.6 Data Organization

Each interview received a code to avoid identification to organize the interview and its related questionnaire data. In *Rio de Janeiro*, "RIOG" is for *gardeners*, and "RIOE" is for *experts*. In *Berlin*, "BERG" is for *gardeners*, and "BERE" is for *experts*. It is important to reinforce that the interviewees were distributed in multiple gardens and in the city hall. Then, they were not a unique group gardening in the same community garden, but a group of people interviewed for the same study. Each code was followed by a unique number representing a sequence of interviews. For example, RIOG7 meant the 7th interviewed gardener in *Rio de Janeiro*, while BERE3 meant the 3rd expert interviewed in *Berlin*. The questionnaire data was organized on Excel sheets following the same logic.

Considering the amount of collected data, the limitation of time, and the lack of human resources, the complete audios were uploaded into MAXQDA qualitative data analysis[52] software to facilitate the extraction of the *relevant* data. This means only the audio frames of themes linked to answer the central question and sub-questions according to the categories presented in the next section. The next step was the transcription of these relevant extracts. When necessary, they were translated into

[49] It divided the German population into Reich citizens, "citizens of German or related blood", on the one hand, and into "simple" nationals, "members of a non-racial nationality."

[50] Lakato (2023, p. 202).

[51] Lakato, loc. cit.

[52] Software program designed for computer-assisted qualitative and mixed methods data, text and multimedia analysis in academic, scientific, and business institutions. Available on: https://www.maxqda.com/. Accessed on 1 Feb. 2024.

English (Google Translate), reviewed by the author, and adapted to preserve the expressions of the original language as much as possible. The noisy background, parallel talk, linguistic errors, repetition of words, and long pauses on the extraction were not considered during the transcription. Subsequently, there was the phase of data organization in Word files by groups. The data collected was ordered according to the codes "RIOG," "RIOE," "BERG," and "BERE."

Regarding documentary material, the data complemented the lack of information on gardens. The necessary information was separated by the garden to produce texts, tables, and illustrations. Another possibility was to advance or illustrate the results, especially with photography.

Summarising, the data collected was organized into data from interviews of *gardeners*, data from interviews of *experts*, data from questionnaires of *gardeners*, data from questionnaires of *experts*, and data from documents.

1.7 Data Analysis

The strategy for data analysis was a combined approach between **case study**[53] and **content analysis**[54] methods to produce information, insights, and arguments from the sources of evidence by combining deductive and inductive reasoning. This mix was necessary to overcome gaps generated by restrictively following just the case study analysis method (general analytical strategies, main methods of analysis, secondary methods of analysis)[55] for investigating data collected by the case study strategy. Also, the variant methodological approach is approved to investigate the commons.[56] However, it is notable that the case study demands the definition of *units of analysis*[57] to "offer an empirical interpretation of the theoretical subject of study."[58] It guides the discussion with previous studies with similar units of analysis to identify close or divergent results.[59] They also generate the research validation.[60] Moreover, "for collective action on the commons, the main unit of analysis can be defined as either the potential participants in collective action or the central objects of collective action."[61]

---

[53] Yin, op. cit., p. 131.

[54] Bardin (2011).

[55] Yin, op. cit., loc. cit.

[56] Poteete, op. cit., p. 78.

[57] Yin, op. cit., p. 133.

[58] Poteete, op. cit., p. 79.

[59] Yin, op. cit., p. 46.

[60] Yin, op. cit, p. 56.

[61] Poteete, op. cit., loc. cit.

In the similar meaning of coding *register and context units*, the **content analysis method** proposes the **thematic analysis,**[62] where **thematic coding**[63] is a necessary step.[64]

Succinctly, the case study and content analysis are qualitative traditional proposals that follow the same crucial coding step differently. Integrating these views, terms, and processes, it was possible to systematically investigate empirical data to identify *patterns* in the coded data and build arguments to confirm or reject the hypothesis.

In light of that, the coding followed the division of the central research question (How do notions of the human right to food connect to food sharing activities in community gardens in Berlin and Rio de Janeiro, and how can these connections' similarities and differences within and between cities be explained?) in three sub-questions: (1) **What are** the community gardeners' urban food sharing activities connected to the human right to adequate food? (2) In what ways are there **similarities** and **divergences** among these activities within each city and between them? (3) **Why** are there commonalities and distinctions among these activities within each city and between them? These sub-questions guided the search for evidence on the empirical data.

To answer the **first sub-question** (What are the community gardens' urban food sharing activities connected to the human right to adequate food?), deductive coding was developed according to the integration of two pillars.

The first pillar was the conceptual legal framework of the key central components of the human right to food. This means an organization in four **themes**: (1) Food availability, (2) Food accessibility, (3) Food acceptability, and (4) Food sustainability.

The second pillar, the **codes**, was established according to the adaptation of the urban food sharing activities in urban commons' initiatives to community gardens. In the original version, these activities can be organized in a matrix[65] composed of *sharing elements*—foodstuff (including seeds, plants, compost), food

---

[62] Thematic analysis is the "data reduction and analysis strategy by which qualitative data are segmented, categorized, summarized, and reconstructed in a way that captures the important concepts within the data set. Thematic analysis is primarily a descriptive strategy that facilitates the search for patterns of experience within a qualitative data set; the product of a thematic analysis is a description of those patterns and the overarching design that unites them." Ayres (2008, p. 867).

[63] "Thematic coding is the strategy by which data are segmented and categorized for thematic analysis. Thematic coding is a strategy of data reduction […]. In thematic coding, the analyst frequently begins with a list of themes known (or at least anticipated) to be found in the data. When data for thematic analysis are collected through semi-structured interviews, some themes will be anticipated in the data set because those concepts were explicitly included in data collection. Codes may also come from a beginning conceptual model, the review of the literature, or professional experience. At this stage of the analysis, coding categories are more heuristic than analytic; that is, coding categories serve as a receptacle for promising ideas. Promising ideas become coding categories through a rigorous process of analytic induction that includes both within- and across-case comparisons. First, an idea must show importance within an individual account. In coding, portions of data are separated from their original context and labeled in some way so that all data bearing the same label can be retrieved and inspected together." Ayres, op. cit., loc. cit.

[64] Ayres, op. cit., loc. cit.

[65] Davies et al. (2018, p. 18).

spaces (including sites for shared growing, areas for food redistribution), food skills (including sharing knowledge and experiences about food growing, eating, redistribution or disposal)—through different *sharing modes*—informal, illicit, or unorganized (IIU) activities (foraging, gleaning), collecting, gifting (voluntarily granting something without expecting any form of compensation), bartering (trading goods or services directly without the use of currency), selling (the exchange of goods or services for monetary payment) for profit or not.

However, the original matrix includes activities not done in the exact same sense that is proposed by community gardens ("providing spaces for supper clubs," "selling home-cooked food that generates income beyond the costs of production," and "providing opportunities for travellers to experience home-cooked meals with locals") because the list includes other initiatives, such as community kitchens, and food banks. Additionally, similar topics have a logic of division for the original study that makes no difference here, such as separating "providing skills around growing gifting" from "providing workshops around nutrition or growing" and "providing spaces for growing for free" to "providing spaces for people to grow food on a not-for-profit basis." Then, the original matrix is only helpful in dealing with the research question after some modification.

After explaining that, the conceptual integration and the matrix's adaptation generated the link of **(1) Food availability** to (a) transforming vacant land in (public) open spaces for growing on a not-for-profit basis, including the offer of acquiring food in exchange for labor; (b) establishment of a gardens' restaurant or café; and (c) learning and practicing nutrition, how to co-produce food, identifying places where gleaning or foraging might occur, and swapping seeds; **(2) Food accessibility** to (a) self-produced foodstuff, sharing it for free, buying it for a symbolic price, or acquiring it by swapping; and (b) income generation opportunities by gardening, social, administrative work, and vegetable sales; **(3) Food acceptability** to (a) agroecological food production (regarding no use of artificial chemicals, fertilizers, pesticides, etc.), and (b) knowledge transfer about food culture, and **(4) Food sustainability** to (a) sharing of the excess foodstuff; (b) gifting and swapping foodstuff; and (c) provision of (public) spaces for growing by the transformation of vacant land. This can be observed in the following Table 1.1.

The **second sub-question** (In what ways are there similarities and divergences among urban food sharing activities connected to the human right to adequate food within each city and between them?) originated from deductive reasoning based on the literature review affirmation of existing multiple possibilities related to community gardens that are similar and divergent from different cities[66] and the same city.[67] Then, based on interviews, questionnaires, and documents, the thematic analysis of each community garden's urban food sharing activity in relation to the right to food (theme) was conducted according to four codes of similarities/divergences within a city/between cities. Illustrating that, on food *availability*, there was study of the establishment of a gardens' restaurant or café. This activity was similar in *Berlin*

[66] Göttl and Penker (2020, pp. 30–43) and Jackisch (2012).

[67] Lima (2019, p. 119 et seq.); Zanotto, op. cit.; Silva, op cit.

Table 1.1 Community gardens' urban food sharing activities in relation to human right to food key components

Theme (legal components of the human right to food)	**Code** (adaptation of community gardens' urban food sharing activities in urban commons' initiatives)	**Result** (integration and adaptation of theme and codes)
1. Food availability	(a) transforming vacant land into (public) open spaces for growing on a not-for-profit basis, including the offer of acquiring food in exchange for labour	Community gardens' urban food sharing activities in relation to food **availability**
	(b) establishment of a garden restaurant or café	
	(c) learning and practicing nutrition, how to co-produce food, identifying places where gleaning or foraging might occur, and swapping seeds	
2. Food accessibility	(a) self-produced foodstuff, sharing it for free, buying it for a symbolic price, or acquiring it by swapping	Community Gardens' urban food sharing activities in relation to food **accessibility**
	(b) income generation opportunities through gardening, social, administrative work, and vegetable sales	
3. Food acceptability	(a) agroecological food production (regarding no use of artificial chemicals, fertilizers, pesticides, etc.)	Community gardens' urban food sharing activities in relation to food **acceptability**
	(b) knowledge transfer about food culture	
4. Food sustainability	(a) sharing the excess of foodstuff	Community gardens' urban food sharing activities in relation to food **sustainability**
	(b) gifting and swapping foodstuff	
	(c) provision of (public) spaces for growing by transforming vacant land	

Source Jardim (2024)

and *Rio de Janeiro*. However, there were differences regarding the payment for the meal. In the case of *Berlin*, these places offer non-profit sales of meals, such as in Prinzessinengarten,[68] while in *Rio de Janeiro*, there is no sale, just gifting in public schools.[69]

Differently from the previous sub-questions, in reply to the **third sub-question** (Why are there commonalities and distinctions among these activities within each city and between them?), there was an inductive reasoning from the collected empirical material and the theoretical framework. The explanation for this change is that a deductive coding system would be imprecise or not embrace the multiple motivations for numerous similarities and divergences in a way that generated patterns, as required by a thematic analysis.[70] Then, the inductive study was done based on the theoretical framework, interviews, questionnaires, and documents. Exemplifying it, following the previous sample, the possible reason for the similarity of establishing a garden restaurant or café could be the nutritional role of a community garden. At the same time, the difference could have ground on the funding origin/institutional relations. On the one hand, the gardens with that type of establishment in *Berlin* are a private non-profit organization. On the other hand, in *Rio de Janeiro*, the gardens in public schools offering meals have public funding.

1.8 Why Berlin and Rio de Janeiro?

The empirical part concerns two cities, *Berlin* and *Rio de Janeiro*. The city level was chosen to be investigated not only because of the method's viability for a time-limited case study but also in view that the local government has an essential (not exclusive) role in governance to face distortions, exclusions, and inequalities of food such as regulating and enforcing the use of urban soil, financing societal actions, and offering institutional support.[71]

Despite their differences, *Berlin* and *Rio de Janeiro* share similarities. They are participants of the Milan Urban Food Pact (international agreement of Mayors)[72] and Sustainable Development Goals Agenda 2030 and both cities are catalogued as urban food sharing initiatives.[73] Further, Germany and Brazil[74] adopted a constitutional social democratic welfare. Both states embraced a federalist mode of political organization and signed the Universal Human Rights Declaration and many agreements on the human right to food and environmental-related issues.

[68] Prinzessinnengarten Kollektiv Berlin.

[69] Rio de Janeiro.

[70] Ayres, op. cit., loc. cit.

[71] Wegelin and Borgman (1995, pp. 131–152) and FAO (2017).

[72] Milan (2019).

[73] Davies (2017, pp. 136–149).

[74] Brazil (2013).

What is crucial to note is that they represent **global cities facing problems connected to vacant land and right to food**. To fight that, one of the **solutions presented** by them is the **land use repurposing** promoting urban and peri-urban agriculture, including **community gardens** as public policies. This strategy means **food as a social function of property and city.** This has been happening especially since the initial decade of the **twenty first century**.

After **2009** the community gardens started to expand in the whole *Berlin*. Currently, there are more than 200 community gardens in *Berlin*'s urban areas and the city government is developing a community gardens program to map and organize activities *(Gemeinschaftsgarten-Programm).*[75] This follows an important historical case with urban agriculture tradition since the end of the nineteenth century by the *Kleingarten* system (in general, a rented allotment garden for private use related to leisure).[76]

The city in the most populated city of Germany, with 3.645 million people (2019), and *Berlin* has a high development level[77] in a German context of low food insecurity level,[78] while *Rio de Janeiro* has a growing population of around 6.6 million inhabitants (2022),[79] of which 2.5 million live in extreme poverty.[80] To reduce the intermediate food insecurity[81] and poverty impacts, the city has a program of 56 community gardens in extremely poor urban areas, Hortas Cariocas.[82] It has been organized and promoted by the city government since **2006**. In 2019, the program was elected by the United Nations as a **model** of action to achieve the Sustainable Development Goals (SDG).[83] Additionally, in 2023, using vacant land under energy transmission lines etc., the city hall of *Rio de Janeiro* started to build "the biggest urban garden of the world" (11 hectares), from Madureira's Park to Guadalupe, in a partnership with public (Embrapa) and private agents (Light, energy company).[84]

Considering the above and in line with the research question, these cities play a crucial role in conducting a cross-country analysis of a common societal phenomenon from different contexts: community gardens. This role aids in elucidating the links between concepts of the right to food and food sharing practices within and across these urban settings. Moreover, the similarities and disparities facilitate an exploration of socioeconomic inequalities, cultural dynamics, community engagement and organization, the right to food stakeholders' involvement, and the methods and significance of realizing the human right to food.

---

[75] Berlin.

[76] Berlin.

[77] City Development Index.

[78] Economist Impact (2022).

[79] IBGE (2022).

[80] Lucena (2021).

[81] Economist Impact (2022).

[82] Rio de Janeiro.

[83] United Nations.

[84] Diário do Rio (2021).

1.9 Summary of Results and Contributions

As a **result**, several similarities and differences in urban food sharing activities were observed within and between the same city. For example, in *Berlin*, the food *availability* motivation was primarily centered on socialization and environmental concerns, while in *Rio de Janeiro*, food security was the primary focus, followed by economic and environmental purposes. An **unexpected finding** was the role of employment opportunities in enhancing food *accessibility* and the economic dimension of food *sustainability* in *Berlin*. In *Rio de Janeiro*, an interesting outcome was the use of a community garden as a tool for gender empowerment. **The results confirmed the hypothesis**. **However**, **agroecological food production** (cultural food *acceptability*) **emerged as a unifying factor across both cities**, demonstrating a shared commitment to *sustainable* practices regardless socioeconomic scenarios and specific urban challenges. This suggests a significant international step toward social-ecological transformation in urban food and land management. The findings expanded the existing literature on the role of urban agriculture and raised awareness of the necessary promotion and protection of community gardens.

The study was able to generate results and draw conclusions, providing room for **reproducibility** and **innovation** in further qualitative and quantitative research, even using or adapting the same interview guidelines. The conclusions of this book are policy recomendations, so they are useful for policymakers around the world.

The findings also **contribute** to **Law** and **Sociology** because the human right to food is an abstract and complex director for life and well-being. The good governance of the right to food is essential to achieve other human rights. Nevertheless, despite the unquestionable significance of society having established food as a human right, it is registered as *words* internationally recognizing rights and duties in *papers*. Hence, society must know and discover how to *practically* apply those words efficiently for individuals and groups to tackle their violations. Stated another way, different bridges must be constructed with many theoretical and empirical pillars to comprehend and act against infringing on the right to food in the concrete world. This runs through the innovation and adaptation of social initiatives, such as community gardens. Filling the research gap is valuable because it represents a different perspective from the regular fulfillment of the right to food through the problematic agri-food system.

Finally, the insights were interpreted in the context of the theoretical framework,[85] trends, or ruptures to existing literature to provide unprecedented contributions to Law and Sociology. This generated generic insights that can be applied in different contexts beyond *Berlin* and *Rio de Janeiro*.

---

[85] "The use of theory, when carrying out case studies, not only represents an immense help in defining the research project and collecting adequate data, but also becomes the main vehicle for generalizing the results of the case study." Yin, op. cit., p. 54.

1.10 Limitations

The study had several limitations to consider when interpreting the results. It cannot be claimed that the study represented all activities in community gardens in Rio de Janeiro and Berlin, nor can the findings be generalized to urban and peri-urban agriculture as the whole Global North and Global South. This limitation arises from the relatively small sample size of participants and territories investigated. Additionally, the study did not include other important stakeholders, such as the real estate market and neighbors, and had limited participation from public agents. Some participants faced difficulties during interviews, including language barriers and digital access issues, leading to incomplete responses. Factors like seasonal challenges and the **COVID-19 pandemic** further complicated empirical data collection. The study was developed from 2019 to 2023, so there were many travel and contact restrictions. Lack of digital data about the gardens and language barriers also posed obstacles. Online interviews had technical issues, such as internet connection, while in person interviewees were more focused, despite complicated to be achieved. It is also important to acknowledge that subjective data interpretation may vary between researchers.

Furthermore, it is crucial to acknowledge that the understanding of subjective data can vary based on the reflexivity and background of different researchers. Consequently, the interpretation of the data may diverge from that of others, potentially yielding disparate results. To understand the starting point of **subjective perspective**, the author declares to be born and raised in Brazil, male, cisgender, gay, lower middle class, without political or religious affiliation, starting doctoral studies at 24 years old, with a bachelor's degree in Law, and a master's degree in Urban Development. Moreover, it is important to announce the lack of gardening experience and no participation in any community gardens' decision processes, nor being an official member of any garden association. Finally, it is pertinent to cite the one year living in *Rio de Janeiro* (2019) and no period as *Berlin*'s inhabitant, just some short field visits of a few days.

To mitigate potential discrepancies and ensure the quality control of the interview guide and sociodemographic questionnaire were developed with the support and insights of the researchers from the Mentalities in Flux Junior Research Group (Flumen) at Friedrich-Schiller University in Jena, Germany, drawing upon their previous experience. In addition, the initial literature review and theoretical framework informed the construction of these materials. After that, the research project underwent a thorough review and approval process by the ethics committee of *Plataforma Brasil* (Process Id. CAAE P 49263021.4.0000.5282), as mandated by Brazilian law for conducting interviews in Brazil. This submission also encompassed details related to the case study protocol. Regarding the selection of bibliographic sources, a meticulous approach was adopted, considering criteria such as quality (peer-reviewed, research credibility), authenticity (geographical and temporal context of the text's creation), and institutional provenance.

1.11 Structure of the Book

After this Introduction, in Chapter 2, the text is divided into several sections that trace the evolution of land use and property rights in urban areas, as well as their relation to agriculture. The *first section* examines the historical shift from common property and agricultural land in early civilizations to the dominance of private property and exchange-value in more recent times, leading to a reduction in urban agricultural space. The *second section* covers the Modern Age and the twentieth century, highlighting the emergence of an economic perspective that prioritizes land as an asset for accumulation rather than for communal benefit. The *third section* delves into the social and functional consequences of this perspective, including the exclusion of agriculture from urban spaces, the proliferation of vacant land, and the development of substandard living conditions. The *fourth section* discusses the reintroduction of food production into urban areas following World Wars and the establishment of the Universal Declaration of Human Rights, emphasizing the revival of communal resources. The *fifth section* addresses contemporary challenges in the urban food system, spanning from agricultural production to waste management, and calls for urgent social-ecological transformation. The *sixth section* introduces urban agriculture as a potential solution to these challenges.

In summary, the chapter sets the groundwork for theoretical pillars that will guide this transformative approach. This means the concepts of urban commons, the human right to adequate food, and the transformation of vacant land through community gardens.

Given the above, Chapter 3 has four sections. The *first section* focuses on the concept of the human right to adequate food, exploring its definition, the associated responsibilities, and its interconnection with other human rights. The *second section* delves into the concept of commons and its relevance in urban contexts, particularly in the context of urban commons. The *third section* provides a comprehensive overview of community gardens worldwide, including various aspects such as motivations, territorial characteristics, profiles of gardeners, and the range of activities they engage in. The *fourth section* acts as a synthesis, bringing together key elements from each section to create a cohesive theoretical foundation.

It serves as the basis for conducting empirical research, which will investigate the profiles of territory, gardeners, and experts involved in community gardens in *Berlin* and *Rio de Janeiro*, as well as their food sharing activities related to *food availability, accessibility, acceptability, and sustainability*. This empirical investigation is crucial in addressing the central research question.

The results are presented and discussed in Chapter 4. Initially, there are two important sections involving each city investigated. *First*, there is an overview of socioeconomic and urbanistic data relevant to the analysis. This is *followed* by territorial, socioeconomic, and demographic information on community gardens (urban commons), gardeners, and experts (commoners) participating in the empirical research. Closing this chapter, there is a brief discussion of side results.

Chapter 5 has a section for the urban food sharing activities (commoning) related to each of the human rights to food's key components (food availability, accessibility, acceptability, and sustainability). Within each topic, the generic argument's structure is composed of an urban food sharing activity happening in both cities, the evidence (interview extract, data from public documents, theoretical framework, etc.) that each case realizes the activity, and a reason for the similitude within the same city, and between cities. Moreover, the presentation includes eventual differences within the same city and between cities, along with their possible reasoning. The arguments are also exploring the already mentioned sources of evidence.

Concluding the study, Chapter 6 is structured into two main components. The *first part* answers the research question and presents unexpected results. *Finally*, the study is concluded by prepositive guidelines for a policy that promotes and protects community gardens and the right to food.

References

Amato-Lourenco LF et al (2021) Building knowledge in urban agriculture: the challenges of local food production in Sao Paulo and Melbourne. Environ Dev Sustain 23(2):2785–2796. https://www.webofscience.com/wos/woscc/full-record/WOS:000520070800001. Accessed 16 May 2024

Ayres L (2008) Thematic coding and analysis. In: The SAGE encyclopedia of qualitative research methods, vol 1–2. University of Alberta, California, p 867. http://www.yanchukvladimir.com/docs/Library/Sage%20Encyclopedia%20of%20Qualitative%20Research%20Methods-%202008.pdf. Accessed 1 June 2024

Bardin L (2011) Content analysis. Edições, São Paulo

Beck V (2018) Iniciativas urbano sustentáveis no Rio de Janeiro: a experiência da horta carioca do Jardim Anil. In: Correia FA (ed) Direito da Regularização Fundiária Urbana Sustentável. Pesquisa, teoria e prática em torno da Lei Federal n. 13.465/2017. 1th edn. Editar, Juiz de Fora-MG, vol 1, pp 9–383. https://nepec-uerj.com.br/wp-content/uploads/2021/12/Direito-Regularizac%CC%A7a%CC%83o-Fundia%CC%81ria-Final-com-capa.pdf. Accessed 23 May 2024

Berlin. Government. Gemeinschaftsgärten in Berlin. https://www.berlin.de/special/sharing/urban-gardening/4763927-7854814-gemeinschaftsgaerten.html. Accessed 25 Mai 2024

Berlin. Government. Senatsverwaltung für Mobilität, Verkehr, Klimaschutz und Umwelt. Kleingärten. https://www.berlin.de/sen/uvk/natur-und-gruen/stadtgruen/gaertnern-in-der-stadt/kleingaerten/. Accessed 25 May 2024

Biazoti AR et al (2021) The Impact of COVID-19 on urban agriculture in Sao Paulo, Brazil. Sustainability, São Paulo, Brazil, 13(11). https://www.webofscience.com/wos/woscc/full-record/WOS:000660719100001. Accessed 16 May 2024

Brazil (2013) Constitution of the Federative Republic of Brazil of 1988. The Federal Senate, Special Secretariat for Printing and Publishing Undersecretariat of Technical Publications, Brasília. https://www2.senado.leg.br/bdsf/item/id/243334/. Accessed 25 Mai 2024

City Development Index. Index score. https://cdindex.net/world/list//. Accessed 25 May 2024

Colding J et al (2013) Urban Green Commons: Insights on urban common property systems. Glob Environ Chan 23(1):1039–1051. https://www.sciencedirect.com/science/article/abs/pii/S0959378013000800?via%3Dihub. Accessed 16 May 2024

Davies AR, Cretella A, Franck V (2019) Food sharing initiatives and food democracy: practice and policy in three European cities. Polit GovAnce 7(4):8–20. https://www.cogitatiopress.com/politicsandgovernance/article/view/2090. Accessed 26 May 2024

Davies AR, Legg R (2018) Fare sharing: interrogating the nexus of ICT, urban food sharing, and sustainability. Food, Culture & Society, p 18. https://www.tandfonline.com/doi/abs/https://doi.org/10.1080/15528014.2018.1427924. Accessed 16 May 2024
Davies A et al (2017) Making visible: interrogating the performance of food sharing across 100 urban areas. Geoforum 86:136–149. https://www.sciencedirect.com/science/article/pii/S00167 1851730266X. Accessed 1 June 2024
Davies A et al (2018) Fare sharing: interrogating the nexus of ICT, urban food sharing, and sustainability. Food Cult Soc 18. Available on: https://www.tandfonline.com/doi/abs/10.1080/15528014.2018.1427924. Accessed 16 May , 2024
Deflorian M (2022) Crowdsourcing infrastructures of green everyday life: how sustainable sharing, swapping and gardening initiatives in Vienna tackle the lack of transformative agency in eco-politics. Environmental politics. https://www.tandfonline.com/doi/full/10.1080/09644016.2022.2164212. Accessed 26 May 2024
Demo P (2012) Pesquisa e informação qualitativa: aportes metodológicos. Papirus, São Paulo, p 8
Diario do Rio (2021) Com 110 mil metros quadrados, Parque Madureira terá a maior horta urbana do mundo. https://diariodorio.com/com-110-mil-metros-quadrados-parque-madureira-tera-a-maior-horta-urbana-do-mundo/. Accessed 25 May 2024
Economist Impact (2022) Global Food Security Index Germany. https://impact.economist.com/sus tainability/project/food-security-index/explore-countries/germany. Accessed 25 May 2024
FAO (2017) Cities and local policies, key to eradicate hunger and eliminate food waste. https://www.fao.org/news/story/en/item/1045957/icode/. Accessed 4 Oct 2024
Ferrari E et al (2023) Towards an integrated garden. Gardeners of all types, unite! Urban Forestry & Urban Greening, vol 81. https://www.sciencedirect.com/science/article/pii/S16188 66723000286. Accessed 26 May 2024
Firmin M (2008) Themes. In: The SAGE encyclopedia of qualitative research methods, vol 1–2. University of Alberta, California, p 869. http://www.yanchukvladimir.com/docs/Library/Sage% 20Encyclopedia%20of%20Qualitative%20Research%20Methods-%202008.pdf. Accessed 01 June 2024
Fox-Kämper R et al (2028) Urban community gardens: an evaluation of governance approaches and related enablers and barriers at different development stages. Landsc Urban Plan 170(1):59–68. https://www.sciencedirect.com/science/article/pii/S01692046173 01615?via%3Dihub. Accessed 16 May 2024
Gil A (2008) Métodos e técnicas de pesquisa social. Atlas, São Paulo, p 27
Gobster PH, Stewart SI, Bengston DN (2004) The social aspects of landscape change: protecting open space under the pressure of development. Landsc Urban Plan 69:149–151. https://www.sci encedirect.com/journal/landscape-and-urban-planning/vol/69/issue/2. Accessed 23 May 2024
Göttl I, Penker M (2020) Institutions for collective gardening: a comparative analysis of 51 urban community gardens in anglophone and German-speaking countries. Int J Commons 14(1):30–43. https://thecommonsjournal.org/articles/10.5334/ijc.961. Accessed 16 May 2024
Guttmann A (2023) Plateformes de développement urbain, villes de la connaissance et développement durable: l'économie politique des biens communs urbains dans le contexte du changement climatique. https://theses.hal.science/tel-04160619/document. Accessed 13 Sept 2024
Halder S (2017) Gemeinsam die Hände dreckig machen: Aktionsforschungen im aktivistischen Kontext urbaner Gärten und kollektiver Kartierungen. Dissertation an der Freien Universität Berlin. https://katalog.dnb.de/EN/resource.html?hit=2&t=gemeinsam+Landwirtschaft+&fD=fmt.hss&key=all&sp=dnb&th=5&tk=F83EFEEC49340E77BD8177FD0B844C927AD1 7C35&pr=0&sortA=bez&sortD=-dat&v=plist. Accessed 23 May 2024
IBGE. Prévia da população calculada com base nos resultados do Censo Demográfico 2022 até 25 de dezembro de 2022. https://ftp.ibge.gov.br/Censos/Censo_Demografico_2022/Previa_da_Populacao/RJ_POP2022.pdf. Accessed 25 May 2024
Jackisch J (2012) Cultivating well-being. A study on community gardening and health in Berlin and Paris. Master thesis. Department of Medical and Health Sciences, Health

and Society, Linköpings University. http://liu.diva-portal.org/smash/record.jsf?pid=diva2%3A579216&dswid=-4110. Accessed 16 May 2024

Karge T (2015) Neue urbane Landwirtschaft: Eine theoretische Verortung und Akteursanalyse der Initiative Himmelbeet im Berliner Wedding. Universitätsverlag der TU Berlin, Berlin. https://d-nb.info/1156274923/34. Accessed 23 May 2024

Lakato E (2023) Fundamentos de Metodologia Científica. 9rd edn. Atlas, São Paulo, p 202

Landman T, Silverman BW (2019) Globalization and modern slavery. Polit GovAnce 7(4):275–290. https://www.cogitatiopress.com/politicsandgovernance/article/view/2233. Accessed 26 May 2024

Lima C (2019) Agriculturas na cidade do Rio de Janeiro: dicotomias e as especificidades da agricultura urbana. Dissertação (Mestrado em Desenvolvimento Territorial e Políticas Públicas) – Seropédica, Instituto de Ciências Sociais Aplicadas, Universidade Federal Rural do Rio de Janeiro, p 119 et seq. https://tede.ufrrj.br/jspui/bitstream/jspui/5596/2/2019%20-%20Caren%20Freitas%20de%20Lima.pdf. Accessed 23 May 2024

Lucena F (2021) Mais de 2 milhões de pessoas estão em situação de pobreza extrema no estado do RJ. Diário do Rio de Janeiro. https://impact.economist.com/sustainability/project/food-security-index/explore-countries/brazil. Accessed 25 May 2024

Magalhães, Mariano J. (2021) Hortas comunitárias in the favelas of Rio de Janeiro: how new i deas are adopted and spread across communities. In: TRAPANI, F. et al. (ed.) Advanced studies in efficient environmental design and city planning. Cham: Springer International Publishing. Available on: https://link.springer.com/chapter/10.1007/978-3-030-65181-7_21. Accessed 20 May 2024

Mayrhofer R (2018) Co-creating community gardens on untapped terrain – lessons from a transdisciplinary planning and participation process in the context of municipal housing in Vienna. Local Environ 23(12):1207–1224. https://sci-hub.hkvisa.net/10.1080/13549839.2018.1541345. Accessed 16 May 2024

Milan (2019) Urban food policy pact. Berlin signature. https://www.milanurbanfoodpolicypact.org/wp-content/uploads/2020/12/GOV-Berlin_2019.pdf. Accessed 8 Apr 2024

Morley J (2014) Academic Phrasebank. The University of Manchester, Manchester. https://graduate.iupui.edu/doc/support/gmc/Academic-Phrasebank.pdf. Accessed 8 Oct 2024

Nagib G, Nakamura AC (2020) Urban agriculture in the city of Sao Paulo: New spatial transformations and ongoing challenges to guarantee the production and consumption of healthy food. Global food security-agriculture policy economics and environment, vol 26. https://www.webofscience.com/wos/woscc/full-record/WOS:000603578100007. Accessed 16 May 2024

Ochoa J et al (2019) Sustainable Community gardens require social engagement and training: a users' needs analysis in Europe. Sustainability 11(14). https://www.mdpi.com/2071-1050/11/14/3978. Accessed 16 May 2024

Pernes FG, Oliveira AJ, Cipolla CM (2019) Design de serviços para inovação social e sustentabilidade: um estudo sobre as hortas comunitárias no Rio de Janeiro. Dissertação de Mestrado – Departamento de Artes e Design, Pontifícia Universidade Católica do Rio de Janeiro, Rio de Janeiro, p 131 et seq. https://www.maxwell.vrac.puc-rio.br/46572/46572.PDF. Accessed 16 May 2024

Poteete K, Janssen M, Ostrom E (2009) Working together: collective action, the commons, and multiple methods in practice. Princeton University Press, New Jersey, p 78

Prinzessinnengarten Kollektiv Berlin. Prinzessinnengarten Café & Restaurant. https://prinzessinnengarten-kollektiv.net/gartencafe/. Accessed 25 May 2024

Rekow L (2017) Urban Agriculture in the Manguinhos Favela of Rio de Janeiro: Laying the Groundwork for a Greener Future. In: Leal Filho W, Pociovalisteanu DM, Al-Amin A. (eds) Sustainable economic development. World Sustainability Series, Springer, Cham. https://link.springer.com/chapter/10.1007/978-3-319-45081-0_10. Accessed 16 May 2024

Rekow L (2015) Fighting insecurity: experiments in urban agriculture in the favelas of Rio de Janeiro. Field Actions Science Reports, vol 8. https://journals.openedition.org/factsreports/pdf/4009. Accessed 16 May 2024

Rio de Janeiro. Prefeitura. Hortas Cariocas. https://carioca.rio/servicos/hortas-cariocas/. Accessed 25 May 2024

Rogge N, Theesfeld I (2018) Categorizing Urban commons: community gardens in the Rhine-Ruhr Agglomeration, Germany. Int J Commons 12(2):255. https://www.jstor.org/stable/26511528. Accessed 28 Aug 2024

Rosol M (2012) Community volunteering as neoliberal strategy? green space production in Berlin. Antipode 44(1):239–257. https://onlinelibrary.wiley.com/doi/abs/10.1111/j.1467-8330.2011.00861.x. Accessed 26 May 2024

Silva SHC et al (2014) Plantas medicinais: tradições e saberes de mulheres de uma comunidade urbana do Rio de Janeiro, RJ, Brasil. https://www.arca.fiocruz.br/handle/icict/11037. Accessed 23 May 2024

Siniscalchi M (2020) Semeando o comum na metrópole contemporânea: as hortas urbanas comunitárias no Rio de Janeiro (RJ). Dissertação de Mestrado - Departamento de Geografia e Meio Ambiente, Pontifícia Universidade Católica do Rio de Janeiro, p 241 et seq. https://www.maxwell.vrac.puc-rio.br/49639/49639.PDF. Accessed 23 May 2024

Steuri B, Vignola G (2022) Towards productive and socio-natural urban landscapes: tapping urban agriculture's potential as a tool for sustainable development. Universitätsbibliothek der HafenCity Universität Hamburg (HCU), Hamburg. https://repos.hcu-hamburg.de/bitstream/hcu/650/2/2022-06-01_steuri-bettina_vignola-gionatan_masterarbeit.pdf. Accessed 23 May 2024

United Nations. Hortas Cariocas (Urban Green Gardens). https://sdgs.un.org/partnerships/hortas-cariocas-urban-green-gardens. Accessed 25 May 2024

Véron O (2023) 'We're Just an ambulance at the bottom of the cliff': Strategies and (a)politics of change in Berlin's community food spaces. Environ Plan A: Econ Space. https://journals.sagepub.com/doi/10.1177/0308518X231158101. Accessed 26 May 2024

Viriato M (2020) Semeando o comum na metrópole contemporânea: as hortas urbanas comunitárias no Rio de Janeiro (RJ). Dissertação de Mestrado - Departamento de Geografia e Meio Ambiente, Pontifícia Universidade Católica do Rio de Janeiro, p 241 et seq. https://www.maxwell.vrac.puc-rio.br/49639/49639.PDF. Accessed 16 May 2024

Visoni C, Nagibi G (2019) Reappropriating urban space through community gardens in Brazil. Field Actions Sci Rep 20:88–91. https://journals.openedition.org/factsreports/5778. Accessed 16 May 2024

Wegelin E, Borgman K (1995) Options for municipal interventions in urban poverty alleviation. Environ Urban 7(2):131–152. https://journals.sagepub.com/doi/pdf/10.1177/095624789500700219. Accessed 4 Oct 2024

Zanotto LC (2016) Semeando o almoço na laje: manual de implementação de hortas urbanas em comunidades de baixa renda, uma alternativa frente a problemas de desigualdade social. (Dissertação) Programa de Pós-Graduação em Práticas em Desenvolvimento Sustentável. Universidade Federal Rural do Rio de Janeiro. https://tede.ufrrj.br/handle/jspui/1397. Accessed 23 May 2024

Chapter 2
Precedents and the Current Crises of Urban Food and Land

2.1 The Space for Agriculture During the Urban Expansion: From Common to Private Land

The city is the product of human existence at a certain historical time. Since the **Neolithic** (3,500 BC–3,000 BC) and its agricultural revolution in Europe, the development of techniques and the social and natural conditions of the work are a few reasons that allowed the growth of food production and expansion of territorial occupations and invasions worldwide leading to the current agriculture.[1] Also, "the beginnings of food production represent a strategic shift in human behavior, towards the manipulation of the soil environment and through an influence on the composition of plant populations grown in that soil, via preferential seeding and tending of one or a few species."[2] This **agricultural revolution** potentially started with crops in vegetable gardens near the dwellings, which had already been deforested and were fertilized with domestic waste or on land recently inundated by river floods.[3] With increased

[1] "Agriculture is the most comprehensive word used to denote the many ways in which crop plants and domestic animals sustain the global human population by providing food and other products. The English word agriculture derives from the Latin *ager* (field) and *colo* (cultivate) signifying, when combined, the Latin *agricultura*: field or land tillage. But the word has come to subsume a very wide spectrum of activities that are integral to agriculture and have their own descriptive terms, such as cultivation, domestication, horticulture, arboriculture, and vegeculture, as well as forms of livestock management such as mixed crop-livestock farming, pastoralism, and transhumance. Also agriculture is frequently qualified by words such as incipient, proto, shifting, extensive, and intensive, the precise meaning of which is not self-evident. Many different attributes are used too to define particular forms of agriculture, such as soil type, frequency of cultivation, and principal crops or animals. The term agriculture is occasionally restricted to crop cultivation excluding the raising of domestic animals, although it usually implies both activities." Harris and Fuller (2014). The discussion in this book aligns with this comprehensive interpretation, but excludes the animal's creation.

[2] Harris and Fuller. op. cit.

[3] Mazoyer and Roudart (2010, p. 131).

F. Jardim, *Right to Food in Community Gardens*, LITES - Legal Issues in Transdisciplinary Environmental Studies 6,
https://doi.org/10.1007/978-3-032-19612-5_2

needs, the agricultural area required more space, so the land occupation was *divided into spaces* with different functions, such as housing, agriculture (especially using the slash-burn system), animal husbandry, religion, and military defense.[4] Then, the past brought two important ways of city development and view that influenced the world into how it is nowadays.

During Greek Classical **Antiquity**, the agricultural revolution was related to the cultivation of cereals using the scarifier plow for the most superficial layer of soil.[5] The *polis* (city-state) represents a unity of three zones: private areas (occupied by the dwelling houses), sacred areas (temples of the gods), and public areas (intended for political meetings, commerce, theater, and sports games).

Regarding property, according to Aristotle, the moral, a reason for justice, would be found in the good of others, doing what is advantageous to others. This arises in the proportionality between the subjects' things and the perception of the good to others. This would be an integrated worldview of totality that seeks harmony.[6] Aristotle treated property as a requirement for the virtuous life of the citizen, an instrumental element for the development and performance of functions inherent to it (and not the functions of the owner), which must be acquired in a natural and non-commercial way. As for the property right, it has three combinations between the property and its use: (i) private property and **common use**, (ii) **common property** and private use, and (iii) **common property and use**.[7] His preference was for the first since the common property would stimulate negligence and generate discussions about the way things are distributed, while private property would serve as a stimulus to the dedication to self-love, friendship, generosity, and moderation. The reason is that without private property, individuals could not use it to benefit others to meet the needs of friends, partners, and strangers.[8]

Aristotle illustrated Sparta, where property ownership is individual, but its usage is commonly shared when needed. While every citizen possesses their property, a portion is designated for the benefit of friends and another piece for the benefit of all. Lastly, a third portion is reserved for personal use exclusively.[9] Thus, the good of the *polis* depended on a key element: the virtue of the citizen, an item inherent in property, since there would be no virtue without property, in the same way that there would be no property without virtue. Therefore, despite the intimate connection of home as an economic unit and the city, the unlimited commercial acquisition of the property would be incompatible with ethics and virtue-oriented political life. Consequently, private property depended on the common interest generated by education,[10] a task of the *polis*, and the laws, which must promote the "virtues of character, punishing, when necessary, the behaviors considered vile and exhorting people to obey righteousness,

[4] Benevolo (2001, p. 16).

[5] Mazoyer and Roudart, op. cit., p. 44.

[6] Aristotle (2001, p. 93).

[7] Aristotle (2002, pp. 19–31).

[8] Brito (2007, p. 73).

[9] Mota (2009, p. 14).

[10] Brito, op. cit., p. 88.

imposing the necessary correctives on those who deviate from it," because "only in the good and just city could men be good and righteous; and only good and righteous men are able to institute a good and just city."[11]

Throughout Roman Antiquity, the **activities associated with food production were expelled.**[12] In Roman Empire law (27 AC–1453), the classification of assets is highlighted, adopting elements of ownership differentiation to define the legal regime of protection. The first group, *res in patrimonio*, would be the things that make up the patrimony of a private individual. The second group, *res extra patrimonium,* was composed of goods that had no correspondence in exchange currency, so humans could not appropriate them because of the destination or material impossibility for this: (i) *res humani juris*, as the **common** things (air, sea), universal (forum, stadiums, theaters, in which the administrators are not owners) and public (things belonging to the State, public use); and the goods of divine law, (ii) *res divini juris,* such as sacred things (temples), religious things (tombs) and saints (city gates, walls).[13]

The commons were also noticed by Caio Júlio César (100 BC–44 BC) on barbarians' resources administration.[14]

Only on post-classical law (Diocletian until the death of Emperor Justinian, 565 AD), the property was the absolute right to use, enjoy, dispose, and claim the good. The exteriorization of the domain is a strong indication of the existence of the property, and the property in Rome would have an absolute, unlimited character, operable to other individuals, exclusive and perpetual, transmitted by tradition. Then, the right-holder could exclusively link the property to his interests, regardless of social or collective demand. The property was seen as the exclusive center of the entire system, turning it around the economic and legal order, which supported the characteristics of a person's strongest power over an object.[15]

Later, a remarkable phenomenon for the **medieval city** was the fall of the Roman Empire and the consequent dispersion of the inhabitants through the fields, where they could extract their sustenance supported by an **agricultural revolution** related to the cultivation in crop rotation of cereals with the use of a plow in the deepest layers of the soil.[16] Due to the barbaric invasions, the Roman lords abandoned the urban centers. They went to live on their properties in the countryside, forming rural centers and fostering the emergence of medieval fiefdoms. In them, other less wealthy Romans

[11] Mota, op. cit., p. 16.

[12] Benevolo, op. cit., p. 143.

[13] Verás (2008, p. 128).

[14] "None has a field restricted or owned by them, but the magistrates and the principals assign each year to the people and kindred, who live in common as much field space to plow, as and where it seems convenient, and oblige them in the following year to move to another part. There are many reasons given for this use, such as: – not to change, driven by habit, the warrior ardor for agriculture, not to seek to expand each one his field, the more powerful at the cost of the weaker, not to occupy themselves in constructions own to keep them from the cold and calm, not to give birth among them the ambition of money, whence factions and discords proceed, and to contain the plebs by a principle of equity, seeing each one equal in wealth to the most powerful." César (2006).

[15] Verás Neto, op. cit., p. 133; Wolkmer (2008).

[16] Mazoyer, Roudart, loc. cit.

sought protection and work on the land, but to do so, they should give the owner part of the production. The servile system of production came into force.[17] In the center of the field, there was the residence of the landowner (cathedral, abbey, castle), and in the extensions of land, there were the barns, stables, personal and administrator dwellings, and there was the hierarchy of lands in different centers (food production, religious, civil, and commercial). The land organization for agriculture used to have **common space**, and traditionally, there was soil **care** by rotation system to extend its use. Of the ancient cities, only ruins remained after the barbarian invasions and reconstructions. They are studied and visited but no longer function as part of the current city. However, many medieval towns are still inhabited and preserve original customs and traditions, with repercussions in the contemporary city, such as the London division between economic seat (city) and political seat (Westminster).[18]

In the Middle Ages, there was a general change in the paradigms of property established in Roman law. The domain was an overlay of rights between the overlord, the feudal lord, and the vassal, which depended on it because of the protection of the land against barbarian invasions. This shows that the subdivision of the land was also a matter of survival of the population since the feudal lord was responsible for the free people who worked there. However, this fact represented a legal uncertainty for the development of the economy since, in addition to the partition of the land, each feudal lord commanded, punished, and applied justice differently.[19] Consequently, landowning was an element of power and exploration on the property hierarchies.

Since the eleventh century, the social system was grounded on feudal lords (rich men), peasants (free farmers or enslaved people, taxpayers, the majority of the population), and clergy. The church was a holder of large amounts of land, with great religious influences, such as Saint Ambrose (337–397 AD) and Saint Augustine (354–430 AD). They promoted the adequacy of the individual initiative but condemned the abuses of property, underscoring the **social function**. In addition to them, Saint Thomas Aquino (1225–1274) resumed ancient Greek thought by considering that human nature acts for a purpose, such as **good to others**. Thus, the interest of the collective would be the greater end. To him, property is founded as a natural law, a rational guide to the human being, good, and justice.

Furthermore, Saint Thomas Aquino followed Aristotle's statement about the need for private property for the **common good** and for "guiding goods to order, efficiency, security, and peace, not disconnected from the instrumental values of modern freedom."[20] However, the legitimacy of the property remained on managing it according to the moral duty of common use: "Man should not have things outside as his own, but as **common**, in this sense that, willingly, each one **shares them with the needy people**."[21] It balances the powers of use in line with the community virtue, a true obligation characteristic of property. In the same space, thus, the public and

---

[17] Benevolo, op. cit., p. 252.

[18] Benevolo, op. cit., p. 256.

[19] Benevolo, loc. cit.

[20] Mota, op. cit., p. 21.

[21] Thomas of Aquino S.

the private coexist, the individual and the common interest, social, cultural, and ideological connotations that make it unique.[22] Following that, during Feudalism, part of the agricultural land and other resources such as forests and water were reserved for collective use. Around the twelfth and thirteenth centuries, the commons were institutionalized[23] as **rural** associations with collective representation and a system of decision.[24] This was possible due to different reasons. Among them are population growth, the need for new social organization forms,[25] and resource depletion (wood and grazing area).[26]

In the Middle Ages, cities started to grow the traits of exchange centers, such as the merchant settlements of **Berlin** (a city officially founded in 1237) and Cologne. With the masses of artisans and merchants, the town grew, forming the suburbs larger than the original core and forcing the expansion of the walls of the villages. Consequently, the physical frontiers and concepts of urban and rural changed, and**food production was pushed away from urban areas again.**

The artisanal and mercantile population (bourgeois) is associated, developed, and strengthened as a public power guiding personal and economic freedom, judicial and administrative autonomy, and more balanced taxation. The urgent need for defense, the scarcity of resources, the lack of specialists, and the new spirit of freedom formed spontaneous, carefree urbanism and variable constructions. With the European economic renaissance (tenth century), agricultural production increased, and industry and trade moved to a new level. Maritime cities such as Venice, Genoa, and Pisa gained prominence as shopping centers.[27]

Also, new cities were formed for economic and military reasons, but urban growth was cut in the mid-fourteenth century by the plague and the decline in economic activity. In general, in medieval cities, unlike the ancient cities, public spaces do not form contiguous and separate areas but rather a **common**, complex, and unitary space: the result of an **equilibrium** between public law and private interests to regulate the various centers. Unlike antiquity, in which Athens, Rome, and Constantinople deserved to stand out, in the medieval period, hundreds of median cities appeared (300 to 600 hectares of surface and 50,000 to 150,000 inhabitants), such as Milan, Florence, Barcelona, Paris, and London.[28]

---

[22] Coulanges (1987).

[23] De Moor (2008, pp. 179–212).

[24] Le Goff (2007).

[25] De Moor, op. cit.

[26] Brakensiek (2002, pp. 225–245).

[27] Benevolo, op. cit., pp. 255–256.

[28] Benevolo, op. cit., pp. 259–263.

2.2 The Economic Value of Land and Food

Later, **modern cities** had population growth, redistribution in the territory (migration from the countryside to the town), and technological innovation, which diversified the goods and services of agriculture, industry, and tertiary activities. There was the construction of toll roads, railways, and the emergence of the steamboat, making the scope of the movement of goods wider. The housing of the countryside, which had plenty of space around with multiple functions (living, animal breeding, space for children), was replaced by a place in the city with no space for outdoor practices and cramped houses with low-quality materials, with brick walls and a firmer roof, but still with primitive or non-existent furniture and service. The construction on the soil was seen as a temporary manufactured good without incorporation into the land. Then, replaceable by another construction. It means that **the land started to have economic value** according to location, demand, etc. At that time, traditional forms of public control of the built environment were devalued, such as urban plans and regulations. In addition, there are economic teachings of limitation of public intervention in social and urban life. The elites explored the freedom of private initiative in the real estate field.[29]

The Renaissance (fourteenth to seventeenth century) is an important mark of the beginning of the Modern Age since Humanism was established, when the human being is the center of philosophy, arts, politics, etc. (anthropocentric view), surpassing the medieval theocentric position that legitimized the power of kings. During this period, scientific discoveries opened room for the **first agricultural revolution of the modern ages**, from the sixteenth to the nineteenth century. It was a period based on polyculture focused on cereal farming associated with animal husbandry and without crop rotation.[30] The productivity growth followed and supported the development of industrialization and overseas expeditions, searching for more resources and consumers. This generated **exploration of natural wealth** and charted the course of history in many areas, especially in Africa, Australia, and the Americas, where pre-existing agricultural systems were replaced by very specialized systems (sugar cane, cotton, coffee, cocoa, palm trees for oil extraction, banana, etc.).

With the most intense colonization, the metropolis limited and controlled administratively, economically, and politically the urban potential of the colony and the role of the rural, such as in **Rio de Janeiro** (officially founded in 1565). The metropolis and the median cities, such as Paris, grew up and made urban changes, intensifying the **remoteness of rural activities to give space for houses and industries**. For example, the periphery was developed, an initiative free of luxury neighborhoods, poor neighborhoods, industries, deposits, and social and architectural homogeneity.[31]

With the emergence of Absolutism, the organizational forms related to commons suffered more and more pressure to "intensify economic production and centralize

[29] Benevolo, op. cit., p. 552.

[30] Mazoyer and Roudart, loc. cit.

[31] Cruz (2019, p. 18).

the management of resources with the purpose of enriching the royalty."[32] After the Absolutism, the Liberal State regarded the commons as a type of property on the brink of vanishing,[33] primarily because they were seen as a contributor to rural poverty, often attributed to the absence of unrestricted entrepreneurial activities.

In the eighteenth century, the ideals of the Enlightenment intellectual and philosophical movement fundamental rights were formed. However, there were different reasoning lines related to **private property**. From one point of view, for Voltaire, it was necessary to respect the accumulation of property, even if it generated inequalities and luxury.[34] From another perspective, for Montesquieu, ostentation and luxury corrupted virtue and compromised the idea of equality from a democratic government,[35] and for Rousseau, private property generated **inequalities** between men and ruined the political body.[36] Following this view, Adam Smith pointed out that the main source of wealth was work and not the earth. For him, "whenever there is much property, there is great **inequality**." He illustrated that "for every rich man, there will be at least five hundred poor men" and that "the property of a few presupposes the indigence of many."[37]

In the **Late Modern Period**, in the eighteenth century, the French Declaration of the Rights of Man and the Citizen (1789) was responsible for reinforcing the absolute and exclusive character of **private property** in Roman law, as observed in Article 2 ("The purpose of every political association is the preservation of the natural and unenforceable rights of man. These rights are freedom, property, security, and resistance to oppression"), as well as in words "inviolable" and "sacred" of Art. 17 ("As property is an inviolable and sacred right, none of it may be deprived, except when legally proven public need requires it and on condition of just and indemnification.").[38]

In 1804, the Napoleonic Code (Civil Code) became an important element of Roman and French inspiration that contributed to law beyond its jurisdiction (France), even reaching **Brazilian** law. With this legal instrument, property rights were categorized as a branch of civil law. The Napoleonic Code followed the principles of the French Revolution (1789), from which the liberal bourgeoisie, who wanted to destroy the ancient privileges of the clergy and nobility, emerged victorious. Thus, he was responsible for eliminating the frequent exemptions and other benefits given by kings to feudal lords. Consequently, the remnants of the feudal monarchies declined in favor of strengthening the absolutist states. There was an excessive preoccupation with **safeguarding individual property**, which became accessible to anyone and

[32] Relly (2022).

[33] Alfonsi et al. (2023, pp. 294–330).

[34] Beuchot (1833, p. 122).

[35] Montesquieu (2024).

[36] Rosseau (1754).

[37] Smith (2014).

[38] France (1789).

with equal treatment. It was a right considered sacred because it was the result of the liberation of the French lands of the former feudal lords.[39]

With the semantic evolution and causing sensitive changes in the content of the proprietary law, in 1851, Auguste Comte, followed by León Duguit, stated that property, although private, had a **social function**. Forty years later, in the papal encyclical *Rerum Novarum*, Pope Leo XVIII defended the thesis (1891) that "private and personal property is, for man, of natural law."[40]

Despite the initial statement of the social function of the property, after the French Revolution and the First Industrial Revolution, the modern city was consolidated as a liberal city, a **disordered and uninhabitable environment**, which can be defined as

> Superposition of many unregulated and non-coordinated public and private initiatives. Individual freedom, required as a condition for the development of the industrial economy, proves insufficient to regulate the transformations of construction and urbanism produced precisely by economic development. The poor classes suffer more directly from the inconveniences of the industrial city, but the rich classes cannot think of running away from them altogether.[41]

For instance, there were epidemics, such as cholera, in 1830, when rulers were forced to correct hygienic defects and begin the clash with freedom of initiative. France, **Germany,** and England abandoned the thesis of non-state intervention in life, replacing it with other mechanisms of control of the new city model, in which there is coordination between business people, land owners, and state participation in large public works.

The liberal city became post-liberal, allowing the reorganization of European cities, such as Paris, and the foundation of colonial cities worldwide. This model is marked by the management agreement on urban spaces: the public administration deals with the essential scan for the city functioning, such as streets, squares, railways, aqueducts, sewers, gas, electricity, telephone, etc. and behaving as landowners when building schools, and hospitals, for example, while the real estate managed the land served by this infrastructure. The post-liberal model is also characterized by the dependence of public or private owners on the use of urbanized land, in which the administration's influence is primarily indirect, exerted through regulations that impose limitations on building measurements to public spaces and establish relationships between adjacent buildings. However, it is important to note that the owners **retain all the financial gains from urban development** (such as increased property value), preventing the administration from recovering the funds invested in constructing public services.

During the nineteenth and twentieth centuries, the "free" worker (without a permanent bond to the ground as in medieval cities, getting distance from nature and food production) was within an open market, including the labor market, resulting in two main consequences.

---

[39] Souza (2004, p. 39).

[40] Leão XIII (1891).

[41] Benevolo, op. cit., p. 567.

With a Marxist basis, the first consequence is the "metabolic rift." The idea concerns the relationships between the capitalist economic system and the natural environment. In summary, there is an ecological imbalance between how society[42] produces and consumes resources and the environment's capacity to regenerate and sustain these resources. During the process of pursuing economic growth and profit, there are ruptures due to the **exploitation and depletion of natural resources in an unsustainable manner**, and the outcomes are environmental degradation, including climate change, biodiversity loss, soil mortification, and pollution, and the disconnection of society from natural metabolism.[43] The metabolic rift turns people, their power, and nature into **commodities**.[44]

The second result is the **urban population growth and spread**. The suburbs, a mix of countryside and urban areas, were driven to areas increasingly far from urban centers. Public parks (artificially bringing the country's experience) and popular housing built with public money arise, but without solving the serious problems of excessive density in the center, such as the precariousness of housing. The city's growth brought the overlap of the medieval town and open space for industries and cars. Indeed, the modern city, industrial and capitalist, was focused on factories (fueled by the consistent domination of the colonies and concentrated in the same place given the emergence of steam), mining, railways, buildings, and real estate speculation.

Consequently, agriculture was **again pushed away from the urban areas**.[45] The scientific advances of the second industrial revolution enabled the **second agricultural revolution of the modern period**: "motorization (explosion engines or electric motors, tractors and increasingly powerful automotive devices), large mechanization (increasingly more complex and efficient machines) fossil-fuel-powered; and chemification (mineral fertilizers and treatment products)."[46] The aim was to produce specialized agricultural products that would bring more financial benefits and support industrialization.[47] Nevertheless, this vigorous progression of the Second Agricultural Revolution was not a general and harmonious development process.[48] Therefore, the city represented a territory of many social problems and an increased **imbalance** between work activities, **agriculture**, commerce, religion, arts, and fun. This was a division of the space as it has already figured in the classical and feudal cities.

---

[42] "Counter to common sense notions, society is not the sum of all individuals and social groups, or of their actions. In theoretical terms, it is more adequately conceived as a structured totality of relations between people, other people and extra-human nature, and since those relations only exist through their constant practical (re)production, ought to be seen as the dynamic outcome of processes of 'societalization.' Eversberg et al. (2022, pp. 389–419).

[43] Foster (1999, pp. 366–405).

[44] Angelis (2007, p. 152).

[45] Mazoyer and Roudart, op. cit., p. 508.

[46] Mazoyer and Roudart, op. cit., p. 420.

[47] Benevolo, op. cit., p. 574.

[48] Mazoyer and Roudart, op. cit., p. 421.

2.3 The Social and Functional Division of the Space, Urban Vacant Land, Favelas and Urban Communities

The commons played a "significant role in shaping modern **Germany**"[49] and fostering "the communal organization as an inherent characteristic of Germanic peoples."[50] Then, the commons were kept alive as part of German agrarian politics until the end of World War II. This can be noticed even as part of the immigration process. For instance, in the South of Brazil, original agents of commons (such as Indigenous and other traditional communities) were substituted by German (and other European nationalities) collective forms of rural soil use.[51] Subsequently, interest in the commons dwindled,[52] and forms of communal land management gradually disappeared because of capitalist development.[53]

To better understand the urban crises generated by the growing capitalist accumulation of urban space, especially in the **post-war period**,[54] it is necessary to investigate economic-social relations (the difference in classes) regarding land. One of the possibilities is through the theory of urban land income.[55] It is an economic operator that produces and reproduces urban space's social division.[56] They are crucial

[49] Brakensiek, op. cit.

[50] Silva (2006).

[51] Relly, op. cit.

[52] Relly, op. cit., p. 38.

[53] Engels (2003, pp. 147–163).

[54] Lefebvre (1999).

[55] Originated from the general theory of land income in the works of David Ricardo (Principles of Political Economy, 1817), Karl Marx, and Friedrich Engels (The Capital, vol. III, 1895). Despite focusing on rural areas, Marx briefly analyzed the role of income in urban land for construction, and it would be characterized as: "1) by the decisive influence of localization on differential income; 2) by the owner's exploitation of the progress of social development to which nothing contributes and in which nothing risks; 3) by the predominance of the monopoly price. Urban land income would be high by the rapid and intense population growth in large cities, and by the consequent growing need for housing resulting therefrom and by the implementation of fixed capital that would be incorporated into the land (such as buildings, railways, highways, warehouses, manufacturing and commercial establishments, docks, etc.). In high-growth cities, what would be the main object of speculation in the real estate sector would not be the property built, but the land income charged by the owners." Botelho (2010, pp. 24–45). Marx (1989). Other applications of urban land income can be classified as follows: "a) Absolute Income: results from the difference between the market price and the prices of the housing production, b) Differential Income I: generated by the supplementary profit obtained by the production of housing (sometimes identical) under different conditions of accessibility and reduced expenses, c) Differential Income II: generated by urban zoning, enabling certain areas to demand more investments - here understood as work - than others, because they need, according to the demands of capital, to be more luxurious and/or larger and better equipped. For Differential Income II, we consider the price of constant spatial production, where the increase in income goes parallel to the development of the mode of production, and d) Monopoly Income: is the determinant of urban land price measures, achieved through monopoly prices, resulting in the power conferred on those who own the land in establishing prices." Gonzales (1985, pp. 93–114), Lipietz (1988, p. 209), and Souza (1994, p. 257).

[56] Oliveira (2005).

parameters for determining the pricing of urban soil and justifying the allocation of land uses. They enable the owners of urban land to appropriate a portion of the appreciation generated by the social production of urban space. The appropriation amount depends on the scarcity produced by the social investment made and to make around the property, the significant impact of the localization factor, the predominance of the monopoly price, and the potential uses and competitors for land use dictated by the market and urban legislation.[57]

Two agents are crucial in this process: the private sector and the state. The private sector pressures the government to invest in already well-equipped places. This leads to an expansion of income derived from urban land in these localities, causing an increase in land pricing (land valuation in cities). A significant portion of the accumulated urban land income is appropriated by those who have ownership or control over the properties, even if they have not directly contributed to the land valuation process from which they will benefit.[58] As another repercussion, the state's action in different forms: "through fiscal imposition; investment in urban infrastructure works, equipment and improvements; the instance of law, in the form of urban plans and laws [protecting private property]; and action as a real estate agent."[59]

These factors conflict with the interests of those who seek the city as a **use-value** (determined by its usefulness) and not as an **exchange-value** (possibility of buying and selling transmitted by the commodity).[60] **With the prevalence of the exchange-value, the city is transformed into a commodity**. Understanding this is relevant because commodities can be sold at prices necessary to realize the full value and surplus value embedded in them. Consequently, "the commodification of urban land as a private capital impedes the right to the city as a social good."[61] During commodification,[62] **the market price of the land will constitute an effective mechanism of spatial organization** where the land income submits access to land in urban space at a value higher than its production cost,[63] even when it means no use at all (vacant urban land).

Nowadays, the city is a production and consumption center where almost no space is left without the market's interference.[64] Indeed, it has a commercial function and is a commerce insert in a local, regional, or global competition with other cities to attract more people and investments. Limited resources and conditions generate a territory of social, political, environmental, and economic daily conflicts.[65] From this standpoint, private property keeps guiding the wish to individually enjoy a status or have more access to infrastructure and services.

---

[57] Santos (1982, p. 43).

[58] Cruz, op. cit.

[59] Barreto (2013, p. 88).

[60] Maricato (1997) and Harvey (1980).

[61] Pagani et al. (2015, pp. 167–183).

[62] Basu (2018, p. 241).

[63] Cruz, op. cit., p. 34.

[64] Rolnik (2004).

[65] Hall (2004, pp. 117–132).

Nonetheless, considering the soil's irreproducibility and less available privileged spaces, the unparalleled land creates market conditions to **increase capital accumulation** (either through speculation and real estate development or through the circulation of capitalized income in the financial market such as mortgage and real estate securities),[66] which is often connected to production and maintenance of **urban vacant land** until a more profitable use is possible (land financial speculation). This could consist of the disruption of the public land's social functions.[67]

The vacant land concept has been developed since the early decade of 1940,[68] and so far, there is no unique international categorization of its types. However, the literature recently treated them, for example, in the United States of America, as post-industrial, derelict, unattended with vegetation, natural, and related transportation. Another classification is the one regarding Chinese cities. It stated the typology of vacant land as wild grassland, wild grass mixed with shrub and tree land, bare land, abandoned building mixed with rough grassland, abandoned building combined with empty land, and left building land.[69]

In brief, **urban vacant land** can be developed in three ways: **1. Unused land**, the one that is not currently in full use. They may be disused or, in the case of constructions, in a state of disrepair, possibly on the verge of ruin or already in ruins. Conversely, if the land's condition does not render it unfeasible for use, it is classified as "closed;" **2. Underutilized land** is the one that still has potential for use and/or occupancy, even if such use is partial or temporary. However, their usage falls below the parameters defined by applicable laws, such as the Master Plan or construction codes. The state of conservation of these flatlands may or may not be compromised, but due to their partial utilization, they are typically considered as partially closed; and **3. Unbuilt land** is completely unoccupied parcels of land with no structures. They can be further classified as closed or abandoned based on their current status.[70]

In addition to being associated with land financial speculation, urban vacant land can be attributed to various socioeconomic factors. Among them, there is population decline, the rapid expansion of cities, economic globalization, deindustrialization, suburbanization, inadequate investment, an oversupply of land, haphazard land division, irregularly shaped land parcels, and **environmental concerns**,[71] such as stormwater volume retention,[72] and bee's conservation in cities.[73]

Vacant land can be a problem related to multiple dimensions. From the economic perspective, it could be associated with maintenance costs, not collected taxes, and lower surrounding property value. From an ecological view, irregular waste deposits,

---

[66] Botelho, op. cit., p. 29.

[67] Moura (2017, p. 353 et seq) and Borde (2006, p. 14).

[68] Emerson (1942).

[69] Song et al. (2020, pp. 669–687).

[70] Jardim (2018), Clemente (2012), Borde, op. cit., and Sousa (2010).

[71] Song, op. cit.

[72] Kelleher et al. (2020).

[73] Turo (2020, pp. 58–69).

soil contamination, and loss of green areas.[74] Moreover, it reinforces the **dispute of urban land uses,**[75] generates the **fragmentation and hierarchization of urban land functions** (commercial, industrial, residential, etc.),[76] and **socio-spatial segregation.**[77] Another result is the city peripheralization[78]: "opposition between center and periphery: the richest social classes are established in the most central areas, equipped with infrastructure and with higher prices; the poor classes are relegated to the peripheries, distant and devoid of equipment and services,"[79] such as basic sanitation systems, electricity, mobility, etc. In some cases, these problems have territorial expansion to other municipalities, becoming a common issue in metropolitan areas.[80] Moreover, there is the "separation between the areas occupied by residences of the popular classes and by residences of the most privileged classes."[81] The non-deterministic result is a "significant influence in the **social interactions** that form the basis of any political mobilization."[82] Thus, the **socio-environmental use of urban vacant land is urgent.**

The continuous urban population growth without urban planning and mismanagement resulted in environmental degradation,[83] generated cities with circulation problems, **without adequate green spaces and leisure**[84] for the entire population, in addition to "ineffectiveness or even the non-existence of an urban policy that addressed the housing needs of the low-income population."[85] Consequently, the urban poor population is forced to distribute itself in inadequate places, environmentally unsafe, and without basic infrastructure, the **slums**. It is "mainly through informal shelter and informal income-generation strategies."[86] The slums can be seen from two *generic* perspectives. The first of which is positive:

> Slums are the first stopping point for immigrants – they provide the low-cost and only affordable housing that will enable the immigrants to save for their eventual absorption into urban society. As the place of residence for **low-income employees**, slums keep the wheels of the city turning in many different ways. The majority of slum dwellers in developing country cities earn their living from informal sector activities located either within or outside slum areas, and many informal entrepreneurs operating from slums have clientele extending to the rest of the city. Most slum dwellers are people […] living within the context of extensive urban poverty and formal unemployment. Slums are also places in which the vibrant mixing of different cultures frequently results in new forms of artistic expression. **Out of unhealthy,**

---

[74] Németh and Langhorst (2014, pp. 143–150).

[75] Jaramillo (2010, p. 178).

[76] Teixeira et al. (2022).

[77] Botelho, loc. cit.

[78] Cruz, op. cit., p. 34; Pagani, op. cit., p. 167–183.

[79] Teixeira, op. cit.

[80] Santos et al. (2020).

[81] Teixeira, op. cit.

[82] Oliveira (1996, p. 72).

[83] Biehl (2017).

[84] Barros (2019).

[85] Santos and Cruz (2018).

[86] United Nations Human Settlements Programme (2003).

> **crowded, and often dangerous environments can emerge cultural movements and levels of solidarity** unknown in the suburbs of the rich. Against all odds, slum dwellers have developed economically rational and innovative shelter solutions for themselves.[87]

Nevertheless, the negative side stands:

> Slums have the most intolerable urban housing conditions, which frequently include tenure insecurity; lack of basic services, especially water and sanitation; inadequate and sometimes unsafe building structures; overcrowding; and location on hazardous land. In addition, slum areas have high concentrations of **poverty** and social and economic deprivation, including broken families, unemployment, and economic, physical, and social exclusion. Slum dwellers have limited access to credit and formal job markets due to stigmatization, discrimination, and geographic isolation. Slums are often recipients of the city's nuisances, including industrial effluent and noxious **waste**, and the only land accessible to slum dwellers is often **fragile, dangerous, or polluted – land that no one else wants**. People in slum areas suffer inordinately from water-borne diseases such as typhoid and cholera, as well as more opportunistic ones that accompany HIV/AIDS. Slum women – and the children they support – are the greatest victims of all. Slum areas are also commonly believed to be places with a high incidence of crime, although this is not universally true since slums with strong social control systems will often have low crime rates.[88]

Earth is believed to host over 250,000 slums, with the five largest metropolises in South Asia (Karachi, Mumbai, Delhi, Kolkata, and Dhaka) that accommodate a population exceeding 20 million residents.[89] Worldwide, they assume different names and forms, with distinction in the access to certain essential services. This land is "dangerous terrain that is not suitable for construction – very steep slopes, riverbanks, and flooded areas. Likewise, they settle in the deadly shadow of refineries, chemical industries, toxic waste dumps, or alongside railways and highways."[90]

In **Brazil**, they are represented under the concept of Favelas and Urban Communities. The concept is based on

> Predominance of households with degrees differentiated from legal insecurity of ownership; and at least one of the other criteria below: absence or incomplete and/or precarious provision of public services; predominance of buildings, streets and infrastructure that are usually self-produced and/or guided by urban and constructive parameters different from those defined by public bodies; and/or location in areas with restrictions on occupation defined by environmental or urban planning legislation.[91]

This includes irregular settlements called by "different names such as **favelas** [the term is probably related to an area named as a plant (*Cninodoscolus quercifolius*)],[92] *ocupações, comunidades, quebradas, grotas, baixadas, alagados, vilas, ressacas, mocambos, palafitas, loteamentos informais, vilas de malocas*, among

---

[87] United Nations Human Settlements Programme, loc. cit.

[88] United Nations Human Settlements Programme, loc. cit.

[89] Davis (2006, p. 202).

[90] Davis, op. cit.

[91] IBGE (2024).

[92] Filho (2011, pp. 33–48).

others."[93] In these places, "the growing socio-environmental injustice prevents or hinders the realization of human rights."[94]

For instance, in the case of **Rio de Janeiro**, they were established before the real estate market interests and the densification of urban land occupation following the slavery abolition (late 1880s)[95] and public policies as housing solutions especially based on economic motives,"[96] but also involving the ethnic factor. Then, the slums have a pattern of concentrating a group of low-income and majority Black people,[97] even nowadays.[98] As a worldwide phenomenon, the twentieth century was genetically characterized by verticalization and urban expansion. To develop this, the constructions resulted in vulnerability to displacement[99] and gentrification,[100] affecting more Black people.[101] Later, for economic reasons, the slums in the industrial Rio de Janeiro attracted migrants from Brazil's northern and northeastern areas,[102] confirming the above "first stopping point."[103] Further, the social segregation in Rio de Janeiro can be associated with fear and violence[104] due to a "situation marked by the activities of drug trafficking and the dangers and prohibitions arising from it"[105] and the consequences of police actions.[106]

Additionally, the cities were (re)organized according to rationalist or functionalist urbanism that influenced urban planning during the late nineteenth and early twentieth centuries, generally reinforcing the urban space division, fragmentation, and hierarchization. This period was particularly notable for introducing the Athens Charter in 1933, in which the private and public[107] urban property should attend collective interests regarding housing, work, leisure, and transportation.[108] This reinforced the **exclusion of food production as an urban social function**.

---

[93] IBGE (2024).

[94] Schonardie (2017, pp. 1363–1382).

[95] Oliveira (1996), op. cit., p. 74.

[96] Oliveira (1996), op. cit.

[97] Oliveira (2021, pp. 1–27).

[98] Oliveira (1996), op. cit.

[99] Figueira and Costa (2018, pp. 2143–2163), Lira (2017, pp. 1383–1932), and Oliveira (2023, p. 192 et seq).

[100] Oliveira (2016, p. 23 et seq).

[101] Oliveira (2023), op. cit.

[102] Oliveira (1996), op. cit.

[103] United Nations Human Settlements Programme, op. cit. p. 6.

[104] Wermuth and Campos (2022, pp. 2608–2636).

[105] Amoroso (2006, p. 164).

[106] Amoroso (2019, pp. 129–157).

[107] Moura (2017).

[108] Le Corbusier (1933).

2.4 The Re-Entry of Food Production to the City and Legal-Urbanistic Context After World Wars

Representing a step of agriculture's return to the city, the **allotment gardens** have been registered as a source of food since the end of the nineteenth century, especially during economic crises, such as the "garden of the poor" as **German** governmental strategy of using public vacant spaces to overcome the malnutrition of rural migrant families and unemployed people, instead of paying financial support. The vegetable gardens were also responsible for food security in the post-war period. The pioneer legal approach is from 1919, but in 1983 came the first federal law to approach the duties and rights related to allotment gardens in Germany.[109] The allotment gardens are part of the food security history and culture in Europe, such as in France (*salons du Pauvre*), Austria, and England. The same is valid for the United States of America (Victory Garden).[110] After the economic recovery of **Germany**, the remaining *Kleingarten* or *Schrebergarten* were mostly used as private (with some fees and fences) scape-places of the industrialized city,[111] and the special role of leisure for family and friends. Nowadays, they are more connected to leisure and environmental concerns. Food production is still part of the *Kleingarten*. However, a great potential for food production could be explored.[112]

The period after the World Wars increased the **Law** functionalization[113] by institutionalizing the crucial rights to guide the future of humanity on the Universal Declaration of Human Rights.[114] **Human Rights** can be understood as a rights' composition (not only in the Universal Declaration of Human Rights of 1948) to which every person, independently of jurisdiction, must contribute and enjoy equally without discrimination as a common standard to establish freedom, justice, and peace in the world.[115] They are inalienable, indivisible, interdependent, and interrelated. Human Rights must be promoted, recognized, and protected by the rule of law. They are

> a common standard of achievement for all peoples and all nations, to the end that every individual and every organ of society, keeping this Declaration constantly in mind, shall strive by teaching and education to promote respect for these rights and freedoms and by progressive measures, national and international, to secure their universal and effective recognition and observance, both among the peoples of Member States themselves and among the peoples of territories under their jurisdiction.[116]

The freedom mentioned above reveals a crucial part of their importance.[117] However, the concept is not unique. There is a complex evolution and involution

---

[109] Germany (1983).

[110] Stoetzer (2018, pp. 295–323).

[111] Nilsen (2016, pp. 124–125).

[112] Ferrari et al. (2023).

[113] Bobbio (2007, p. 92).

[114] United Nations (1948).

[115] Sarlet (2022).

[116] United Nations (1948), op. cit.

[117] Sen (2004).

of theories and practices in time and variation of society in a theological, philosophical, and juridical position. For example, in July 2022, access to a clean, healthy, and sustainable environment was declared a human right.[118] Thus, investigating human rights is complex in multidisciplinary and updated debates. For instance, the concept of human rights is not always understood, which triggers contestation between pro- and anti-human rights actors.

Moreover, international relations are also affected by conflicts and humanitarian crises connected to the violation of rights. When a violation happens, responsibility can be required in the legal system to establish adequate legal protection for individuals and vulnerable groups. This involves creation, adaptation, extinction, and application of laws from local to international level. In addition, it is necessary to develop and implement policies, monitoring systems, and laws. When the implemented instruments are insufficient, discriminatory, non-participative, or fail to protect people, it could be considered a transgression of human rights. In addition, Human Rights are an abstract and complex director for good governance that people must know and discover how to apply[119] in the cities because a city "must be an area for the realization of all human rights and fundamental freedoms, ensuring the dignity and collective well-being of all people, on a level playing field, equity, and justice, as well as full respect for the social production of habitat."[120] The concept of social rights guarantee was adopted by Italy (1948), **Germany** (1949), Spain (1978), Chile (1981), and **Brazil** (1988).

In the last decades, Human Rights critics have developed a sense of cultural bias and imperialism,[121] overcoming social and economic issues,[122] complex application of universalism,[123] and limited protection.[124] Consequently, limitations and challenges to Human Rights were exposed. Naturally, not all negative aspects have been solved so far. Still, their continuous refining is an ongoing process to experiment with better ways to address the world's diverse social and environmental needs. This reasoning led to urban social and legal organizations against violating rights and multidisciplinary investigations on urban land use. This has given rise to various concepts, including the **Right to the City.** This emerged in 1968 when Henry Lefebvre proposed that the city should be shaped by democratic decisions made collectively by its inhabitants. It should serve as a space for social interaction and the expression of creativity.[125]

As with other conceptual perspectives, the Right to the City also can focus on access to information and communication technologies,[126] emphasis on the right to

---

[118] United Nations (2022).

[119] Nussberger (2022).

[120] Carta Mundial pelo Direito à Cidade.

[121] Benhabib (2002), Mutua (2001), and Baxi (2012).

[122] Moyn (2012).

[123] Donnelly (2013).

[124] Anaya (2004).

[125] Lefebvre (1968, 1991).

[126] Castells (1989) and Castells (1996–1998).

housing, and the need for social and spatial justice to distribute the benefits of the city to all citizens.[127] In addition, it can highlight the importance of political participation and the transformation of the city's social and spatial structures.[128] There is also the understanding of **the city as a common good** as an element of the Right to the City.[129]

Other contributions to the debate came from different international conferences that proposed an agenda for specific problems, such as housing (United Nations Conference on Human Settlements in 1976, 1996, and 2016) and environment (United Nations Conference on Environment and Development in 1972, 1992, 2012). To the city, this was an essential integration between "rural" topics related to the effects of the **third agricultural revolution** (Green Revolution) between 1950 and 1960 and the urban problems. Then, the "environmentalism of the rich"[130] resulted in international funds, organizations, and political parties, especially during the 1960s and 1980s, focusing on environmental problems, including acid rain, nuclear worries, and life conservation. Examples are the World Wide Fund for Nature (WWF) (Switzerland, 1961), Greenpeace (Canada, 1971), and the political party *Die Grünen* (**Germany**, 1979).[131] Through the different environmentalism, "detractors of ecology always say that concern for the environment is something like a **hobby** for citizens of rich countries who, since they do not have to worry about survival until the end of the month or teacher strikes, decide to protect whales from the South Atlantic or Chinese pandas."[132]

Later, the decade of 1990 was marked by "environmentalism of the poor" (also in richer countries, such as the United States of America) regarding "actions and concerns in situations where the environment is a source of livelihood"[133] as part of the global **environmental justice** movement,[134] to obtain the "basic needs for life, including water, energy, and shelter"[135] in risk-society[136] with different vulnerabilities and resiliencies. For instance, the Rome Declaration on World Food Security (World Food Summit of 1996) agreed to "implement policies aimed at eradicating poverty and inequality and improving physical and economic access by all, at all times, to sufficient, nutritionally adequate and safe food and its effective utilization." The goal of implementing this was, "by governments, in partnership with all actors of civil society," "to ensure that food supplies are safe, physically and economically accessible, appropriate and adequate to meet the energy and

[127] Rolnik (1988), Rolnik (2019), and Maricato (1985, pp. 405–411).

[128] Harvey (2008).

[129] Júnior and Libório (2021, pp. 1466–1494).

[130] Folchi (2019, p. 96).

[131] Folchi, op. cit.

[132] Alier (2010).

[133] Alier (2014, pp. 239–241).

[134] Alier, op. cit., 2014.

[135] Alier (1994).

[136] Beck (1992).

nutrient needs of the population." One of the ways of realizing that was by encouraging "where appropriate, **school gardens** and **urban agriculture**, using sustainable technologies."[137]

2.5 In-Process Agrifood System Pressures

Urban food inequalities and problems have been intensified since the third agricultural revolution in the mid-twentieth century. It is common knowledge that the Green Revolution, through the upgrade in irrigation, fossil-fuel-powered mechanization, and chemical inputs, especially in developing countries—(such as **Brazil**, India, and Mexico) brought the necessary increase in food production for world population growth. In the last decades, these advances were incremented by precision agriculture technologies (Global Position System, harvest monitors and equipment for dosing seeds, irrigation, and fertilizers, drones, genetic modification, roboticization, etc.). Nonetheless, the benefits were not equally distributed, and there were many environmental side effects, so the current urban food supply chain (production, post-harvest handling, and storage, processing, distribution, consumption, waste)[138] based on the **agri-industrial business has many problems**.

One of them is a barrier to the self-provision of food, the restricted access to productive land due to real estate speculation (land price), bureaucracy (documents, fees), and legal prohibitions. Another problem is the expulsion of original occupants. The large-scale invasions, deprivation, and violation of the Indigenous right to land represent a historical example of **land-grabbing**.[139] This had a substantial increase in the last decades because of various factors. One of the motivations is that the urbanization process requires more and more land from rural areas. When this was not enough to sustain logic until the breaking point (such as the 2008 global financial

---

[137] FAO (1996).

[138] "Before food reaches our plates, it travels a long way. And every stage of that journey makes up our agrifood systems. But what are agrifood systems? They are a set of actions that are interlinked. Farming, harvesting, fishing, livestock-rearing, storing, processing, transporting, selling, buying, eating, and disposing of our food are all part of these complex systems. Sustainable agrifood systems can offer a variety of sufficient nutritious, safe food at an affordable price to everyone. The systems also include all the non-food products that come from agriculture like cotton and forest products. Our actions and choices can help these systems become more sustainable. The food and products we choose make all of us an integral part of the way an agrifood system works. If we make these systems more sustainable, we can achieve better production, better nutrition, a better environment and a better life, for all. We can all be food heroes." FAO.

[139] "The 'land grabbing' has many different definitions but what they all have in common is the idea that it involves the large-scale acquisition of land for commercial or industrial purposes, such as agricultural and biofuel production, mining and logging concessions, big infrastructure development or tourism.6 Most definitions agree that it involves acquiring more than 200 hectares, with some pushing for a threshold of 1,000 hectares, many involving more than 10,000 hectares and several more than 500,000 hectares.7 In any case, it concerns large-scale land acquisition. It also involves land being acquired by investors rather than producers, very often foreign investors." Gilbert (2017).

crisis), the global search for land was intensified as a target.[140] This is related to the rush to promote the globalization of agricultural production and the growing demand for resources from emerging centers of global capital.[141]

Additionally, land-grabbing is connected to the "efforts of replacing the fossil base of modern societies through the intensified use of biomass sources, one of the last concepts of bioeconomy policies,"[142] with many practical consequences for societies and environments, especially for global peripheries.[143] There are "well-intended and ambitious blending targets for the proportion of agrofuels to be reached in coming years," however, the "targets far exceed the agricultural capacities of developed countries in Europe and North America."[144] Then, for instance, the European bioeconomy strategy and policy papers of bio-based ecological development are "essentially built on the prerequisite of the subordination, devaluation, appropriation and/or exploitation of (1) different geographical regions, (2) ecological foundations, and (3) prevalent bioeconomy practices."[145] As a result, the production of resource-intensive bioenergy (instead of choosing other sustainable energy sources) generated a greater competition between food and non-food (cereals, oilseeds, and sugarcane) because of their increased use as biomass or biofuels. Consequently, it "intensified the interdependence between food, feed, and energy markets"[146] for heating and cooking.[147] While seeking new natural resources, governments, and public agencies legitimize the "unoccupied" land transfer to national or foreign investors without considering the previous user rights and having no compensation.[148]

More than that, the search for land is connected to the **degradation of the current farmland.** Approximately one-third of the world's farmland is moderate to highly degraded[149] because of ongoing human activities, such as deforestation, urbanization, and agricultural intensification, along with the negative consequences, including loss of soil organic matter (SOM) or soil organic carbon (SOC), soil compaction, surface sealing, soil acidification, nutrient imbalance, pollution, salinization, sodification, desertification, wildfires, erosion, and landslides, are progressively undermining the vital role of soil biodiversity in sustaining ecosystem functioning and delivering ecosystem services.[150]

---

[140] Gilbert, loc. cit.

[141] Gilbert, loc. cit.; Backhouse and Lehmann (2019, pp. 373–388).

[142] Backhouse et al. (2021, p. 3).

[143] Backhouse et al. (2022), Backhouse and Lorenzen (2021), and Backhouse (2020).

[144] FAO (2007, p. 1).

[145] Pungas (2023, pp. 689–706).

[146] FAO (2007), loc. cit.

[147] FAO (2017a), op. cit.

[148] FAO (2011).

[149] FAO (2017a).

[150] FAO (2020c, 2022a). FAO (2020c) State of knowledge of soil biodiversity: Status, challenges and potentialities. Rome: FAO. https://doi.org/10.4060/cb1928en. Accessed: 5 July 2024. FAO (2022a) The State of World Fisheries and Aquaculture 2022: Towards Blue Transformation. Rome: FAO. https://doi.org/10.4060/cb9910en. Accessed: 14 April 2024.

In addition, **climate change** already affects food production, and the future scenario is not positive.[151] Climate change "may significantly reduce yields" (wheat, maize, rice, and soybeans) "in the long run."[152] In addition, climate change is related to the disruption of "complex interactions among species, potentially affecting ecosystem services such as pollination and the control of crop pests by natural predators,"[153] and the supplies of freshwater are also expected to be affected[154] with a "direct impact on animal health and reducing the quality and supply of feed and fodder."[155] Thus, "food systems have particular vulnerabilities to the adverse impacts of climate change."[156] It threatens "the safeguarding food security and ending hunger," which means a "direct impact on the realization of the right to adequate food"[157] because it "will critically determine the future state of natural resources, as well as the future conditions of and constraints to agricultural production, thereby affecting food availability and the stability of food supplies."[158]

Moreover, the rural population suffers from differentials in employment opportunities, access to public services and infrastructure, and environmental differentials that impact agricultural production and demographic factors (e.g., flood, drought, land access restriction). This scenario ordinarily leads to **rural migration**, from a totally voluntary search for opportunities to totally forced displacement by conflicts and crises, international or internal in the country, to urban or another rural area.[159] For example, the 2013 five-year internal migration intensity is estimated at 10 percent globally, with 6 percent migrating to urban areas, especially in highly urbanized countries such as Latin America, the Caribbean, the Near East, and North Africa.[160] Naturally, mobility is part of human history, and it has benefits and challenges to personal and collective growth, local economies, national development, labor shortages, and knowledge sharing to the origin and destination.[161]

151 Vogel et al. (2019).

152 Porter et al. (2014, pp. 485–533).

153 Porter et al., loc. cit.

154 Hoffman (2012).

155 FAO (2011), op. cit.

156 United Nations (2016).

157 United Nations (2016), op. cit. The Special Rapporteur on the right to food has indicated that climate change poses a serious threat to the enjoyment of the right to food and threatens all aspects of food security, with 600 million additional people potentially vulnerable to malnutrition by 2080 (A/70/287, para. 82). United Nations (2015).

158 Vuuren et al. (2012, pp. 21–35).

159 FAO (2018a).

160 FAO (2018a), loc. cit.

161 FAO (2018a), op. cit., p. xix.

Nevertheless, the rising **growth of the urban population**[162] puts pressure on the food chain[163] (from production to marketing) and "on basic, administrative, and social services, infrastructure, housing supply, health and education services and to facilitate decent livelihood." It raises the host area's vulnerability and the urban poor level and "forces more people to live in informal settlements or inadequate housing, with associated environmental consequences."[164] Given that, demographic structures and spatial location dynamics of the population are expected to influence the future of food demand and dietary preferences,[165] like age, income, or concentration in urban areas, because they affect consumer behavior. For example, young and older adults have different nutrition needs and preferences. Also, the swift rise in income within emerging nations is driving increased demand for resource-intensive items such as meat, fish, dairy products, and more.[166] Consequently, there are effects on food prices. For instance, "in megacities worldwide, urban food prices have risen, as it has become more and more difficult and time-consuming to transport fresh produce to market."[167]

Also, rapid urbanization is related to "increased consumption of processed food and more sedentary lifestyles."[168] The **long distances** of space/time between the distribution-consumption of traditional agriculture to urban centers is a problem because of fossil fuel, gas emissions, food loss, and waste[169] ("each year, one-third of all food produced for human consumption is lost or wasted across the globe").[170]

On the one hand, *food loss* is defined as "all the food produced for human consumption that is not eaten by humans"[171] or "the decrease in mass (dry matter) or nutritional value (quality) of food that was originally intended for human consumption." Food loss "occurs throughout the supply chain – from production to final household consumption," being "mainly caused by inefficiencies along the food supply chain,

[162] Urban population growth is often confused with urbanization but is a distinct concept. Urban growth can take place without any urbanization if urban and rural areas are both growing at the same rate. Urban growth is the increase in the absolute number of people living within defined urban areas. It is defined as "the increase in the proportion of the urban population over time as part of the whole population. Urban growth comes from demographic growth and international and internal migration.

World Migration Report (2015).

[163] FAO (2019).

[164] United Nations (2018).

[165] FAO (2018b, p. 7).

[166] FAO (2018b), op. cit., p. 12.

[167] FAO (2020e, p. 128). FAO (2020e) The State of Food Security and Nutrition in the World 2020: Transforming food systems for affordable healthy diets. Rome: FAO. Available at: https://doi.org/10.4060/ca9692en Accessed: 14 April 2024.

[168] FAO (2017a), op. cit.

[169] FAO (2017a), op. cit.

[170] FAO (2018b, p. 4).

[171] FAO (2018b), loc. cit.

such as poor infrastructure, lack of adequate technology or access to markets, as well as insufficient knowledge and management skills or capacities by actors involved."[172]

On the other hand, *food waste* is "a part of food loss." It is the "food intended for human consumption being discarded or left to spoil as a result of decisions taken by actors along the food supply chain," the "food appropriate for human consumption being discarded, whether or not after it is kept beyond its expiry date or left to spoil." It is "mainly discarding either by choice or spoilage and is closely related to retailers' and consumers' behaviors – oversupply due to market forces or consumers' shopping and eating-related habits." It is "more noticeable at the end of the food chain – retail and final consumption stages," although it may also occur at the post-harvest stage. Food waste could be "the result of a looming 'best by' date or a product that does not comply with certain aesthetic criteria – marketing standards related to size, shape or accepted appearance – whether through consumer preferences, wholesalers, or retailers" which are criteria to discard edible goods not based on safety standards.[173] The moment that food loss and waste happens in the food chain varies by product and region.[174]

Moreover, physical access to affordable, nutritious foods is also problematic due to the "absence or low density of food shops, markets or outlets – particularly fresh foods of short self-life or requiring refrigeration – within a practical traveling distance (referred to as **food deserts**),"[175,176] and "shops and outlets offering an overabundance of energy-dense foods high in fats, sugars and/or salt and few nutritious foods" **(food swamps)**.[177] They represent food environment problems. Both cases of unequal spatial placement of food access happen even in high-income countries, like the United States of America[178] or Canada. Still, they hit more on Black and poor communities,[179] what is also nominated as "**food apartheid**" through "a view at the whole food system, along with race, geography, faith, and economics."[180,181] Lower socio-economic neighborhoods have high geographic access to food retailers

---

172 FAO (2018c), loc. cit.

173 FAO (2018c), loc. cit.

174 FAO (2018c), loc. cit.

175 United States of America (2017).

176 There is no agreed upon definition of a "food desert". The USDA defines it as: "a low-income census tract where either a substantial number or share of residents has low access to a supermarket or large grocery store. "Low income" tracts are defined as those where at least 20 percent of the people have income at or below the federal poverty levels for family size, or where median family income for the tract is at or below 80 percent of the surrounding area's median family income. Tracts qualify as "low access" tracts if at least 500 persons or 33 percent of their population live more than a mile from a supermarket or large grocery store (for rural census tracts, the distance is more than 10 miles) United States of America (2017).

177 FAO (2022).

178 United States of America.

179 Barker et al. (2012).

180 GCAP UCR.

181 "Activist and community organizer Karen Washington has been battling for food justice for three decades. She is opposed to using the expression "food desert", she prefers "food apartheid, "which brings us to the more important question: What are some of the social inequalities that you

perceived as promoting mainly minimally nutritious food options such as fast-food outlets and convenience stores).[182] This can be seen as **environmental racism**, which means "to treat badly other people in pollution or resource-extraction injustices on grounds of membership of particular ethnic groups, social class or caste."[183]

Nonetheless, the mere production and distribution of food do not guarantee people access to it. On a global scale, food systems generate an ample food supply, but due to inequalities, not everyone possesses the **purchasing power** to secure the right to food. This starkly highlights the profound inequality between those who have access to sufficient food and those who are compelled to endure hunger.[184] More exactly, every one percent rise in the cost of food represents 16 million people in a food insecurity situation,[185] with far-reaching consequences for the most susceptible demographics, including smallholder/family agriculture and low-income urban and rural communities. Naturally, the food price construction and variation are related to different reasons. One is that food prices "will be increasingly linked to oil prices" because "as most of the 82 low-income countries with food deficits are also net oil importers, the competing pressure on crop use will increase."[186]

With high prices for nutritious food, the markets usually offer "a wide variety of non-perishable energy-dense foods of minimal nutritional value, often high in unhealthy fats, sugars and/or salt, at lower prices."[187] This results in the consumption of processed food, with more sedentary lifestyles also being part of this increase in obesity,[188] along with diet-related non-communicable **diseases,**[189] given the lack of access to healthy food worldwide. For example, "in Northern America, Europe, and Oceania, 28 percent of adults are classified as obese, compared with 7 percent in Asia and 11 percent in Africa. In Latin America and the Caribbean, roughly one-quarter of the adult population is currently considered obese."[190] Thus, consequences are not only to the individual body but also to the collective, considering that "the **economic price** of malnutrition is billions of dollars lost in productivity and health care costs."[191]

Finally, other problems related to the agricultural food chain crisis reported in 2022 are: **(a) Organized violence and conflict risks:** in Democratic Republic of the Congo, Ethiopia, Nigeria, Mozambique, Sahel, Somalia, South Sudan, Syrian

---

see, and what are you doing to erase some of the injustices? "Food apartheid" looks at the whole food system, along with race, geography, faith, and economics," Karen says. 'When we say 'food apartheid', the real conversation can begin'." GCAP UCR, op. cit.

182 FAO (2011), op. cit., p. 14.

183 Alier et al. (2016).

184 FAO (2018a), loc. cit.

185 FAO (2007), loc. cit.

186 FAO (2007), loc. cit.

187 FAO (2020f), p. 128.

188 FAO (2017a), op. cit.

189 GBD (2016, pp. 1659–1724) and GBD (2017).

190 FAO (2017b).

191 FAO (2017b), op. cit.

Arab Republic, Ukraine,[192] and Yemen; **(b) Natural hazard risks:** in Afghanistan, Somalia, Ethiopia, Kenya, South Sudan, Benin, and Guinea, Nigeria, Cabo Verde, Angola, Madagascar, Mozambique, Zimbabwe, and Haiti; **(c) Economic risks:** in Yemen, Syrian Arab Republic, Lebanon, Haiti, Sri Lanka, Afghanistan, Ethiopia, Kenya, and Ukraine; **(d) Animal and plant pests and diseases**: in Ethiopia, Yemen, and Kenya**; (e) Aggravating factor (humanitarian access constraints):** in Afghanistan, Ethiopia, Mali, Nigeria, Syrian Arab Republic, Democratic Republic of the Congo, Niger, Somalia, and South Sudan.[193]

The **COVID-19 pandemic** also must be listed as part of the crisis because it affected the whole food chain, from production to consumption.[194] The last available evidence suggests a rise of 112 million to almost 3.1 billion in people unable to afford a healthy diet worldwide.[195]

In short, the above problems illustrate the urgent need for a profound **social-ecological transformation of urban food and land.**[196] Among different issues, this change concerns

> societal transformations away from dominant forms of relating to nature in different stages of food systems, as well as in the politics and policies that shape these processes. Even the idea that nature is a resource is disputed. Policymakers have indeed noticed that such a change concerns not only technology and the economy; it requires a societal transformation, and they have thus started to fund research related to societal aspects, such as values, norms, practices, and social conflicts involved in such processes.[197]

---

[192] The war in Ukraine is currently exerting pressure on the world economy, causing disruptions in supply chains and impacting global prices for grains, fertilizers, and energy. This situation has resulted in shortages and is contributing to a further increase in inflation rates. Global prices for both food and energy are skyrocketing, reaching levels that have not been witnessed in decades. FAO (2022) op. cit., p. 53.

[193] The projection from June to September 2022 is 20 countries or situations (including two regional clusters) with acute food insecurity (called hunger hotspots) related to one or more key problems. FAO (2022), loc. cit.

[194] "Movement and transport restrictions led to shortages in agricultural labor and inputs, affecting food production and processing. Limited mobility as well as restricted access to and operation of markets and retail disrupted food supply and increased food loss and waste, especially for perishable products. Remote areas dependent on food imports were especially affected by food shortages due to border closures and limited transportation. Moreover, restaurants, canteens, markets, and street traders were shut down in many cities. Many producers and agri-food businesses were not able to recover from the lockdown restrictions. Confined to their area, urban dwellers dependent on local markets and informal traders in their neighbourhoods experienced limited access to food. Food supply challenges and panic buying led to spikes in food prices in many parts of the world. In addition, the most vulnerable population dependent on school meals and food banks suffered from school closures and disruptions in food relief programmes. While income losses and unemployment led to significant increases in demand for food relief, food banks received fewer donations and movement restrictions limited support by volunteers." FAO (2020a).

[195] FAO (2022), op. cit., p. VI.

[196] Brand (2016, pp. 503–525), Moore et al. (2014), Westley et al. (2013, p. 27), Olsson et al. (2014, p. 1), Masterson et al. (2017, p. 49), and Patterson et al. (2017, pp. 1–16).

[197] Motta (2021).

These transformative practices can be guided by different alternative approaches representing "fresh societal conventions that govern access to essential resources, aiming to free such access from the constraints of market forces or government assistance,[198] including feminist and decolonial epistemologies and critical studies of science and technology.[199] Also, the commons and Human Rights are possible theoretical and legal approaches to guide it.[200] Urban agriculture is one of the practical ways that does not exclude the other approaches.

2.6 Contemporary Urban Agriculture

The twenty-first century started with important contributions to the Right to the City through the World Social Forums after 2001. Moreover, the New Charter of Athens of 2003 (for European development), in the chapter on Environmental Coherence, is an alert that toxic substances can compromise **food** and health. Furthermore, the New Charter highlights the diminishing presence of agriculture, diminishing open spaces, and declining biodiversity as illustrative instances of detrimental factors jeopardizing the urban living environment and public areas' quality. Concerning agricultural initiatives, cities should actively encourage the development of local markets and the adoption of organic production methods.[201] Despite the advances and worries, the charter maintained the **exclusion of food as an urban social function**. Even so, the food could be seen included in education, health, natural and cultural patrimony, (social, economic, and environmental) sustainability, and part of the housing as social and ecological functions of the city and property broader than the previous Charter version.

In 2006, the World Charter for the Right to the City established responsibilities and actions that civil society, local and national governments, parliamentarians, and international organizations must undertake to ensure that all individuals can live with dignity in cities. The concept of the Charter is that

> The Right to the City is defined as the equitable usufruct of cities within the principles of sustainability, democracy, equity, and social justice. It is a collective right of the inhabitants of cities, especially vulnerable and disadvantaged groups, which gives them the legitimacy of action and organization based on their uses and customs, with the aim of achieving the full exercise of the right to free self-determination and an adequate standard of living. **The Right to the City is interdependent with all human rights** internationally recognized and fully conceived and, therefore, includes all civil, political, economic, social, cultural, and environmental that are already regulated in treaties regarding international human rights. This assumes the inclusion of the right to work in conditions equitable and satisfactory; to found and join trade unions; access to social security and public health; **adequate food,**

[198] Guttmann (2022, p. 38).

[199] Motta, op. cit. Plomwood (2004).

[200] Cortez et al. (2022), FAO (2021), Mcgreevy (2022), and Weston and Bollier (2013a, p. 87; 2013b, pp. 215–225).

[201] The New Charter of Athens (2003).

clothing, and housing; access to potable water, electricity, transportation, and other social services; to quality public education; right to culture and information; political participation and access to justice; the acknowledgment the right to organize, assemble and demonstrate; public safety and coexistence peaceful. It also includes respect for minorities and ethnic, racial, sexual, and cultural plurality, and respect for migrants. The territory of cities and their rural surroundings is also a space and place for the exercise and fulfillment of **collective** rights as a way to ensure the **distribution and enjoyment of equitable, universal, just, democratic, and sustainable use of resources**, wealth, services, goods and opportunities offered by cities. For this reason, the Right to the City also includes the right to development, a healthy environment, the enjoyment and **preservation of natural resources**, participation in urban planning and management, and historical and cultural heritage.[202] (Bolded by the author)

This represents a dialogue with the Universal Declaration of Human Rights stakeholders and rights to be guaranteed, with special detach for adequate food. Moreover, the World Charter for the Right to the City is important to indicate that in cities, the **realization of human rights should be aligned with the common interest.** This considers that the **social functions of the city and of property** point that cities' public and private spaces and properties are collective goods to be used in a social and environmental balance that prioritizes the communal interest. This is a condition to assure dignity, collective well-being, equality, justice, and the social production of the habitat.[203]

Following that, for the planning and managing urban spatial development section, the United Nations Habitat New Urban Agenda (2017) final report presents the commitment "to support **urban agriculture** and farming, as well as responsible, local and sustainable consumption and production, and social interactions, through enabling and accessible networks of local markets and commerce as an option for contributing to sustainability and food security."[204] In 2020, urban agriculture was listed as making cities healthier and more sustainable.[205] Indeed, in the last decades, urban agriculture has been encouraged and internationally recognized as a tool to achieve key elements of the right to food because it has the potential to promote **food security**, food system resilience, and sustainability[206] by the "production, processing and marketing of food on all types of publicly and privately held land and water bodies dispersed throughout urban and peri-urban areas, mostly destined to consumers residing in these areas,"[207] like 800 million people (1996) worldwide have been doing.[208] In addition, in 2023, FAO recently published this about urban and peri-urban agriculture:

It can be defined as practices that yield foods and other outputs from agricultural production and related processes (transformation, distribution, marketing, recycling, etc.) taking place

---

[202] World Charter for the Right to the City (2001).

[203] World Charter for the Right to the City, op. cit.

[204] United Nations (2017).

[205] FAO (2020d).

[206] Opitz et al. (2016, pp. 341–358), Clinton et al. (2018), and Walsh et al. (2022).

[207] Pearson et al. (2010, pp. 7–19) and Smit et al. (2001a).

[208] FAO (2020d), op. cit.

Fig. 2.1 Location of urban agriculture (UA), peri-urban agriculture (PUA), and rural agriculture (RA) within the urban–rural continuum. *Source* Opitz et al. (2016)

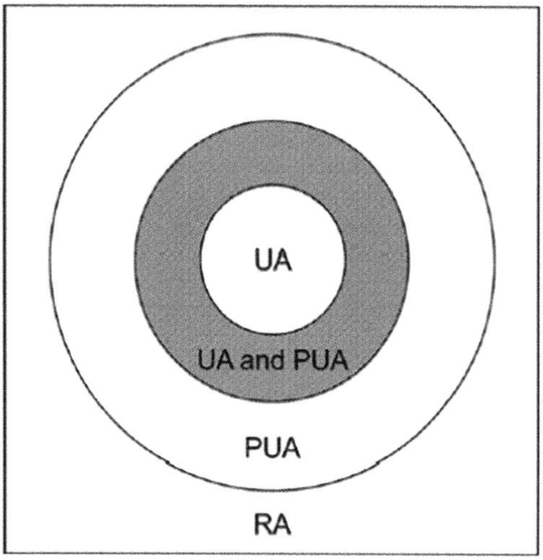

> on land and other spaces within cities and surrounding regions. These involve **urban and peri-urban** actors, communities, methods, places, policies, institutions, systems, ecologies, and economies, largely **using and regenerating local resources** to meet the changing needs of local populations while serving **multiple goals and functions.**[209] (Bolded by the author)

Regarding the above information, three main considerations are crucial for this research. The first is the conceptual and practical notions' differentiation between urban and peri-urban agriculture. **Urban agriculture** is "predominantly located in the densely settled areas of a city." It is usually "performed on land that is not agriculturally zoned"[210] by residents, migrants, and children without formal agricultural education. In contrast, **peri-urban** agricultural landscapes reside within a transitional zone, bridging the gap between urban and rural domains. These zones, situated at the edges of urban areas, embody a blend of urban and rural characteristics with limited available agricultural and natural space. This form of agriculture, existing in residual capacity, contends with urban pressures while also capitalizing on its proximity to urban centers and markets. The practice is done mainly by agricultural professionals. Importantly, the distinction between these two regions is not fixed or absolute; rather, intersecting regions often exist, as depicted in Fig. 2.1. This diagram illustrates how rural agriculture is positioned beyond the bounds of urban or metropolitan expansions.[211]

The second fundamental approach of the previous citation[212] is that urban agriculture ordinarily is a strategy to **transform vacant urban land** (totally or partially not used or underutilized land) with human and natural resources regenerating potential. This has scientific recognition worldwide, especially for former industrial cities.

[209] FAO (2023) and Barrett et al. (2022, pp. 1316–1377).

[210] Mceldowney (2017).

[211] Mceldowney, op. cit.

[212] FAO (2023, p. 250), and Barret et al. (2022, pp. 1316–1377).

Moreover, it is extremely relevant due to the **increasing vacant land scenario**.[213] For example, around Shenyang, China, a real estate company broke up in 2010, and this resulted in an abandoned luxury complex of 260 mansions. Nowadays, the streets give place to agriculture.[214]

The third highlight of the urban agriculture concept[215] is its multiple goals and benefits. In summary, they can be categorized regarding *society* (community building, education, sense of pride, aesthetic improvement, sense of security), *health* (physical activities, mental health, nutrition, food literacy), *ecology* (stormwater management, urban hydrology, organic waste and nutrient recycling, biodiversity, urban climate, air quality, urban climate, air quality, and energy consumption savings), and *economy* (economic savings on food, tourism, employment opportunities and entrepreneurial endeavors, increased property values, savings for municipal agencies).[216] Also, it has a role in addressing *social-ecological justice*.[217]

Between these functions, urban agriculture in the **Global North** typically serves to promote a more sustainable lifestyle or foster community bonds. Research in developed countries primarily emphasizes the positive impacts on social connections, health, emotional well-being, and education. Conversely, in the **Global South**, the focus tends to lean towards the economic advantages of urban agriculture. Urban agriculture plays a crucial role in meeting food security and nutritional requirements in developing nations. In regions like Latin America and Africa, individuals employ innovative methods to cultivate crops in extremely limited spaces to ensure their families' sustenance and survival. Addressing this disparity can facilitate mutual learning. For instance, developing nations can draw inspiration from developed countries on how urban agriculture can enhance urban dwellers' social, physical, and mental well-being. Meanwhile, developed nations can glean insights from developing countries on how urban agriculture practices can yield significant economic benefits.[218]

Urban agriculture draws attention to the fact that conceptual delimitations are not unique because of their multiple designs, uses, and local regulations. In **Brazil**, the new National Program of Urban Agriculture (Federal Decree Number 11.700, on 12th **September 2023**) understands that the concept of urban and peri-urban agriculture as "activities and small animal husbandry carried out in urban areas or peri-urban regions, which include: I - the stages of production, processing, distribution and commercialization of food, medicinal plants, aromatic and ornamental plants, herbal medicines and inputs, for self-consumption or commercialization; and

---

213 For instance, in Brazil, the 2022 Census also counted 11.4 million vacant permanent private homes, representing 12.6% of the total number of permanent private homes—an increase compared to 2010, 9.0%. IBGE (2022a, b).

214 FRANCE 24 (2024).

215 FAO (2023), loc. cit., Barrett, op. cit.

216 Steuri and Vignola (2015, p. 55) and FAO (2020b, p. 7).

217 Andrés (2017).

218 Beck (2018), Hamilton et al. (2014, pp. 45–73), Lima (2019), p. 119 et seq, Orsini et al. (2013, pp. 695–720), Poulsen et al. (2015, pp. 131–146), Siniscalchi (2020), p. 241 et seq, Smit et al. (2001b), Steuri and Vignola, op cit., Taguchi and Santini (2019), Zezza and Tasciotti (2010, pp. 265–273), and Zanotto (2016).

II - organic waste management processes."[219] This decree is important for institutionalizing national-level urban agriculture through the combination of efforts among different public spheres, such as Federal (Agrarian Development and Family Farming; Development and Social Assistance, Family and Fight against Hunger; Environment and Climate Change; and Labor and Employment), state and local governments, in addition to civil society and private sector. Their efforts must follow principles[220] and prioritize vulnerable populations, with a highlight of the human right to adequate food and the right to the city. This represents a legal bond between urban agriculture, the human right to adequate food, the right to the city, collective forms of organization, and social, economic, and sustainable food co-production.

Even so, the decree requires complement by the legal-institutional system centered on local urban planning, the tax system (different between urban and rural), and the responsibility of specific public agencies, such as the National Institute for Colonization and Agrarian Reform (INCRA), Brazilian Institute of Geography and Statistics (IBGE), and Brazilian Agricultural Research Corporation (EMBRAPA). On one hand, according to IBGE,[221] an agricultural establishment is any unit of production or exploitation dedicated, totally or partially, to agricultural, forestry, or aquaculture activities, regardless of its size, legal form (whether it belongs to a producer, several producers, to a, to a set of companies), or its location (urban or rural area), with the objective of production, whether for sale (commercialization of production) or subsistence (support of the producer or his family). On the other hand, EMBRAPA defined urban agriculture as "the exercise of various activities related to food production and conservation of natural resources within urban centers or in their respective peripheries."[222] It has three main contribution areas: well-being, environment, and economy.

> The increase in food security, improving nutrition, and human health in poor communities added to better sanitary conditions reduces diseases and is related to the well-being of the population, environmental conservation of natural resources, mitigation of environmental impact resulting from human occupation, and communities transformation seeking sustainability, reuse, and recycling; increase in the generation of jobs and the incentive to the young people, adults, and elderly with job opportunities. Urban agriculture strengthens the economic base, reduces poverty, and fosters entrepreneurship, generating work for women and other marginalized groups.[223]

However, the local legal institutional system can also be exclusionary and outdated, generating problems for the development of urban agricultural activity due

---

219 Brasil (2023).

220 "The principles of the National Urban and Peri-Urban Agriculture Program are: the human right to adequate food; the right to health; the right to the city; popular and social participation; the popular and solidarity economy; cooperativism and associations; agroecology and organic production; healthy and sustainable food systems; short marketing circuits; the sustainable use of soil, water, ecosystems and agro-sociobiodiversity; respect for socio-environmental and cultural diversity; food as a cultural and social practice; the bioeconomy." Brasil, op. cit., Art. 4.

221 IBGE (2017).

222 Machado A.

223 Machado, op. cit., p. 23.

to the lack of reach of public policies. In view of that, recent studies on urban agricultures in **Brazil** proposed an academic categorization into *a. traditional farmers*, which occupy the transition zone where the urban gives way to the rural to preserve agrobiodiversity or replicate conventional agriculture; *b. backyard agriculture*, a small extension of land related to those classified in the category of traditional farmers. There is a significant production both for self-production; *c. initiatives by urban collectives*, different social profiles that seek to preserve green spaces in the city, environmental education, and food production in public areas; and *d. agriculture promoted or linked to the government*, like public policies to provide work or gardening educational activities in schools and business and commercial agriculture.[224]

Regarding **urban agriculture**, the **European Parliament** calls attention to the difference between urban farming and urban gardening. Urban gardening can be related to "agricultural activities with low economic dependence on material outputs while using the production of food for achieving other, mostly social, goals."[225] In urban gardening, a clear distinction has emerged between zones dedicated to individual cultivation, like allotments and family gardens, and spaces where collective endeavors occur, such as educational, therapeutic, and **community gardens**.[226] In a critical sense, urban gardening "can be traced back to the 1970s in New York, when communities re-appropriated green space for building projects and the enjoyment of nature."[227] In contrast to urban gardening, urban farming "is based on a business model that takes advantage of proximity to a city by offering local or regional agricultural products or services."[228] Regarding urban farming, the territories have been categorized into various types. This includes areas associated with on-site services, like leisure and educational gardens and local food farms.

Additionally, the European Parliament recognizes that **urban agriculture** is divergent from conventional rural agriculture due to the smaller scale of the method's implementation (limiting the competition against industrialized production),[229] the need for alternatives to soil-based practices to overcome urban soil contamination, and urban agricultures' possibility to offer more connectivity between food growers and consumers, which is an important step to advancement in the food citizenship[230] and is one of the possible ways for the reversion of the **metabolic rift**[231] when observing different spectrums of urban agriculture.

Despite the differences, in general, urban agriculture requires physical and non-physical components to achieve its goals. The physical features are "(legal) growing space, construction, and growing material, including fertilizers, tools, and water."

[224] Lima, C (2019)

[225] Keeffe (2016, pp. 15–37).

[226] Mceldowney, op. cit., p. 6.

[227] Certomà (2015, p. 13).

[228] Mceldowney, op. cit.

[229] Keeffe, loc. cit.

[230] Titarelli et al. (2022, p. 1590).

[231] Mcclintock (2010, pp. 191–207).

The non-physical components are "funds, labor, construction permissions, training, and networks."[232]

In common, urban agriculture tends to face some **challenges,** such as *a. skepticism, sociocultural biases, and institutional constraints* (this includes social, legal,[233] and political issues, such as gender/ethnic/class disparities and low visibility on decision-makers agenda); *b. constrained access to resources, inputs, and financial means* (this embraces natural, political, bureaucratic, and economic conflicts, such as competition with other land uses and constrained access to water, tools, and financial resources); *c. special risks of cultivating in the city* (this counts social and natural limitations, for instance, pollution, vandalism, and driving gentrification); and *d. organizational constraints, considering human resources difficulties* (for example, lack of networking, know-how on gardening or management, and data).[234]

Regarding the **types**, urban agricultural activities can be owned by private individuals, public entities, or commercial enterprises, taking on diverse forms. For instance, there are school gardens, urban farms, community gardens, backyard gardens, and edible landscapes. Furthermore, urban agriculture is integrated into buildings or facilities, for example, aquaponics (aquaculture and hydroponics), edible walls, indoor farms, vertical farms, rooftop greenhouses, and open-air rooftops[235] (Fig. 2.2).

The above figure gives a view of the panorama of multiple possibilities urban agriculture offers as an alternative food system. While they are more socially relevant and environmentally sustainable than the agri-industrial food system, alternative agricultural methods still face certain constraints, including land access, property rights, and the expenses associated with implementation and maintenance. Consequently, the quest for means to promote the human right to adequate food in urban areas through no or low-tech, cost-effective solutions directs our attention toward a different approach to urban agriculture, the Public Access Urban Community (Edible/Vegetable) Gardens or **Community Gardens**.

[232] Steuri et al., op. cit., p. 56.

[233] Wegelin and Borgman (1995, pp. 131–152).

[234] Steuri et al., op. cit., pp. 59–79, 121.

[235] Santo et al. (2016).

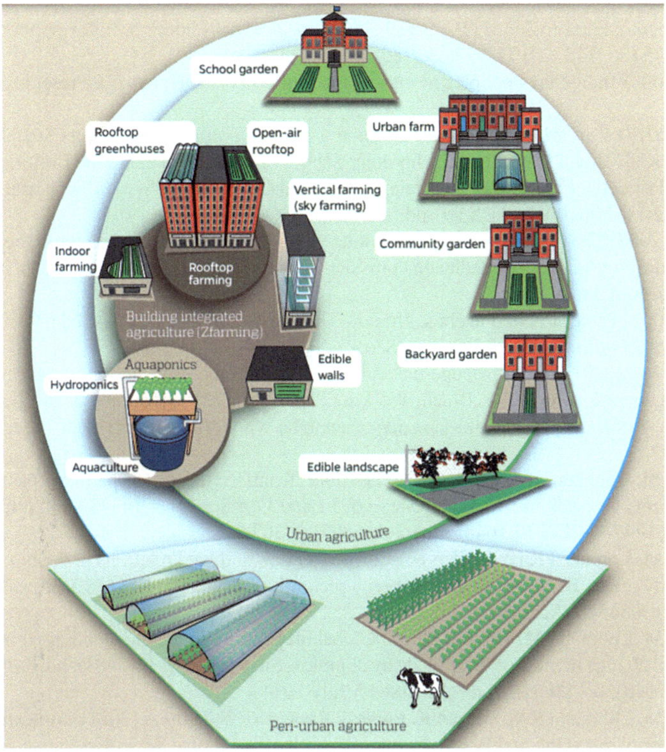

Fig. 2.2 Urban agriculture types. *Source* Santo et al. (2016, p. 2)

References

Alfonsi B de M et al (2023) Do cercamento das terras comuns ao Estatuto da Cidade: a colonialidade do direito de propriedade como obstáculo para a efetivação do direito à cidade no Brasil. Revista de Direito da Cidade 15(1):294–330. https://www.e-publicacoes.uerj.br/index.php/rdc/article/view/64045. Accessed 9 June 2024

Alier J (1994) De la economía ecológica al ecologismo popular. Icaria Editorial, Barcelona, Espanha

Alier J (2010) El ambientalismo de los pobres, una agenda de supervivência, La capital, Buenos Aires. https://www.lacapital.com.ar/economia/el-ambientalismo-los-pobres-una-agenda-supervivencia-n343751.html. Accessed 19 Aug 2024

Alier J (2014) The environmentalism of the poor. Geoforum 54:239–241. https://www.sciencedirect.com/science/article/pii/S0016718513000912. Accessed 19 Aug 2024

Alier J et al (2016) Is there a global environmental justice movement? The Journal of Peasant Studies. https://www.tandfonline.com/doi/full/10.1080/03066150.2016.1141198. Accessed 20 Aug 2024

Amoroso M (2006) Nunca é tarde para ser feliz? A imagem da favela pelas lentes do Correio da Manhã. Dissertação de Mestrado, Universidade Fluminense, Departamento de História, Niterói, p 164. https://www.historia.uff.br/academico/media/aluno/1167/projeto/Dissert-mauro-henrique-de-barros-amoroso.pdf. Accessed 3 Oct 2024

Amoroso M (2019) A tropa e a cidade: a Polícia Militar no Rio de Janeiro durante a abertura e seus impactos negativos futuros para a consolidação de um universo de direitos para as favelas. Tempo e Argumento, Espírito Santo 11(27):129–157. https://revistas.udesc.br/index.php/tempo/article/view/2175180311272019129. Accessed 3 Oct 2024

Anaya S (2004) Indigenous peoples in international law. Oxford University Press, Oxford, Reino Unido

Andrés J (2017) Can urban agriculture become a planning strategy to address social-ecological justice? KTH Royal Institute of Technology School of Architecture and the Built Environment. Degree Project in Environmental Strategies, Second Cycle. https://www.diva-portal.org/smash/get/diva2:1153064/FULLTEXT01.pdf. Accessed 4 Oct 2024

Angelis M (2007) The beginning of history: Value struggles and global capital. Pluto Press, London, p 152. http://www.lamarre-mediaken.com/Site/COMS_630_files/Beginning%20of%20History.pdf. Accessed 3 Oct 2024

Aristotle (2001) Ethics to Nicomachus. 4rd edn. University of Brasilia, Brasilia, p 93

Aristotle (2002) Politics. Martins Fontes, São Paulo, pp 19–31

Backhouse M (2020) The knowledge-based bioeconomy in the semi-periphery. A case study on second-generation ethanol in Brazil, Working Paper No. 13, Bioeconomy & Inequalities, Jena. https://www.bioinequalities.uni-jena.de/sozbemedia/wp/workingpaper13.pdf. Accessed 5 July 2024

Backhouse M, Lehmann R (2019) New 'renewable' frontiers: contested palm oil plantations and wind energy projects in Brazil and Mexico. J Land Use Sci 15(2–3):373–388. https://doi.org/10.1080/1747423X.2019.1648577.Accessed05July2024

Backhouse M, Lorenzen K (2021) Knowledge production and land relations in the bioeconomy. A case study on the Brazilian sugar-bioenergy sector. In: Sustainability, vol 13. https://doi.org/10.3390/su13084525. Accessed 5 July 2024

Backhouse M, Lühmann M, Tittor A (2022) Global inequalities in the bioeconomy: thinking continuity and change in view of the global soy complex. Sustainability 14(5481). https://www.mdpi.com/2071-1050/14/9/5481/pdf. Accessed 5 July 2024

Backhouse M, Lühmann R, Lorenzen K, Puder J, Rodríguez F, Tittor A (2021) Contextualizing the Bioeconomy in an Unequal World: Biomass Sourcing and Global Socio-Ecological Inequalities. In: Backhouse et al. (eds) Bioeconomy and global inequalities: socio-ecological perspectives on biomass sourcing and production, 1st edn, p 3

Barker C et al (2012) Unshared bounty: How structural racism contributes to the creation and persistence of food deserts. New York Law School. Unshared Bounty. https://digitalcommons.nyls.edu/cgi/viewcontent.cgi?article=1002&context=racial_justice_project. Accessed 20 Aug 2024

Barreto CGP (2013) Land rent, urban legislation, land use dispute: the transformation of Avenida 17 De Agosto into a commercial axis over the last decade. Master (thesis) in Urban Development. Universidade Federal de Pernambuco, Recife, p 88. https://repositorio.ufpe.br/bitstream/123456789/17709/1/DISSERTA%c3%87AO%20Claudia%20Paes%20Barreto.pdf. Accessed 9 June 2024

Barrett C, Reardon T, Swinnen J, Zilberman D (2022) Agri-food value chain revolutions in low- and middleincome countries. J Econ Lit 60(4):1316–1377. https://doi.org/10.1257/jel.20201539. Accessed01Sept2024

Barros JL de (2019) Racismo ambiental e direito ao lazer no espaço público: um estudo sobre o Parque Santana Ariano Suassuna. Dissertação (Mestrado em Desenvolvimento Urbano), Universidade Federal de Pernambuco, Recife. https://repositorio.ufpe.br/handle/123456789/39968?locale=es. Accessed 19 Aug 2024

Basu D (2018) Marx's analysis of ground-rent: theory, examples and applications. UMASS Amherst Economics Working Papers, p 3. https://scholarworks.umass.edu/cgi/viewcontent.cgi?article=1242&context=econ_workingpaper. Accessed 9 June 2024

Baxi U (2012) The future of human rigths. Oxford University Press India, New Delhi

Beck U (1992) Risk society: Towards a new modernity. Sage Publication, California

Beck V (2018) Iniciativas urbano sustentáveis no Rio de Janeiro: a experiência da horta carioca do Jardim Anil. In: Direito da Regularização Fundiária Urbana Sustentável.

Correia AF (ed). Pesquisa, teoria e prática em torno da Lei Federal n. 13.465/2017. Editar, Juiz de Fora-MG, v 1, pp 9–383

Benevolo L (2001) City history. 3rd edn. Editora Perspectiva, São Paulo, p 16

Benhabib S (2002) The claims of culture: equality and diversity in the global era. Princeton University Press, Princeton, New Jersey. https://www.jstor.org/stable/j.ctv346pnd. Accessed 28 Aug 2024

Beuchot M (1833) Oeuvres Voltaire, vol 14. Lefèvre, Paris, p 122

Biehl J (2017) A expansão irregular dos municípios como forma de degradação ambiental: a necessidade de planejamento para ocupação e uso do solo. In: Função socioambiental da propriedade, vol II. Bühring MA (ed). https://www.ucs.br/site/midia/arquivos/ebook-funcao-ambiental.pdf. Accessed 19 Aug 2024

Bobbio N (2007) Da Estrutura à Função: Novos Estudos da Teoria do Direito. Manole, Barueri, p 92

Borde ALP de (2006) Vazios urbanos: perspectivas contemporâneas. Tese (Doutorado em Arquitetura e Urbanismo) – Faculdade de Arquitetura e Urbanismo, Universidade Federal do Rio de Janeiro, Rio de Janeiro, p 14. http://www.prourb.fau.ufrj.br/integrantes/andrea-de-lacerda-pessoa-borde/. Accessed 19 Aug 2024

Botelho A (2010) Urban land rent: a still valid analysis category. GEOgraphia 10(19):24–45. https://periodicos.uff.br/geographia/article/view/13551/8751. Accessed 9 June 2024

Brakensiek S (2002) The management of common land in northwestern Germany. In: De Moor M, Taylor L, Warde P. The management of common land in north-west Europe, c. 1500–1850. Brepols, Turnhout, Bélgica, pp 225–245

Brand U (2016) How to get out of the multiple crisis? Contours of a critical theory of social-ecological transformation. Environ Val 25(5):503–525. https://doi.org/10.3197/096327116X14703858759017.Accessed20Aug2024

Brasil (2023) Governo Federal. Decreto Nº 11.700. Institui o Programa Nacional de Agricultura Urbana e Periurbana e o Grupo de Trabalho do Programa Nacional de Agricultura Urbana e Periurbana. http://www.planalto.gov.br/ccivil_03/_ato2023-2026/2023/decreto/D11700.htm. Accessed 23 Sept 2024

Brito M (2007) The justification of private property in a constitutional democracy. Almedina, Coimbra, p 73

Carta Mundial pelo Direito à Cidade. Artigo II, item 1.1. https://www.suelourbano.org/wp-content/uploads/2017/08/Carta-Mundial-pelo-Direito-%C3%A0-Cidade.pdf. Accessed 28 Aug 2024

Castells M (1989) The informational city: information technology, economic restructuring, and the urban-regional process. Basil Blackwell, Oxford

Castells M (1996–1998) The information age: economy, society and culture, vol 1: the rise of the network society, vol 2: the power of identity, vol 3: end of millennium. Blackwell, Oxford

Certomà C (2015) Critical urban gardening. RCC Perspectives, 1:13. http://www.jstor.org/stable/26241301. Accessed 27 Aug 2024

César CJ (2006) Comentários: De Bello Gallico. Ebooks Brasil, São Paulo. E-book. http://www.ebooksbrasil.org/eLibris/cesarP.html. Accessed 7 Feb 2024

Clemente J (2012) Vazios urbanos e imóveis subutilizados no centro histórico tombado da cidade de João Pessoa - PB. Dissertação de mestrado, Universidade Federal da Paraíba, Programa de pós-graduação em engenharia urbana e ambiental, João Pessoa. https://repositorio.ufpb.br/jspui/handle/tede/5472?mode=full. Accessed 19 Aug 2024

Clinton N et al (2018) A global geospatial ecosystem services estimate of urban agriculture. Earth's Future, vol 6. https://agupubs.onlinelibrary.wiley.com/doi/full/10.1002/2017EF000536. Accessed 1 Sept 2024

Cortez RP et al (2022) Beyond urban-rural linkages, the defense of territories and cities for life. Barcelona. https://www.right2city.org/wp-content/uploads/2022/11/07_Right-to-the-City-Rural_EN_OK2.pdf. Accessed 20 Aug 2024

Coulanges D (1987) The ancient city. Martins Fontes, São Paulo

Cruz CES (2019) Desenvolvimento e periferia: análise sobre possibilidade de eficácia de instrumentos de política urbana em periferias intramunicipais. Dissertação de Mestrado – Centro de Ciências Sociais, Faculdade de Direito, Universidade do Estado do Rio de Janeiro, Rio de Janeiro, p 18. https://www.bdtd.uerj.br:8443/bitstream/1/9508/1/Carlos%20Eduardo%20Souza%20Cruz%20%20TOTAL%20PROTEGIDO.pdf. Accessed 9 June 2024
Davis M (2006) Planeta de favelas: A involução urbana e o proletariado informal. Boitempo Editorial, São Paulo, p 202. https://edisciplinas.usp.br/pluginfile.php/4126351/mod_resource/content/1/Mike%20Davis%20-%20Planeta%20de%20Favelas.pdf. Accessed 3 Oct 2024
De Moor T (2008) The silent revolution: a new perspective on the emergence of commons, guilds, and others forms of corporate collective action in western Europe. Int Rev Soc Hist 53:179–212
Donnelly J (2013) Universal human rights in theory and practice. Cornell University Press, New York
Emerson RG (1942) Problems of vacant land in the in-town area. Dartmouth College. Massachusetts Institute of Technology. https://dspace.mit.edu/bitstream/handle/1721.1/74376/28952000-MIT.pdf?sequence=2. Accessed 3 Oct 2024
Engels F (2003) A marca. Crítica Marxista, Campinas 17:147–163. www.unicamp.br/cemarx/criticamarxista/critica17-D-engels.pdf..
Eversberg D et al (2022) Social relationships with nature: elements of a framework for socio-ecological structure analysis. Innov Eur J Soc Sci Res 35(3):389–419. https://www.tandfonline.com/doi/full/10.1080/13511610.2022.2095989. Accessed 17 Aug 2024
FAO (1996) Declaration on world food security. Rome. https://www.fao.org/3/w3613e/w3613e00.htm. Accessed 4 Oct 2024
FAO (2007) Right to food and bioenergy, p 1. https://www.fao.org/3/a1614e/a1614e.pdf. Accessed 5 July 2024
FAO (2011) Land Tenure, Investments and the Right to Food. https://www.fao.org/3/i2418e/i2418e.pdf. Accessed 5 July 2024
FAO (2017) The future of food and agriculture—trends and challenges. www.fao.org/3/a-i6583e.pdf. Accessed 5 July 2024
FAO (2017a) The state of food security and nutrition in the world 2017: building resilience for peace and food security. Rome. https://www.wfp.org/publications/2017-state-food-security-and-nutrition-world-sofi-report. Accessed 20 Aug 2024
FAO (2018a) The state of food and agriculture 2018: migration, agriculture and rural development. Rome, p XVII. https://www.fao.org/documents/card/en/c/I9549EN. Accessed 20 Aug 2024
FAO (2018b) Alternative pathways to 2050. Rome, p 7. https://www.fao.org/3/I8429EN/i8429en.pdf. Accessed 20 Aug 2024
FAO (2018c) Food loss and waste and the right to adequate food: Making the connection, p 4. https://www.fao.org/3/ca1397en/CA1397EN.pdf. Accessed 20 Aug 2024
FAO (2019) Framework for the Urban Food Agenda: Leveraging sub-national and local government action to ensure sustainable food systems and improved nutrition. Rome. https://www.fao.org/3/ca3151en/ca3151en.pdf. Accessed 20 Aug 2024
FAO (2020a) Cities and local governments at the forefront in building inclusive and resilient food systems: key results from the FAO survey "Urban Food Systems and Covid-19". https://www.fao.org/3/cb0407en/CB0407EN.pdf. Accessed 5 July 2024
FAO (2020b) COVID-19 and the role of local food production in building more resilient local food systems. p 7. https://www.fao.org/3/cb1020en/CB1020EN.pdf. Accessed 4 Oct 2024
FAO (2020c) State of knowledge of soil biodiversity: Status, challenges and potentialities. Rome: FAO. https://doi.org/10.4060/cb1928enAccessed 5 July 2024
FAO (2020d) The future of food and agriculture: trends and challenges. Rome. https://www.fao.org/3/i6583e/i6583e.pdf. Accessed 1 Sept 2024
FAO (2020e) The State of Food Security and Nutrition in the World 2020: Transforming food systems for affordable healthy diets. Rome: FAO. Available at: https://doi.org/10.4060/ca9692enAccessed 14 April 2024.

FAO (2020f) The state of the world's land and water resources for food and agriculture 2021. https://www.fao.org/3/cb9910en/cb9910en.pdf. Accessed 5 July 2024

FAO (2021) Consumer organizations and the right to adequate food—making the connections. Rome. https://www.fao.org/3/cb3685en/cb3685en.pdf. Accessed 5 July 2024

FAO (2022) The state of food security and nutrition in the world. https://www.fao.org/documents/card/en/c/cc0639en. Accessed 20 Aug 2024

FAO (2022a) The State of World Fisheries and Aquaculture 2022: Towards Blue Transformation. Rome: FAO. https://doi.org/10.4060/cb9910enAccessed 14 April 2024

FAO (2023) The state of food security and nutrition in the world 2023: urbanization, agrifood systems transformation and healthy diets across the rural–urban continuum. Rome, p 250. https://www.fao.org/3/cc3017en/cc3017en.pdf. Accessed 4 Oct 2024

FAO. https://www.youtube.com/watch?v=eEH2TvJRsa4/. Accessed 19 Aug 2024

Ferrari E et al (2023) Towards an integrated garden. Gardeners of all types, unite! Urban Forestry & Urban Greening, vol 81. https://www.sciencedirect.com/science/article/abs/pii/S1618866723000286. Accessed 3 Oct 2024

Figueira L, Costa P (2018) Deslocamentos urbanos involuntários e a remoção da favela Metrô-Mangueira: a produção do espaço a partir das noções de centro e periferia. Involuntary urban displacements and the removal of metrô-Mangueira slum: the production of the space considering the ideas of downtown and outskirts. Revista de Direito da Cidade, São Paulo, 10(4):2143–2163. https://www.e-publicacoes.uerj.br/rdc/article/view/31597. Accessed 3 Oct 2024

Filho AP de Q (2011) Sobre as origens da Favela. Mercator, Santa Catarina, Brasil. 10(23):33–48

Folchi M (2019) Ecologismo de los pobres: conflictos ambientales y justicia ambiental. In: Social-ecological Systems of Latin America: Complexities and Challenges. Delgado LE, Marín VH (eds). Springer Nature Switzerland, p 96. https://www.researchgate.net/publication/337224098_Ecologismo_de_los_pobres_conflictos_ambientales_y_justicia_ambiental. Accessed 19 Aug 2024

Foster JB (1999) Marx's theory of metabolic rift: classical foundations for environmental sociology. Am J Sociol 105(2):366–405. https://www.jstor.org/stable/10.1086/210315. Accessed 17 Aug 2024

France (1789) Declaration of the rights of man and of the citizen. National Constituent Assembly, Paris

France 24 (2024) Chinese ghost town of mansions reclaimed by farmers. https://www.france24.com/en/live-news/20230720-chinese-ghost-town-of-mansions-reclaimed-by-farmers. Accessed 4 Oct 2024

GBD (2016) Global, regional, and national comparative risk assessment of 79 behavioural, environmental and occupational, and metabolic risks or clusters of risks, 1990–2015: a systematic analysis for the global burden of disease Study 2015. Lancet 388(10053):1659–1724. https://doi.org/10.1016/S0140-6736(16)31679-8. Accessed 4 July 2024.

GBD (2017) Global, regional, and national disability-adjusted life-years (DALYs) for 333 diseases and injuries and healthy life expectancy (HALE) for 195 countries and territories, 1990–2016: a systematic analysis for the Global Burden of Disease Study 2016. The Lancet. https://www.thelancet.com/journals/lancet/article/PIIS0140-6736(17)32130-X/fulltext. Accessed 20 Aug 2024

GCAP UCR. Environmental Justice: Food Deserts. https://www.gcapucr.com/environmental-justice-food-deserts. Accessed 20 Aug 2024

Germany (1983) BKleingG – Bundeskleingartengesetz. https://www.gesetze-im-internet.de/bkleingg/BJNR002100983.html. Accessed 3 Oct 2024

Gilbert J (2017) Land grabbing, investments & indigenous peoples' rights to land and natural resources: case studies and legal analysis. Copenhagen. https://www.iwgia.org/images/publications/new-publications/land-grabbing-indigenous-peoples-rights.compressed.pdf. Accessed 5 July 2024

Gonzales S (1985) Urban land rent: hypotheses to explain its role in the evolution of the city. In: Farret R (ed) The space of the city: contribution to urban analysis. Projeto, São Paulo, pp 93–114

Guttmann A (2022) Plateformes de développement urbain, villes de la connaissance et développement durable: l'économie politique des biens communs urbains dans le contexte du changement climatique. Sociology. Université Paris-Nord, Paris XIII, p 38. https://theses.hal.science/tel-04160619. Accessed 4 Oct 2024

Hall P (2004) Megaciudades, ciudades mundiales y ciudades globales. In: Lo urbano en 20 autores contemporáneos. Ramos AM (ed), pp 117–132

Hamilton AJ et al (2014) Give peas a chance? Urban agriculture in developing countries: a review. Agron Sustain Dev 34(1):45–73. https://link.springer.com/article/10.1007/s13593-013-0155-8. Accessed 4 Sept 2024

Harris D, Fuller D (2014) Agriculture: definition and overview. https://www.researchgate.net/publication/301345493_Agriculture_Definition_and_Overview#fullTextFileContent. Accessed 17 Aug 2024

Harvey D (1980) Social justice and the city. Hucitec, São Paulo

Harvey D (2008) The right to the city. New Left Review, vol 53. https://newleftreview.org/issues/ii53/articles/david-harvey-the-right-to-the-city. Accessed 19 Aug 2024

Hoffman MT (2012) Climate change impacts on African rangelands. Rangelands 30(3). https://www.researchgate.net/publication/305199366_Climate_Change_Impacts_on_African_Rangelands. Accessed 20 Aug 2024

IBGE (2017) Censo agropecuário. https://www.ibge.gov.br/estatisticas/economicas/agricultura-e-pecuaria/21814-2017-censo-agropecuario.html?=&t=conceitos-e-metodos. Accessed 4 Oct 2024

IBGE (2022a) Censo Demográfico 2022: População e domicílios, p 27. https://biblioteca.ibge.gov.br/visualizacao/livros/liv102011.pdf. Accessed 4 Oct 2024

IBGE (2022b) Favelas e Comunidades Urbanas. https://www.ibge.gov.br/geociencias/organizacao-do-territorio/tipologias-do-territorio/15788-aglomerados-subnormais.html?=&t=o-que-e. Accessed 3 Oct 2024

IBGE (2024) Favelas e Comunidades Urbanas. https://biblioteca.ibge.gov.br/visualizacao/livros/liv102062.pdf. Accessed 3 Mar 2024

Jaramillo S (2010) Hacia uma teoria de La renta Del solo urbano. 2rd edn. Ediciones uniandes, Bogotá, p 178

Jardim F (2018) IPTU progressivo no tempo ou arrecadação de bem vago abandonado?: aplicabilidade de instrumentos jurídico-urbanísticos em imóveis ociosos do bairro do Recife. Mestrado em Desenvolvimento Urbano – UFPE, Recife. https://repositorio.ufpe.br/handle/123456789/32193. Accessed 19 Aug 2024

Júnior NS, Libório DC (2021) Questões chave sobre a noção jurídica do direito à cidade. Revista de Direito da Cidade 13(3):1466–1494. https://www.e-publicacoes.uerj.br/rdc/article/view/43832. Accessed 3 Oct 2024

Keeffe G (2016) Hardware software interface: A strategy for the design of urban agriculture. In: Roggema R (ed) Sustainable urban agriculture and food planning. Routledge, pp 15–37

Kelleher C et al (2020) Urban vacant lands impart hydrological benefits across city landscapes. Nat Commun 11(1):1563. https://pubmed.ncbi.nlm.nih.gov/32218437/https://www.webofscience.com/wos/woscc/full-record/WOS:000522450900002. Accessed 19 Aug 2024

Le Corbusier (1933) The Athens charter. https://jasonsedar.files.wordpress.com/2011/03/the_athens_charter.pdf. Accessed 19 Aug 2024

Le Goff J (2007) As raízes medievais da Europa. 2rd edn. Vozes, São Paulo

Leão XIII (1891) Rerum Novarum: On the condition of workers. Roma. https://www.vatican.va/content/leo-xiii/pt/encyclicals/documents/hf_l-xiii_enc_15051891_rerum-novarum.html. Accessed 9 June 2024

Lefebvre H (1968) Le droit a la ville. Anthropos, Paris

Lefebvre H (1991) The production of space. Blackwell, Oxford

Lefebvre H (1999) The urban revolution. University of Minnesota Press, Minnesota

Lima C (2019) Agriculturas na cidade do Rio de Janeiro: dicotomias e as especificidades da agricultura urbana. Dissertação (Mestrado em Desenvolvimento Territorial e Políticas Públicas), Instituto de Ciências Sociais Aplicadas, Universidade Federal Rural do Rio de Janeiro, Seropédica, p 119 et seq. https://tede.ufrrj.br/jspui/bitstream/jspui/5596/2/2019%20-%20Caren%20Freitas%20de%20Lima.pdf. Accessed 23 May 2024

Lipietz A (1988) Capital and its space. 2rd edn. Nobel, São Paulo. p 209

Lira R (2017) Remoção de favelas / Removal of slums. Revista De Direito Da Cidade, São Paulo, 9(3):1383–1932. https://www.e-publicacoes.uerj.br/rdc/article/view/29022. Accessed 3 Oct 2024

Machado A. Agricultura urbana. Embrapa. https://www.embrapa.br/busca-de-publicacoes/-/publicacao/565842/agricultura-urbana. Accessed 4 Oct 2024

Maricato E (1985) Direito à terra ou direito à cidade? Revista de Cultura Vozes 79(6):405–411. https://www.academia.edu/42297879/Direito_%C3%A0_terra_ou_direito_%C3%A0_cidad. Accessed 19 Aug 2024

Maricato E (1997) Housing and city. 7rd edn. Atual, São Paulo

Marx K (1989) The capital, vol III. Bertrand Brasil, Rio de Janeiro

Masterson VA et al (2017) The contribution of sense of place to social-ecological systems research: a review and research agenda. Ecol Soc 22(1):49. https://doi.org/10.5751/ES-08872-220149. Accessed04Oct2024

Mazoyer M, Roudart L (2010) History of agriculture in the world: from the Neolithic to the contemporary crisis. Editora UNESP, São Paulo, p 131

Mcclintock N (2010) Why farm the city? Theorizing urban agriculture through a lens of metabolic rift. Camb J RegNs, Econ Soc 3(2):191–207. https://academic.oup.com/cjres/article/3/2/191/441835?login=true. Accessed 4 Oct 2024

Mceldowney J (2017) Urban agriculture in Europe: patterns, challenges and policies. https://www.europarl.europa.eu/RegData/etudes/IDAN/2017/614641/EPRS_IDA(2017)614641_EN.pdf. Accessed 4 Oct 2024

Mcgreevy SR (2022) Sustainable agrifood systems for a post-growth world. Nature Sustainability. https://www.nature.com/articles/s41893-022-00933-5. Accessed 20 Aug 2024

Montesquieu (2024) On the corruption of the principle of democracy. Accuel, The Spirit of Law. Book VIII. ENS Lyon. https://montesquieu.ens-lyon.fr/spip.php?article2677. Accessed 19 Aug 2023.

Moore M et al (2014) Studying the complexity of change: toward an analytical framework for understanding deliberate social-ecological transformations. Ecol Soc 19(4). https://doi.org/10.5751/ES-06966-190454. Accessed 4 Oct 202

Mota M (2009) Theoretical foundations of the social function of property: property in Thomas Aquinas. Revista Jurídica da Presidência 10(92):14. https://revistajuridica.presidencia.gov.br/index.php/saj/article/view/210. Accessed 20 June 2024

Motta R (2021) Food for justice: power, politics and food inequalities in a bioeconomy. Preliminary research program. Food for justice working paper series, 1. Berlin. https://refubium.fu-berlin.de/bitstream/handle/fub188/32086/WP_%231.pdf?sequence=1&isAllowed=y. Accessed 4 Oct 2024

Moura E (2017) A função social como elemento estruturante da teoria do domínio público: o dever de funcionalização dos bens públicos. Tese (Doutorado em Direito Civil Constitucional; Direito da Cidade; Direito Internacional e Integração Econômica; Direi) - Universidade do Estado do Rio de Janeiro, Rio de Janeiro, p 353 et seq. https://www.bdtd.uerj.br:8443/handle/1/9365. Accessed 19 Aug 2024

Moyn S (2012) The last utopia: Human rigths in history. Harvard University Press, Cambridge, Massachusetts

Mutua MW (2001) Savages, victims, and saviors: the metaphor of human rights. Harv Int Law J 42(201). https://digitalcommons.law.buffalo.edu/journal_articles/570. Accessed 28 Aug 2024

Németh J, Langhorst J (2014) Rethinking urban transformation: Temporary uses for vacant land. 40(B):143–150

Nilsen M (2016) The working man's green space: allotment gardens in England, France, and Germany, 1870–1919. J Hist Geogr 53:124–125. https://doi.org/10.1016/j.jhg.2015.08.009.Accessed03Oct2024
Nussberger A (2022) Os direitos humanos: História, filosofia, conflitos. Editora Fundação Fênix, Porto Alegre. https://www.fundarfenix.com.br/_files/ugd/9b34d5_b1199b1f46824dc1a0f99379c7848107.pdf. Accessed 18 Aug 2024
Oliveira NS (2023) Produção capitalista racista da espacialidade carioca: uma análise a partir de conflitos fundiários urbanos. PhD thesis. University of the State of Rio de Janeiro.
Oliveira SSR (2021) Informalidade urbana, classe trabalhadora e raça no Rio de Janeiro: a história dos censos de favelas (1948–1960). Revista de História 180:1–27. São Paulo. https://www.revistas.usp.br/revhistoria/article/view/170643. Accessed 3 Oct 2024
Oliveira NS de (2016) Gentrificação e moradia social: como a política urbana pode atuar. Dissertação (Mestrado em Direito), Universidade do Estado do Rio de Janeiro, Rio de Janeiro, p 23 et seq. https://www.bdtd.uerj.br:8443/handle/1/9769. Accessed 3 Oct 2024
Oliveira MRN (2005) Land rent and its somersaults: a discussion on urban land rent, soil as a commodity and the centrality of Iguatemi. GeoTextos, vol 1. https://periodicos.ufba.br/index.php/geotextos/article/view/3029. Accessed 9 June 2024
Oliveira N (1996) 'Favelas and Ghettos: Race and Class in Rio de Janeiro and New York City', Latin American Perspectives, 23(4): 72. Washington. http://www.jstor.org/stable/2634130. Accessed 28 Sept 2024
Olsson P, Galaz V, Boonstra WJ (2014) Sustainability transformations: a resilience perspective. Ecol Soc 19(4):1. https://doi.org/10.5751/ES-06799-190401.Accessed04Oct2024
Opitz I et al (2016) Contributing to food security in urban areas: differences between urban agriculture and peri-urban agriculture in the global North. Agric Hum Values 33:341–358. https://link.springer.com/article/10.1007/s10460-015-9610-2. Accessed 1 Sept 2024
Orsini F et al (2013) Urban agriculture in the developing world: a review. Agron Sustain Dev 33(4):695–720. https://link.springer.com/article/10.1007/s13593-013-0143-z. Accessed 4 Sept 2024
Pagani E, Alves J, Cordeiro S (2015) Socio-spatial segregation and real estate speculation in urban space Argumentum. Argumentum 7(1):167–183. Espírito Santo. https://www.academia.edu/71780234/Socio_spatial_segregation_and_property_speculation_in_the_urban_space. Accessed 20 June 2024
Patterson J et al (2017) Exploring the governance and politics of transformations towards sustainability. Environ Innov Soc Transit 24:1–16. https://www.sciencedirect.com/science/article/pii/S2210422416300843. Accessed 4 Oct 2024
Pearson LJ, Pearson L, Pearson CJ (2010) Sustainable urban agriculture: Stocktake and opportunities. Int J Agric Sustain 8:7–19. https://www.researchgate.net/publication/233555575_Sustainable_urban_agriculture_Stocktake_and_opportunities. Accessed 1 Sept 2024
Plomwood V (2004) Gender, eco-feminism and the environment. In: White R (ed) Controversies in environmental sociology. Cambridge University Press, Cambridge. https://ebin.pub/urban-food-production-for-ecosocialism-cultivating-the-city-1nbsped-9780367674175-9780367674182-9781003131281.html. Accessed 4 Oct 2024
Porter et al (2014) Food security and food production systems. In: IPCC. Climate Change 2014: Impacts, Adaptation, and Vulnerability. Part A: Global and Sectoral Aspects. Contribution of Working Group II to the Fifth Assessment Report of the Intergovernmental Panel on Climate Change, pp 485–533. www.ipcc.ch/pdf/assessmentreport/ar5/wg2/WGIIAR5-Chap7_FINAL.pdf. Accessed 5 July 2024
Poulsen MN et al (2015) A systematic review of urban agriculture and food security impacts in low-income countries. Food Policy 55:131–146. https://www.sciencedirect.com/science/article/abs/pii/S0306919215000809. Accessed 4 Sept 2024
Pungas L (2023) Invisible (bio)economies: a framework to assess the 'blind spots' of dominant bioeconomy models. Sustain Sci, 18:689–706. https://link.springer.com/article/10.1007/s11625-023-01292-6. Accessed 5 July 2024

Relly E (2022) A experiência dos "commons" como via para desenvolver uma ecologia política. [Entrevista concedida a] João Vitor Santos. Instituto Humanitas Unisinos. https://www.ihu.unisinos.br/622765-propriedade-comunal-na-alemanha-pre-moderna-a-experiencia-de-cooperacao-social-e-uso-comum-da-terra-que-pode-inspirar-a-producao-em-nosso-tempo-entrevista-especial-com-eduardo-relly. Accessed 9 June 2024
Rolnik R (2019) Guerra dos Lugares. Boitempo Editorial, São Paulo
Rolnik R (2004) What is city. 3rd edn. Editora Brasiliense, São Paulo. https://arquiteturaeurbanismosite.files.wordpress.com/2016/03/rolnik-raquel-o-que-c3a9-cidade-livro-completo.pdf. Accessed 9 June 2024
Rolnik R (1988) O que é cidade. Editora Brasiliense, São Paulo. https://edisciplinas.usp.br/pluginfile.php/4405239/mod_resource/content/1/O%20que%20%C3%A9%20Cidade%20parte%201.pdf. Accessed 19 Aug 2024
Rosseau JJ (1754) Discourse on the origin of inequality a discourse on a subject proposed by the Academy of Dijon: What is the origin of inequality among men, and is it authorised by natural law? ISN, Zurich
Santos, AMSP et al (2020) O município e os desafios da política urbana em aglomerados urbanos: a experiência da metrópole fluminense. Geo UERJ, Rio de Janeiro. https://www.e-publicacoes.uerj.br/index.php/geouerj/article/view/47268/32232. Accessed 19 Aug 2024
Santo R, Palmer A, Kim B (2016) Vacant lots to vibrant plots. John Hopkins Center for Liveable Future, p 2. https://clf.jhsph.edu/sites/default/files/2019-01/vacant-lots-to-vibrant-plots.pdf. Accessed 4 Oct 2024
Santos AMSP, Cruz CES de (2018) Regularização Fundiária: de seu avanço institucional à reprodução crescente do problema que a originou. In: Direito da regularização fundiária urbana sustentável: pesquisa, teoria e prática sobre a Lei Federal nº 13.465/2017. Correia AF (ed). Editar Editora Associada Ltda, Juiz de Fora, p 40. https://nepec-uerj.com.br/wp-content/uploads/2021/12/Direito-Regularizac%CC%A7a%CC%83o-Fundia%CC%81ria-Final-com-capa.pdf>. Accessed 3 Oct 2024
Santos, B de S (1982) The State, the law and the urban question. Revista Crítica de Ciências Sociais 9:9–86, p 43. https://estudogeral.uc.pt/handle/10316/10792?locale=en. Accessed 9 June 2024
Sarlet I (2022) Conceito de direitos e garantias fundamentais. Enciclopédia jurídica da PUC-SP, 3rd edn. Pontifícia Universidade Católica de São Paulo, São Paulo. https://enciclopediajuridica.pucsp.br/verbete/67/edicao-2/conceito-de-direitos-e-garantias-fundamentais. Accessed 28 Aug 2024
Schonardie EF (2017) A concretização dos direitos humanos e a questão dos aglomerados subnormais nas cidades brasileiras. Revista de Direito da Cidade 9(3):1363–1382. Rio de Janeiro. https://doi.org/10.12957/rdc.2017.27166. Accessed 3 Oct 2024
Sen A (2004) Elements of a theory of human rights. Philos Public Aff 32(4). http://www.mit.edu/~shaslang/mprg/asenETHR.pdf. Accessed 28 Aug 2024
Silva H (2006) Entre o amor ao Brasil e ao modo de ser alemão. Oikos, São Leopoldo
Siniscalchi M (2020) Semeando o comum na metrópole contemporânea: as hortas urbanas comunitárias no Rio de Janeiro (RJ). Dissertação de Mestrado, Departamento de Geografia e Meio Ambiente, Pontifícia Universidade Católica do Rio de Janeiro, p 241 et seq. https://www.maxwell.vrac.puc-rio.br/49639/49639.PDF. Accessed 23 May 2024
Smit J, Nasr J, Ratta A (2001a) Cities that feed themselves: food jobs and sustainable cities. United Nations Development Programme. http://jacsmit.com/book/Chap01.pdf. Accessed 1 Sept 2024
Smit J, Nasr J, Ratta A (2001b) Constraints to Urban Agriculture. In: Smit J, Nasr J, Ratta A (eds) Urban Agriculture—food, jobs and sustainable cities. The Urban Agriculture Network, New York
Smith A (2014) The wealth of nations. Penguin Classics, Nova York
Song XQ et al (2020) Urban vacant land in growing urbanization: an international review. J Geogr Sci 30(4):669–687. China. https://www.webofscience.com/wos/woscc/full-record/WOS:000528559600010. Accessed 19 Aug 2024

Sousa C (2010) Do cheio para o vazio: metodologia e estratégia na avaliação de espaços urbanos obsoletos. Mestrado em Arquitetura, Universidade Técnica de Lisboa, Lisboa. https://fenix.tecnico.ulisboa.pt/downloadFile/395142195938/DO%20CHEIO%20PARA%20O%20VAZIO_versao%20final.pdf. Accessed 19 Aug 2024

Souza, MAA de (1994) The identity of the metropolis. Editora Hucitec, São Paulo, p 257

Souza G (2004) Escrituras Públicas: Teoria e Prática. São Paulo: Juarez de Oliveira.

Steuri B, Vignola G (2015) Towards productive and socio-natural urban landscapes: tapping urban agriculture's potential as a tool for sustainable development. Master's thesis on Resource efficiency in architecture and planning. Hafen City Hamburg University, p 55. https://repos.hcu-hamburg.de/bitstream/hcu/650/2/2022-06-01_steuri-bettina_vignola-gionatan_masterarbeit.pdf. Accessed 13 Sept 2024

Stoetzer B (2018) Ruderal Ecologies: rethinking nature, migration, and the urban landscape in Berlin. Cult Anthropol 33:295–323. https://www.researchgate.net/publication/325460611_Ruderal_Ecologies_Rethinking_Nature_Migration_and_the_Urban_Landscape_in_Berlin. Accessed 3 Oct 2024

Taguchi M, Santini G (2019) Urban agriculture in the Global North & South: a perspective from FAO. Field Actions Science Reports. Institut Veolia: Aubervilliers, France. http://journals.openedition.org/factsreports/5610. Accessed 4 Sept 2024

Teixeira VM de L, Pereira CS, Silva CF (2022) Social division of space and socio-spatial fragmentation. Vol 21. Mercator, Fortaleza. https://www.scielo.br/j/mercator/a/X4mCHxhdMgP7Qy6LcVkRdNz/. Accessed 19 Aug 2024

The New Charter of Athens (2003) The European Council of Town Planners' Vision for Cities in the 21st century. http://www.itc.cnr.it/ba/re/Documenti/The%20New%20Charter%20of%20Athens%202003.htm. Accessed 19 Aug 2024

Thomas of Aquino S. A theological suma II. vol 6, ca 1265–1273. https://www.ccel.org/ccel/aquinas/summa.toc.html. Accessed 9 June 2024

Titarelli F et al (2022) food citizenship as an agroecological tool for food system re-design. Sustainability 14(3):1590. https://www.mdpi.com/2071-1050/14/3/1590. Accessed 4 Oct 2024

Turo KJ et al (2020) Conservation in post-industrial cities: How does vacant land management and landscape configuration influence urban bees? Br Ecol Soc 58(1):58–69. https://besjournals.onlinelibrary.wiley.com/doi/full/10.1111/1365-2664.13773. Accessed 19 Aug 2024

United Nations (2022) The human right to a clean, healthy and sustainable environment. https://digitallibrary.un.org/record/3982508?ln=en. Accessed 28 Aug 2024

United Nations (2018) Habitat bried on migration and cities. Types of migration. p 3. https://unhabitat.org/sites/default/files/documents/2019-05/migration_brochure_10122018.pdf. Accessed 20 Aug 2024

United Nations (2017) Habitat III: new urban agenda. Quito. https://habitat3.org/wp-content/uploads/NUA-English.pdf/. Accessed 1 Sept 2024

United Nations (2016) Paris agreement. https://unfccc.int/process-and-meetings/the-paris-agreement. Accessed 20 Aug 2024

United Nations (2015) Right to food. https://www.ohchr.org/sites/default/files/Documents/Issues/Food/A-70-287.pdf. Accessed 20 Aug 2024

United Nations (1948) Universal declaration of human rights. https://www.un.org/en/about-us/universal-declaration-of-human-rights. Accessed 28 Aug 2024

United Nations Human Settlements Programme (2003) The challenge of slums global report on human settlements. London, p VI. https://unhabitat.org/sites/default/files/download-manager-files/The%20Challenge%20of%20Slums%20%20Global%20Report%20on%20Human%20Settlements%202003.pdf. Accessed 3 Oct 2024

United States of America (2017) Department of Agriculture. Food Desert Locator. Release nº 0191.11. https://www.fns.usda.gov/tags/food-desert-locator. Accessed 20 Aug 2024

Verás Neto F (2008) Classical Roman law: its legal institutes and its legacy. In: Fundamentals of the History of Private Law, p 128

Vogel E et al (2019) The effects of climate extremes on global agricultural yields - IOPscience 14(5). https://iopscience.iop.org/article/10.1088/1748-9326/ab154b/meta. Accessed 20 Aug 2024
Vuuren V et al (2012) A proposal for a new scenario framework to support research and assessment in different climate research communities. Glob Environ Chang 22(1):21–35. https://doi.org/10.1016/j.gloenvcha.2011.08.002. Accessed 5 July 2024
Walsh L et al (2022) Potential of urban green spaces for supporting horticultural production: A national scale analysis. Environ Res Lett 17(1). https://iopscience.iop.org/article/10.1088/1748-9326/ac4730. Accessed 1 Sept 2024
Wegelin E, Borgman K (1995) Options for municipal interventions in urban poverty alleviation. Environ Urban 7(2):131–152. https://journals.sagepub.com/doi/pdf/https://doi.org/10.1177/095624789500700219. Accessed 4 Oct 2024
Wermuth M, Campos P (2022) Livrai-nos de todo mal: medo, controle social e segregação espacial. Revista De Direito Da Cidade 14(4):2608–2636. São Paulo. https://www.e-publicacoes.uerj.br/index.php/rdc/article/view/60193. Accessed 3 Oct 2024
Westley FR et al (2013) A theory of transformative agency in linked social-ecological systems. Ecol Soc 18(3):27. https://doi.org/10.5751/ES-05072-180327.Accessed04Oct2024
Weston B, Bollier D (2013a) Green governance: ecological survival, human rights, and the law of the Commons. Cambridge University Press, New York, p 87. http://students.aiu.edu/submissions/profiles/resources/onlineBook/K9S4V4_Green_Governance_Ecological_Survival-_Human_Rights-_and_the_Law_of_the_Commons.pdf. Accessed 26 Aug 2024
Weston B, Bollier D (2013b) Universal Covenant affirming a human right to commons- and rights-based governance of earth's natural wealth and resources. J Hum Righ Environ 4(2):215–225. https://www.elgaronline.com/view/journals/jhre/4-2/jhre.2013.02.05.xml. Accessed 20 Aug 2024
Wolkmer AC (2008) Fundamentos de história do direito. 4rd edn. Editora Del Rey, Belo Horizonte
World Charter for the Right to the City (2001) Right to the city. Porto Alegre. https://www.right2city.org/document/world-charter-for-the-right-to-the-city/. Accessed 19 Aug 2024
World Migration Report (2015) Migrants and cities, new partnerships to manage mobility. https://www.iom.int/sites/g/files/tmzbdl486/files/country/docs/syria/IOM-World-Migration-Report-2015-Overview.pdf. Accessed 20 Aug 2024
Zanotto LC (2016) Semeando o almoço na laje: manual de implementação de hortas urbanas em comunidades de baixa renda, uma alternativa frente a problemas de desigualdade social. (Dissertação) Programa de Pós-Graduação em Práticas em Desenvolvimento, Universidade Federal Rural do Rio de Janeiro. https://tede.ufrrj.br/handle/jspui/1397. Accessed 23 May 2024
Zezza A, Tasciotti L (2010) Urban agriculture, poverty, and food security: empirical evidence from a sample of developing countries. Food Pol 35(4):265–273. https://www.sciencedirect.com/science/article/abs/pii/S0306919210000515. Accessed 4 Sept 2024

Chapter 3
Standards Towards a Social-Ecological Transformation of Urban Food and Land

3.1 The Right to Food Standard

The **Human Right to Adequate Food** (right to food) is settled in Article 25 of the United Nations Universal Declaration of Human Rights as part of the right to a standard of living,[1] so it is important to ensure health and well-being and a way to fulfill other (human) rights.[2] It goes much further than charity or a restrictive sense of hunger prevention,[3] and according to its **legal** background, it is accomplished when every person,[4] alone or in a community, has physical and continuous economic access to adequate and culturally acceptable food produced and consumed sustainably, preserving access to food for future generations, or the means for its procurement (resources that will enable the person to make, earn or purchase) in dignity.[5] This statement has four essential and **combined** key components that the United Nations recognizes[6]:

[1] United Nations (1948).

[2] Sepúlvida et al. (2004) and FAO (2007b).

[3] United Nations (1999).

[4] FAO (2007a), op. cit.

[5] "There are emergency situations – wars, natural disasters – and persons – disabled, sick or orphaned – who cannot feed themselves and need assistance. People in those circumstances must receive assistance, whether food aid, cash, or any other form." FAO (2007a). "Adequate food must be accessible to everyone, including physically vulnerable individuals, such as infants and young children, elderly people, the physically disabled, the terminally ill, and persons with persistent medical problems, including the mentally ill. Victims of natural disasters, people living in disaster-prone areas, and other especially disadvantaged groups may need special attention and sometimes priority consideration with respect to the accessibility of food. A particular vulnerability is that of many indigenous population groups whose access to their ancestral lands may be threatened." United Nations (1999, p. 4).

[6] United Nations (1999), loc. cit.

F. Jardim, *Right to Food in Community Gardens*, LITES - Legal Issues in Transdisciplinary Environmental Studies 6,
https://doi.org/10.1007/978-3-032-19612-5_3

(a) physical **availability** sufficient to satisfy the dietary needs[7] of individuals according to demand's interest,[8] and involving the freedom of choice regarding production (including food self-provision) and distribution (food available for sale in markets and shops).
(b) economic and physical **accessibility** stable over time, not affecting the satisfaction of human rights and basic needs or the resources for future generations, encompassing intangible qualities linked to food and its consumption, while also delving into the details regarding the availability of food resources.
(c) **acceptability** means food free from adverse substances for a dietary need according to age, living conditions, health, occupation, sex, etc. Additionally, it should be devoid of any impurities or remnants from industrial or agricultural practices, such as pesticides, hormones, or veterinary medications, and should align with cultural acceptability for consumption.
(d) economic, social, and environmental **sustainability**, representing long-term availability and accessibility. The food sustainability principles are:

> Principle 1. Improving efficiency in the use of resources is crucial to sustainable agriculture; Principle 2. Sustainability requires direct action to conserve, protect, and enhance natural resources; Principle 3. Agriculture that fails to protect and improve rural livelihoods, equity, and social well-being is unsustainable; Principle 4. Enhanced people, communities, and ecosystems resilience is key to sustainable agriculture; Principle 5. Sustainable food and agriculture require responsible and effective governance mechanisms.[9]

These above key components of the right to food must be seen together. So, for example, the lack of access to natural resources is a problem that affects production, and without products, there is no or rare food availability. This triggers issues related to prices (accessibility) and acceptability and is challenging for the food chain's long-term perspective (sustainability). Then, the categorization is important to understand what part of the human right to food is observed by individuals and groups from society and government. Otherwise, when not followed, the human right to food is violated. It is also relevant to create specific laws and public policies to achieve the non-observed element that reverberates in other concepts, such as food insecurity and violation of food sovereignty.

---

[7] "Dietary needs implies that the diet as a whole contains a mix of nutrients for physical and mental growth, development and maintenance, and physical activity that are in compliance with human physiological needs at all stages throughout the life cycle and according to gender and occupation. Measures may, therefore need to be taken to maintain, adapt, or strengthen dietary diversity and appropriate consumption and feeding patterns, including breastfeeding, while ensuring that changes in availability and access to food supply, as a minimum, do not negatively affect dietary composition and intake." United Nations (1999), loc. cit.

[8] "Free from adverse substances sets requirements for food safety and for a range of protective measures by both public and private means to prevent contamination of foodstuffs through adulteration and/or through bad environmental hygiene or inappropriate handling at different stages throughout the food chain; care must also be taken to identify and avoid or destroy naturally occurring toxins." United Nations (1999), loc. cit.

[9] FAO (2014).

3.1.1 Stakeholders and Responsibilities

International law establishes, in general terms, human rights as **individual rights**. Specifically, the right to food means that "every individual not only has the right to feed themselves and their family in dignity but also has the responsibility to do everything within their power to do so."[10] This represents access to resources, freedom to realize other human rights, and participation in discussions, decisions, and monitoring programs, policies, and actions.[11] Even so, the "individual-rights approach may be insufficient to defend some crucial collective interests not only from a procedural point of view but also from a substantive one,"[12] such as the indigenous people's primary view of the collective right to food.[13] As "collective," they are ascribed to groups of people and can only be claimed by the joint entity and its authorized agents. Without excluding individual safeguarding of rights (with indirect and cumulative effects on the group), collective rights have a direct and additional value to joint protection.

Sometimes, it is even the case of a better appropriate concept than individual rights. For example, indigenous people "possess **collective rights which are indispensable for their existence, well-being, and integral development as peoples**"[14] as the case of rights on lands, territories, and resources, and subsistence-based activities carried out collectively that are part of their cultural identity, and usually the only source of existence. It would be hard to respect an individual perspective. Thus, the collective right "may be the expression of the collective dimension of a corresponding individual right (e.g., the right to collective property), or it may be inherently collective – new and different in comparison to the rights of the individual (e.g., the right of peoples to self-determination, right to culture, right to development)."[15,16]

Just after "every individual," the Universal Declaration of Human Rights affirms that "**every organ of society**" promotes respect, recognition, and observance of human rights.[17] To organize the general provision, the first presented element is the States in the concept of nations that are duty-bearers with legal obligations according to international treaties they have ratified. To implement the right to adequate food at the national level is necessary, States must

---

[10] FAO (2007c).

[11] FAO (2007c), loc. cit.

[12] United Nations (2007).

[13] "In fact, the Declaration of Atitlán states 'that the content of the right to food of indigenous peoples is a collective right.' Both the United Nations Declaration on the Rights of Indigenous Peoples and the Inter-American Commission on Human Rights (IACHR) Draft Declaration on Indigenous Rights as well as the ILO Convention No. 169 acknowledge certain collective rights." FAO (2009), op. cit., p. 18.

[14] United Nations (2007), loc. cit.

[15] FAO (2009), loc. cit.

[16] (2009), op. cit., p. 18.

[17] United Nations (1948).

> To **respect** existing access to adequate food requires States parties not to take any measures that result in preventing such access; To **protect** requires efforts by the State to ensure that enterprises or individuals do not deprive individuals of their access to adequate food; To **fulfil** (facilitate) or pro-actively engage in activities intended to strengthen people's access to and utilization of resources, and means to ensure their livelihood, including food security; To **fulfil** (provide) the right directly when an individual or group is unable, for reasons beyond their control, to enjoy the right to adequate food by the means at their disposal. This also applies to victims of natural or other disasters.[18]

Thus, nations cannot be inactive. They must take steps to maximize their available resources for the **progressive realization** "by all appropriate means, including the adoption of **legislative measures** and the full effectiveness."[19] For example, the right to food is **constitutionally** applicable by (i) "explicit and direct recognition as a human right in itself or as part of another, broader human right; (ii) the right to food implicit in a broader human right; (iii) explicit recognition of the right to food as a goal or directive principle within the constitutional order; and (iv) indirect recognition, through interpretation of other human rights by the judiciary."[20] Although, there is no legal protection, enforcement, or applicability in many countries. Thus, to be effective, the right to adequate food should extend beyond the confines of constitutional law.[21] **Brazil** is a highlighted case study by the United Nations[22] because it has explicit constitutional provisions on the right to food regarding direct and general statements involving specific groups connected to the standard of living and as directive principles. In contrast, in broader rights, **Germany** has implicit constitutional provisions on the right to food.

On the topic of obligations, there are four **immediate effects** under the International Covenant on Economic, Social and Cultural Rights:

> **The elimination of discrimination** in access to food and related resources based on race, color, sex, language, age, religion, political or other opinion, national or social origin, property, birth, disability, or other status, and the adoption of measures to eradicate discrimination on these grounds. **Obligation to "take steps"**: While the full realization of the right to food may be achieved progressively, steps towards that goal must be taken within a reasonably short time. Such efforts should be deliberate, concrete, and targeted as clearly as possible,

---

[18] The Committee on Economic, Social and Cultural Rights in General Comment No. 12 also defined the obligations that States must fulfill in order. United Nations (1999), loc. cit.

[19] According to Article 2.1 of the International Covenant on Economic, Social and Cultural Rights United Nations (1966).

[20] "Currently, 56 constitutions protect the right to food either implicitly or explicitly as a justiciable right, or explicitly in the form of a directive principle of state. In addition, through the direct applicability of international treaties, the right to food is directly applicable, with a higher status than national legislation, in at least 51 countries, 84 thus reaching a total of 106 countries in which the right to food is applicable. Finally, ten countries have already adopted a framework law on the right to food or food security recognizing the right to food, and a further nine countries are in the process of drafting such legislation." FAO (2010a), op. cit.

[21] "45 countries have recognized the right to adequate food in their constitutions, and almost 30 countries have an explicit recognition of the right to sufficient food in their constitutions." FAO (2022b), op. cit.

[22] Landiva (2012).

using all appropriate means and resources.[23] **Prohibition of retrogressive measures:** States cannot allow the existing level of fulfillment of the right to food to deteriorate unless there are strong justifications.[24] **Protection of minimum essential story of the right to food**: For the right to food, States have to ensure the satisfaction of, at the very least, the minimum necessary level required to be free from hunger, even in times of natural or other disasters. Suppose a State fails to meet these obligations owing to resource restraints. In that case, it must demonstrate that it has made every effort to use all available resources to satisfy these core obligations as a matter of priority. Even if the resources at its disposal are inadequate, the Government must still introduce low-cost and targeted programs to assist those most in need so that its limited resources are used efficiently and effectively.[25]

The State is also responsible for government, laws, policymakers, and inspectors at national and local levels, making isolated or cumulative attitudes to implement, monitor, and enforce the right to food.[26] To give an example, adopting **economically related** measures regarding public budget, household income, food prices, remuneration of labor (wages), expatriated profits that remunerate foreign investors, money transfer (such as pensions or social protection payments), financial incentives, credit lines, taxes exemptions, taxes on international transactions and trade policies (imports and exports), taxes from the production sectors (indirect taxes, net of subsidies), households (income, consumption taxes) and enterprises (corporate taxes). Another way is by the **public management** to promote work, health, education (and other human rights related to the right to food) and public services (including water, gas, and electricity), community kitchens and restaurants, street fairs with agroecological products, restaurants to low-income people, schools' food menu, sanitary measures, society participation in the public budget construction, protection of vulnerable groups, use licensing processes to influence permitted food premises or what outlets are allowed to sell, verify if non-State actor is respecting the right to food, also, through **laws and regulations** of food production, distribution, consumption, and post-consumption, such as land-use policies and zoning laws to support and incentives nutritious foods food chain (including the security of land tenure, allowing urban agriculture, advertising restrictions, and restricting food retail and food service outlets), and imposing advertising limitations, or introducing taxes

[23] Examples of such steps are: "Assessing the state of enjoyment of the right to food, including ensuring adequate mechanisms to collect and assess relevant and suitably disaggregated data; Formulating strategies and plans, incorporating indicators, benchmarks and time-bound targets, which are achievable and designed to assess progress in the realization of the right to food; Adopting the laws and policies necessary for the realization of the right to food or revising the laws and policies which may negatively affect it; Establishing the institutional mechanisms necessary for coordinating multi-sectoral efforts to realize the right to food; Regularly monitoring the progress made in the realization of the right to food; Establishing recourse mechanisms which can provide remedies for violations of the right to food." FAO (2010a), op. cit.

[24] For example, "withdrawing without justification existing services vital for smallholders, such as extension services or support to access productive resources, could constitute a retrogressive measure. To justify it, a State would have to demonstrate that it adopted the measure only after carefully considering all the options, assessing the impact and fully using its maximum available resources." FAO (2010a), loc. cit.

[25] FAO (2010a), loc. cit.

[26] FAO (2011; 2020), op. cit.

on sugary beverages. Instinctively, who applies the Law is also part of the right to food protection. Thus, to promote access to justice, judges and lawyers from internal, regional, or international law or court need to study the elements of the right to food in case the court demands.[27]

Moreover, globalization and interdependence require attention to **other actors** related to the right to food, such as intergovernmental and Non-Governmental Organizations (NGOs) (essential for advocacy, capacity building, and organizing marginalized target groups), responsibilities of States regarding people living in other countries, international organizations and transnational corporations. The multilateral organizations help "to design policies, strategies and programs, delivering assistance, or negotiating trade, finance and investment,"[28] such as the United Nations World Food Program (WFP), Office of the United Nations High Commissioner for Refugees (UNHCR), United Nations Children's Fund (UNICEF), United Nations Food and Agriculture Organization (FAO), United Nations Development Assistance Framework (UNDAF), United Nations International Fund for Agricultural Development (IFAD), International Monetary Fund (IMF), World Bank, and regional development banks.[29]

Although human rights obligations are not directly related to the private sector, the Human Rights Council and regional and international soft-law instruments recognize that corporations and other non-States should not disturb human rights enjoyment and apply effective measures if that happens. From local businesses to transnational corporations, the private sector has a substantial role because most food is produced, processed, distributed, and traded across borders by private entities. This can be positive through guaranteeing food security even if it is not a food-related business, e.g., respecting labor standards (minimum wages and pause time to eat), but also negative. As an illustration, competition over land, resources or market access, contamination and eviction, sale of unsafe food or misleading information, distribution of healthy food to specific areas of the city, speculation in food and productive resources, and price of food.[30]

In summary, urban food's multiple challenges affect the enjoyment of the human right to adequate food. To act against that, the stakeholders have been doing different, individually or in cooperation, actions, programs, investments, and movements, from local to international. For instance, to promote food **availability**, charitable food services such as food banks and pantries play a crucial role in facilitating access to food for individuals and households. They serve as essential resources during emergencies, such as the COVID-19 pandemic, helping uphold food security and promote dietary quality for those in need.[31] In addition, to ensure fair prices for farmers and stabilize the domestic food supply, the Brazilian National Supply Company (Conab) utilizes the Acquisitions mechanism of the Federal Government to purchase food

---

[27] FAO (2011).

[28] FAO (2007c), op. cit.

[29] United Nations (1999), op. cit.; FAO (2010a), op. cit.

[30] FAO (2010a), op. cit.

[31] Bertmann et al. (2021).

that will supply the cities. This practice not only guarantees the minimum price for agricultural products and supports farmers' income but also helps regulate internal supply, mitigating price fluctuations in the market, which tends to guarantee physical and economic food **accessibility**.[32] Various regulatory bodies engage in discussions and guidelines on international food standards on safety and quality to ensure food **acceptability**. These responsible organizations include the Codex Alimentarius Commission, which promotes global food labeling standards,[33] and the European Commission of Food Safety.[34] Furthermore, one example to encourage food **sustainability** is the FAO list of five key principles previously approached to build a common vision.[35]

3.1.2 Interdependence and Interrelation of the Right to Food to Other Human Rights

Human rights are interdependent and indivisible, so the right to food is closely interconnected with other human rights (including those established after the Declaration of 1948). Naturally, food is a fundamental pillar of **life** experience and expectancy.[36] Moreover, "when people cannot feed themselves and face the risk of death by starvation, malnutrition, or resulting illnesses, their right to life would also be at stake."[37] Also, food safe from adverse substances and nutritious food is essential to be **healthy**, body and mind functioning well, with immunological integrity, and reducing the chances of non-communicable diseases (such as diabetes). In addition, "the stress of living with uncertain access to food and going periods without food can lead to physiological changes that can contribute to overweight and obesity."[38] Thus, food is not only essential but also necessary to seek an **adequate standard of living** and to **maintain other human rights**. A person can have it as a transfer or earned way (or both) in return for economic activities, like wage labor, self-employment, providing goods, services, or means of production, and social welfare transfer from the social security system based on the reason that a person's other income is insufficient to provide for an adequate standard of living.[39] Moderately food insecure people have uncertain access to food and might have to sacrifice different basic needs, affecting their dignity, to eat. And "when they do eat, it might be whatever is most readily available or cheapest, which might not be the most nutritious food."[40]

---

[32] Almeida (2024).
[33] FAO (2023a, b).
[34] European Comission (2024).
[35] FAO (2014), op. cit.
[36] Dias et al. (2022).
[37] FAO (2010a, p. 5).
[38] FAO (2023a, b).
[39] Circle of Rights.
[40] FAO (2023a, b).

Equality is another significant human right related to food. It means "being equal in dignity and rights to all other people while recognizing the right of all peoples to be different, to consider themselves different, and to be respected as such."[41] From this statement must be highlighted **self-determination** and **non-discrimination**. Discrimination is distinction, exclusion, or restriction based, for example, on race, color, sex, language, religion, opinion, national or social origin, property, birth, or another status. It has as cause and consequence to invalidate or weaken the equitable ability to enjoy or exercise essential liberties and entitlements granted to humans. This phenomenon is associated with the relegation of certain demographic groups and is typically the underlying cause of significant disparities in societal structures.[42] On the other hand, any prejudicial treatment regarding the ability to obtain food or the resources necessary to acquire it is considered an infringement of human rights. However, non-discrimination and equality do not imply that every situation requires the same treatment. Instead of respecting self-determination, governments must acknowledge and accommodate various groups' requirements and exceptional circumstances, particularly those facing the greatest marginalization, disadvantage, and dissimilar dietary needs or cultural practices.[43] It is the right of all people to go after their economic, social, and cultural development without outside interference or prejudice, primarily not to deprive means of subsistence.[44] It also requires prior and informed consent in government plans and actions.[45]

Self-determination and non-discrimination must consider each **culture**. UNESCO has defined the concept of culture as the "distinctive traits, including the total spiritual, material, intellectual and emotional traits that characterize a society or social group, and that includes, in addition to arts and literature, their ways of life, the manner, in which they live together, their value systems, and their traditions and beliefs."[46] Thus, food selection, procurement, acquisition, preparation, and consumption are often an important part of culture, and cuisine is part of cultural heritage and identity.[47] It means that food is not only part of the individual **recognition of a person as** a **holder of rights** that can be demanded in court but also part of the **personality's development in the community**. While society offers conditions for individuals to follow their aspirations in life, people contribute in different ways to the community, such as through **food sharing initiatives**.

Additionally, an essential element of the right to food is the "substantive **freedom** of the individual and the family to establish ownership over an adequate amount of food, which can be done either by growing the food oneself (as peasants do), or by buying it in the market (as the non growers of food do)."[48] Freedom can also

[41] FAO (2010a), op. cit., p. 20.

[42] FAO (2010a), loc. cit.

[43] FAO (2010a), loc. cit.

[44] FAO (2011), op. cit., p. 14–15.

[45] Doswald-Beck (1986), pp. 371–372.

[46] FAO (2008), op. cit., p. 2.

[47] FAO (2008), loc. cit.,

[48] Sen (2001), p. 161.

be understood as **freedom of movement and residence**. This can be necessary to pursue the right to life in case of violation of the human right to **peace**, including conflicts regarding food or migration to seek new opportunities in life. In both cases, food is essential to guarantee the establishment in a new area.

In another sense, **freedom of opinion and expression** is crucial for full, active, free, meaningful, transparent, social, and political participation is essential in a **democracy**. Without it, there is no peaceful life in common.[49] If a country's democracy is strengthened, it is less likely to experience famine. This is because democracy promotes various elements towards reducing poverty and hunger, such as freedom of the press, dissemination of information, and an open and responsible administration.[50] People must be free to choose their government and take part in formulating and effectuating laws, regulations, and policies that affect them.[51] Consequently, the freedom of opinion and expression has three important links. The first is that **participation** should be ensured at all stages of development, design, implementation, and monitoring of food and nutrition strategies, policies, programs, and all other relevant decisions to not miss out on the real needs of populations.[52] "Simply calling for participation is too vague and may even be counterproductive. Certain standards of participation must also be set and followed,"[53] for example, by legislation to ensure adequate representation[54] and the representation of vulnerable groups[55] in civil society mechanisms.[56] The second is that **freedom of association** must be guaranteed because it is one of the possibilities to make civil voices be heard and their views reflected in public policies relevant to food so that their right to food will be protected.[57] The third is that obtaining, transmitting, and receiving **information** without barriers is crucial to guarantee the freedom of opinion and expression and food security. Information "enables individuals to receive information on food and nutrition, on markets, and allocation of resources. It enhances people's participation and free consumer choice."[58] For that, States should "collect and disseminate information to the public regarding food-borne diseases and food safety matters" and "adopt measures to protect consumers from deception and misrepresentation in the

[49] Hardt and Negri (2004, p. XII).

[50] FAO (2008), op. cit., p.51.

[51] FAO (2005).

[52] FAO (2009), p. 30.

[53] FAO (2009), loc. cit.

[54] FAO (2009), loc. cit.

[55] States should "promote the participation of the poor in economic policy decisions" (Guideline 2.6) and "promote women's full and equal participation in the economy" (Guideline 8.6). Particularly, in developing poverty reduction strategies, "States are encouraged to consult with civil society organizations and other key stakeholders at national and regional levels, including small-scale and traditional farmers, the private sector, women and youth associations, with the aim of promoting their active participation in all aspects of agricultural and food production strategies." (Guideline 3.8). FAO (2005), op. cit., p. 22–23.

[56] FAO (2009), loc. cit.

[57] FAO (2010a), op. cit. p. 5.

[58] FAO (2008), loc. cit.., p. 21–22.

packaging, labeling, advertising, and sale of food and facilitate consumers' choice by ensuring appropriate information on marketed food."[59]

Even extremely relevant information must be connected to education to empower individuals to make informed choices about healthy food and handling. Enhancing **education**, particularly literacy rates among women is a powerful tool to combat hunger and malnutrition. Education prevents the disruption of schooling because of food insecurity and helps to break the cycle of need not only because of the school lunch but also out of school because it equips individuals with the skills to maintain a nutritious diet and secure food for their livelihood, promoting freedom from hunger and malnutrition.[60] In addition, education drives development and opens doors to **economic prosperity** and **dignified employment**. Governments should invest in educational programs, adult literacy initiatives, and training opportunities to improve equal access to the labour market. Work serves to acquire food for sustenance, trade, or income to purchase other food items. Furthermore, food provides the necessary physical and mental conditions to sustain the body for work. Labor rights play a vital role in establishing a connection between food production and respecting, protecting, and valuing the individuals involved in its production. The presence of hunger and malnutrition among children and teenagers renders them more vulnerable to extreme forms of child labor, including forced conscription as child soldiers, involvement in drug trafficking, or being vulnerable to sexual exploration for survival.[61]

The right to food depends on the right to adequate **housing** in at least three senses. First, when a house lacks basic amenities, such as cooking or storing food, its residents' right to adequate food may be undermined. Also, when the cost of housing is too high, people may have to cut down on their food bills.[62] Without **access to land and natural resources**'[63,64] (soil, water, sun) in a **healthy environment, self-provision** of food cannot be possible.[65] For instance, the right to food cannot be realized if people lack access to safe drinking water for personal and domestic uses, defined as water for drinking, washing clothes, food preparation, and personal and household hygiene.[66]

Finally, when there is a human rights violation, everyone has the right to an effective remedy by the competent national and international **tribunals** for acts violating

---

[59] Right to Food Guidelines 9.6 and 9.7. FAO (2005; 2008), op. cit., p. 5.

[60] FAO (2008, 2010a), op. cit.

[61] FAO (2010a), loc. cit.

[62] FAO (2010a), loc. cit..

[63] FAO (2010b).

[64] Land is not a human right per se, but "several instruments cover aspects that are relevant to land, either directly or indirectly, such as, for instance, issues of ownership, management and administration of property, access to and utilization of natural resources, food production, access to agricultural credit and loans, and agrarian reform." They are important "to improve methods of production, conservation and distribution of food." FAO (2010b).

[65] The right to food cannot be realized if people lack access to safe drinking water for personal and domestic uses, defined as water for drinking, washing clothes, food preparation, and personal and household hygiene. FAO (2010a), op. cit.

[66] FAO (2010a), op. cit.

the fundamental rights granted by the constitution or law. Thus, the right to food is connected to **access to justice** and **order**.[67]

3.2 The Urban Commons Standard

The "commons" do not have a unique sense. They have pre-existing contexts and concepts that vary according to the territory and time because "the commons are not static, passive and the same everywhere. They are malleable and adapted to the historical conditions of each time and generation,"[68] as presented in Chapter 2. In the United States of America and England, these forms of expression are referred to as "*commons*," while in **Germany**, they are known as "*Allmende*," in France, they are called "*biens communaux*," in Mexico, they go by "*ejido*." In **Brazil**, they were called "*rossio*." In addition, the management of communal assets has responded reasonably well for centuries and millennia to the life aspirations of millions of people. Even today, most of the Earth's surface and waters are collectively managed.[69]

The commons have been established as a collective resource management alternative in the literature,[70] despite the critics favouring private property exploratory ways.[71] However, in a world with decreasing resources to be dominated, the private property concept is losing its sense.[72]

The commons' importance was recognized by the Nobel Prize in Economics to Elinor Ostrom in 2009.[73] From these studies, it is possible to understand that the commons have an important experimental protective role of common pool resources

[67] United Nations (1948).

[68] Warde (2002, pp. 195–224).

[69] Monterroso et al. (2019, pp. 376–391).

[70] Burke (2001), Feeny et al. (1990, pp. 1–19), Frischmann et al. (2019, pp. 211–228), Ostrom (1990), and Ostrom et al. (1999).

[71] In 1968, Garrett Hardin argued the "tragedy of the commons." Hardin (1968, pp. 1243–1248). Accessed on: Feb. 7th, 2024. According to him, individuals driven by self-interest were seen as likely to deplete shared resources through excessive use. Consequently, proponents of the "neoliberal consensus advocated for private property rights and individual self-interest aligned with profit motives," arguing that this approach would mitigate the risk of human failure associated with commons-based governance. Guttmann (2022, p. 186). Nevertheless, different studies contradicted this theory in total or partially. Burke (1998, pp. 12185–12190), Feeny et al. (1990, pp. 1–19), and Frischmann et al. (2019, pp. 211–228).

[72] Hardt and Negri (2000, p. 302).

[73] "Conventional wisdom says that common ownership is a bad idea. 'That which is owned by all is cared for by none.' Therefore, all scarce resources should either be owned privately by individuals or be regulated by central authorities. Or should they? Elinor Ostrom rejects that conventional wisdom. She concludes that common property is often well tended, based on numerous empirical studies of user-managed fish stocks, pastures, woods, lakes, and groundwater basins. Elinor Ostrom identifies seven keys to successful cooperation: Rules clearly define entitlements; Conflict resolution mechanisms are in place; Duties stand in reasonable proportion to benefits; Monitoring and sanctioning is carried out either by the users themselves or by someone who is accountable to the users; Sanctions are graduated, mild for a first violation and stricter as violations are repeated;

(CPR)[74] in the context of neoliberalism over-exploitation threats[75] and "predatory capitalist behavior."[76] Then, it is important to differentiate that the commons are not the resources, but social practices and community relations around a resource create them.[77] Given that the commons do "not simply exist,"[78] commons are a human creation[79] system based on collective sustainable governance further than a classical dichotomy of exploratory governance of public and private property in pure capitalist systems[80] because this collaborative and sustainable governance can be applied to private,[81] public, or common goods.[82]

This affirmation raises three crucial elements to understanding the commons. The first is that "**social practices and relations**," *commoning*,[83] include the participatory process of accessing, managing, and developing a resource.[84] This way, the group can define shared norms, values, objectives, needs, interests, enforcement, and forms of collective identity. This allows **governance towards sustainability**,[85] the second element, which is crucial in "**tackling social-ecological transition** concerns through experimentation with new provisioning systems."[86] The *commoning* happens in geographical and virtual spaces.[87] The third part is that "**resource**" is a "material or immaterial […] non-commodified means of supplying some good or service to the *commoners*."[88] They are a "group of individuals involved in producing and

---

Decision processes are democratic; and the rights of users to self-organize are clearly recognized by outside authorities". NobelPrize (2024).

[74] "Common pool resources are resource systems that can produce resource units by nature. Those resource units are appropriated by individuals. But their appropriation is managed through collective action among other resource users. Therefore, the resource system would contain collectively managed rules and rights of use that make commons persistent, autonomously organized, and self-regulated." Guttmann, op cit., p. 36.

[75] Junge (2010) and Guttmann, op. cit., p. 186.

[76] Guttmann, loc. cit.

[77] Guttmann, op. cit., p. 36.

[78] Guttmann, loc. cit.

[79] Helfrich (2012, pp. 61–67).

[80] Guttmann, op. cit.

[81] "When we mention the commons, we do refer also to a private property on which the non-owners have certain rights and uses" Antonucci (2020, p. 194).

[82] In public and common goods, everybody has the right to use it without exclusion and without affecting other's use. They can accommodate multiple uses without conflict, such as the air or public lighting. However, the commons goods, when considered the finite and unsustainable character of some resources, introduce certain level of rivalry and exclusivity and open space for the commons' governance. Guttmann, op. cit., p. 48.

[83] Linebaugh (2008) and Helfrich (2012, pp. 61–67).

[84] Dellenbaugh-Losse et al., op. cit., p. 7.

[85] Coriat (2015) apud Guttmann, op. cit., p. 38–39.

[86] Bauwens and Ramos (2020, p. 124).

[87] Coriat (2015) apud Guttmann, op. cit., p. 38–39.

[88] Dellenbaugh-Losse et al. (2020, p. 9).

reproducing commons" because they depend on this resource.[89] They are "organically formed and self-defined" and "responsible for collectively negotiating and enforcing the rules about how the commons resources are managed and used."[90] They have different scales, from a group of neighbours to global communities.[91] In these communities, the essence is non-commercial.

> The essence of the community, its heart and soul, is the **non-monetary exchange of value**: things we do and share because we care about others and the good of the place. The community is made up of things that we do not try to measure, that we do not keep on file, and that we do not ask for a reward for [...] like respect, tolerance, love, trust, and beauty - whose supply is unrestricted and unlimited. The non-monetary exchange of value does not just come from **altruistic motives**. It comes from the deep, intuitive, usually subconscious realization that self-interest is inseparably bound up with the interest of the community, that the individual good is inseparable from the general good, that somehow, generally beyond our comprehension, all things they are, at the same time, independent, interdependent and interdependent – of which the singular 'one' is simultaneously the plural 'one.' (...) Life is not a right. Life is a gift that brings a gift, which is the art of giving. And the community is where we can give our gifts and receive the gifts of others.[92]

Consequently, the commons represent an effort to combat the conversion of essential resources into private property,[93] the commodification, such as the water fountain, that can be seen as public, free, and collective managed good, or economic, profitable, and market managed good.[94] The same could happen to a river[95] or the beach.[96] In this sense of commons, "labour's **use-value** is directed to the production of a community resource, and part of its capacity for surplus labour is returned to the commons."[97] In contrast, in commodities, the "labour's use-value is captured primarily as the use-value for capital."[98] In this way, the commons change the individual perception of itself.

> In a world of commoning, people are quite **emotionally attached** to the "care-wealth" that they **love** and depend upon. They do not have relationships with commodities or resources but with things that belong to them in a deeper sense: ancient lands, beloved traditions, stable livelihoods, and a **sense of purpose and meaning**. People's lives become somewhat more enmeshed with each other; new social circuits emerge and proliferate. **The iron grip of capital recedes, if only a bit, as people recover a sense of the local, affective, and collective**. Life becomes more relational and not merely transactional. Commoning becomes an enactment of Thomas Berry's insight, "The universe is not a collection of objects, but a communion of subjects."[99] **A sense of belonging and shared meaning emerges**.

---

[89] Coriat (2015) apud Guttmann, op. cit., p. 38–39.

[90] Dellenbaugh-Losse et al., loc. cit.

[91] Coriat (2015) apud Guttmann, op. cit., p. 38–39.

[92] Hock (2000).

[93] Bakker (2007, pp. 430–455).

[94] Bakker op. cit.

[95] Nacur (2022).

[96] Costa and Sampaio (2021, pp. 1–36).

[97] Gidwani (2010, p. 43).

[98] Gidwani, loc. cit.

[99] Berry (2015, p. 17).

The significance of commons also extends to **empowering communities**[100] that advocate for their pivotal role as policy instruments in addressing climate change adaptation and mitigation.[101] Additionally, it serves as a political instrument to counteract capitalism's divisive and marginalizing effects on communities.[102] Illustrating that, despite inter and intra-ethnic differences,[103] land is uniformly held as commons by indigenous groups from the Amazonian context.[104] Still, **quilombos,**[105] indigenous, and other traditional communities generally have a particular culture regarding a "traditional way of living and the special relationship they enjoy with their land and natural resources."[106] This has a special sense in fighting against neoliberalism's influence on nature, including **land grabbing** and incorporating genetic resources and traditional knowledge into the global market.[107]

For instance, the Tapajós National Forest (Flona), Brazil, is an environmental conservation area protected by federal law. More than a thousand families reside there, hunting, cultivating, and extracting natural resources solely for sustenance. In the surrounding areas of the Flona, the land adjacent to this conservation zone is utilized for growing soya bean crops. The stark contrast between these two landscapes extends beyond the varying shades of green, which define the scene separated by the asphalt of the federal highway. This dichotomy is further underscored when examining deforestation statistics: over three decades, Belterra, which encompasses a portion of the Flona Tapajós within its boundaries, witnessed 10% of its forest cover succumb to deforestation. Conversely, if we focus solely on the percentage of deforestation within the Flona, it stands at a mere 0.1%.[108]

Moving to a specific part of the commons, a crucial notion for this study is that they can also be related to the city, the **urban commons**.

> The concept of urban commons is based on the idea that public spaces, urban land, and infrastructure ought to be accessible to and able to be utilized by urban communities to

[100] Angelis (2013, p. 603).

[101] Guttmann, op. cit., p. 36.

[102] Guttmann, op. cit., p. 36.

[103] A similar element from the concept of commons' past and nowadays is the "interpersonal agreements concluded between different social groups. They ranged from family relationships and passed through dispositions of rural villages, rules of professional associations, religious groups, and tribal confederations" Relly (2022, p. 17).

[104] Lu (2006, pp. 187–94) and Lauriola (2013, pp. 157–185).

[105] In Brazil, "during its existence, the Quilombo served as a symbol for ethnic and political resistance. As an institution, it retains unique characteristics from its African model. As political practice, it proclaims liberal, emancipatory ideas, which resist the distortions imposed by hegemony at moments of national crisis. For Black people, often figured as docile and subservient, the figure of heroism fortifies everyday struggles against oppression and social inequality. Quilombo is a powerful tool in the process of recognizing a Black Brazilian identity and in moving towards deeper self-affirmation as Black and Brazilian. Alongside other practices which strengthen cultural identity, the history of Quilombo as an actually existing breach in the system of oppression of Black people offers hope that similar institutions can have a similar effect today" Nascimento (1985, pp. 41–49).

[106] FAO (2004, p. 1) and Tzul (2018).

[107] Guetta and Bensusan (2018, pp. 117–140).

[108] Dantas (2019).

produce and support a range of goods and services important for the sustainability of those populations, particularly the most vulnerable people. The founding principles of this movement include sharing, collaboration, civic engagement, inclusion, equity, and social justice. Civic collaborations create and manage urban commons, including participants from local communities, government, business, academic, and nonprofit organizations. In this way, the city is a platform utilized and optimized by citizens from all backgrounds and social statuses.[109]

In that respect, the **urban commons** represent new possibilities for citizens to claim their **right to the city**[110] and **co-produce the social space** given the "articulation of new forms of urban citizenship based on the right to access and inhabit urban spaces and to imagine[111] and shape their future uses"[112] as a "response to market and state failure in maintaining and constructing the infrastructures of social life."[113] Then, urban commons are "vectors of the **ecological transition** while at the same time advancing a new way of understanding capitalism based on resource reusability and abundance"[114] "in an ecological understanding of urban land use"[115] by a "vernacular law." [116,117] This can be illustrated by the case of an environmental conservation park in Rio de Janeiro,[118] where the natural resources from public land are sustainably used by *residents* for ecotourism (*visitants*), environmental education, and income generation.

This example expresses the meaning that commons occupy a "unique space in social organization"[119] with an application in urban spaces[120] due to the cooperation and involvement with *multiple urban actors* in resources **collaborative management**[121] (**polycentrism**, another crucial pillar of urban commons),[122] such as "social innovators, public authorities, businesses, civil society organizations, knowledge

---

[109] Foster, Iaione, op. cit.

[110] Follmann and Viehoff (2015, pp. 1148–1174) and Fernandes (2021).

[111] Messina (2019).

[112] Morrom (2019, pp. 202–212).

[113] Bauwens and Ramos (2020, p. 124).

[114] Guttmann, op. cit., p. 397.

[115] Foster (2013a, b, p. 528).

[116] Bollier (2021, p. 67). and Bollier and Weston (2014, p. 104).

[117] "In effect, commoning is itself a form of law. It serves to organize people into orderly wholes to achieve shared ends. People are able to generate consensual rules, practices, and ethical norms that preserve both shared wealth and the community. This form of law and governance could be called Vernacular Law, a term inspired by Ivan Illich's celebration of vernacular practice as a way to re-humanize people caught up in systems of institutional domination." Bollier (2021, p. 67). In addition, "Vernacular Law," it will be recalled, is the term we use to distinguish informal or unofficial law from what we call "State Law." Vernacular Law originates in the informal, unofficial zones of society and is a source of moral legitimacy and power in its own right." Bollier and Weston (2014, p. 104).

[118] Sinay et al. (2014).

[119] Guttmann, op. cit., p. 48.

[120] Antonucci (2020).

[121] Foster and Iaione (2016).

[122] Flynn (2018).

institutions, and urban residents."[123] They can have different levels of participation, such as event participants, members, core teams, and organizational forms, including informal groups, registered associations, cooperatives, and companies.[124]

In addition, another key concept within the realm of urban commons is the principle of **horizontal subsidiarity**, lying in legal terms for enabling citizens to engage in self-governance by themselves and their representatives.[125] This provides "a progressive platform for active citizen engagement and formation of civil society organizations operating beyond the market logic of capitalism and alongside local government."[126] It is important to highlight that technology is crucial in providing and sharing knowledge and data to support engagement and communication.[127]

Embracing these characteristics could represent problems for the resource's collective management. For example, tensions can appear among users with different social backgrounds and goals.[128] In this case, methods of conflict resolution are crucial. **Conflicts** can also happen between *commoners* (gardeners and municipalities) when there is a lack of public support and different views on resource management, bureaucracy, and legal barriers. Also, the urban commons must overcome the isolation. The exchange of experiences and methods depends on the network's expansion. Another issue is the lack of validation within the regulatory setup and surroundings. As one of the solutions, charters can be an effective way to dialogue with public bodies and neighbourhoods.[129]

Moreover, the urban commons are defined as resources shared by the community and susceptible to rivalry and exclusion problems.[130] Even so, the urban commons can also be highlighted as one of the strategies for **re-appropriating public spaces**,[131] a fight against city commodification. This is important because "urban public space remains the site where public life is consumed, and citizens' imagination and sense of identity are shaped."[132] The process includes "experiences of grassroots movements that give back subjectivity to widespread urban goods threatened by financial or real estate speculation."[133] "Profoundly shaped by the scale of the city, neighbourhood, or block,"[134] these movements can rely on urban resources such as "squares, parks, **abandoned buildings**, **vacant lots**, and streets that can be repurposed for a multitude of uses and functions by their users. They are renewable throughout their life cycle,

---

[123] Guttmann, op. cit., p. 83.

[124] Dellenbaugh-Losse et al. (2020, pp. 111–114).

[125] While the vertical subsidiarity requires a policy from local or other level. Breton et al. (1998, pp. 21–51) apud Guttmann, loc. cit. Iaione (2016).

[126] Guttmann, loc. cit.

[127] Guttmann, op. cit., p. 98.

[128] Iaione (2015) apud Guttmann, p. 398.

[129] Guttmann, op. cit., pp. 381–98.

[130] Foster (2013a, b, p. 57).

[131] Antonucci, op. cit., p. 198.

[132] Antonucci, loc. cit.

[133] Antonucci, op. cit., p. 197.

[134] Linebaugh (2008) apud Guttmann, op. cit., p. 82.

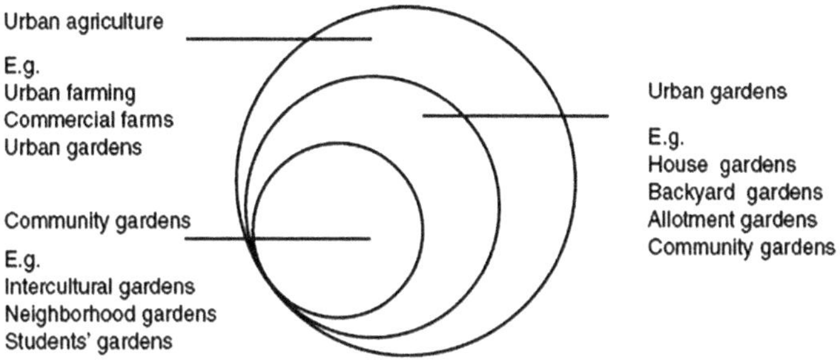

Fig. 3.1 Urban and peri-urban agriculture universe. *Source* Rogge and Theesfeld (2018, p. 255)

remain flexible in usability and durability, and are thus far less exhaustible than natural resources would typically be."[135]

Overall, urban commons **goals** can be "civic (inherited for/by all urban citizens), community (created for a collective use), and club goods with commons-like features (created for personal use/profit)."[136] They can be related to various **focus**, such as "ecological (natural processes and natural resource production), social (human process for equitability and human well-being), immaterial (connectivity, communication, and human development)."[137] Housing, public spaces, labour and public services, artistic endeavours, and urban infrastructure can exemplify this.[138] This investigation highlights the **community gardens** as **urban commons**.[139]

3.3 Community Gardens Standard

In the urban and peri-urban agriculture universe, **community gardens** are one of the urban gardens' subcategories. Around the world, there are many possibilities regarding location, actors, spatial division, institutional affiliation, and property regimes, such as neighbourhood gardens, intercultural gardens (focusing on the migration background), or school gardens,[140] as shown in Fig. 3.1.

Regarding **land ownership**, they are developed in public or private areas. Usually, the occupation of **urban vacant land** (unused, underutilized, and unbuilt soil)[141] has no specific spatial configuration (size and design).[142] Then, there are community gardens on streets' sidewalks, residential (rooftops, inside apartment complexes) or

[135] Guttmann, op. cit., p. 82.

[136] Guttmann, op. cit., p. 140.

[137] Guttmann, loc. cit.

[138] Muller et al. (2015).

[139] Guttmann, loc. cit.

[140] Rogge and Theesfeld (2018, p. 255).

[141] Jardim (2018), Borde (2006), Clemente (2012), and Sousa (2010).

[142] Guttmann, op. cit., p. 122.

school buildings, "along railways and roads, under power lines, on the grounds of community centers, churches, and in public parks and other green areas."[143]

In some cases, the gardens can be situated in vulnerable areas,

> amid economically and socially fragile communities. Many of these lots were left vacant by demolishing buildings abandoned by their original owners or cleared but not redeveloped in the wake of defunct urban renewal programs and whose ownership was assumed by the city through tax foreclosure. These lots had often become "rivalrous" spaces overrun by drug users, car strippers, and illegal dumpers of all kinds of waste. They thus became safe havens for a host of criminal and other illicit activities.[144]

The transformation process "of these abandoned lots to community gardens emerged as a means of 'self-help' for citizens to address a variety of problems related to, and signified by, vacant land in their communities."[145] For instance, "without this cooperation, many of these open, vacant lots would likely have remained blighted and dangerous, threatening the economic and social health of the community."[146] However, "often enough, these community gardens are temporary set-ups before the vacant lots are put under construction."[147]

In general, the **gardener** is a volunteer that joins a self-organized group (neighbourhoods, schools, churches, and Non-Governmental Organisations). Nevertheless, in some cases, there are hired professionals to organize the garden's bureaucratic and financial issues or to promote agricultural and environmental education.[148] "Communal gardens involve poor as well as higher income families, individuals, older people, and recent migrants, among others."[149] The gardener's **background and socioeconomic status vary** greatly from local to local, even within the same country. For example, studies in the United States of America identify Black and poor communities as local gardeners in Washington, D.C. At the same time, other analyses presented in St. Louis showed the predominance of White people, women with high household income, and intermediate or high educational level.[150] Additionally, further study identified a predominance of non-White women with lower income in Los Angeles and Newark, while in New York, there were more White men with high income.[151] In Europe, "community gardeners will usually be residents, migrants and children without formal agricultural education."[152] In Quito, Ecuador, a study demonstrated the predominance of female gardeners. They have low income and education and no immigration status.[153] In Global North, the gardeners can be

---

[143] FAO (2022, p. 16).

[144] Foster (2011, p. 94).

[145] Foster (2013a, b), op. cit., p. 540.

[146] Foster (2011), op. cit., p. 95.

[147] Guttmann, loc. cit.

[148] Ponstingel (2022, pp. 355–376).

[149] FAO (2022), op. cit., p. 16.

[150] Wong et al. (2018, pp. 809–822).

[151] Das and Ramaswami (2022).

[152] Mceldowney (2017).

[153] Audate et al. (2021).

associated with the image of "hip and bohemian citizens,"[154] which dialogues with the "environmentalism of the rich" mentioned in the previous chapter. In addition, not only their backgrounds are multiple, but also the **motivations** for community gardening are diverse. This includes

> providing safe spaces for circumjacent residents and improving the neighbourhood's liveability by cleaning, shaping, and beatifying vacant, underutilized, neglected areas, (re)connection to nature, physical outdoor activities, and mental recreation, building social capital & developing a community spirit, educating people of all ages, participation on urban development and striving for public visibility.[155]

Non-profitable interests exist to achieve the above goals, even when organized as a business. However, the gardeners can adopt diverse bottom-up manifestations to finance the garden maintenance,[156] such as renting plots through small fees or symbolic monetary contributions to courses and events. The creation, organization, development, and maintenance of a community garden happen with or without governmental support, and often there is no specific legal regulation.[157] In some cases there is total or partial top-down governmental funding, such as Hortas Cariocas program in *Rio de Janeiro.*

Not only the administration and maintenance responsibilities are shared, but also the social, economic, and environmentally sustainable use of resources like soil, water, tools, and knowledge. Given this, community gardens are **urban commons with an ecological focus, making the spatial production of social capital possible.**[158] On the one hand, this means that they are created for a collective use community-oriented framework "with some forms of exclusion, but the maintenance and use of those commons are shared by a group of urban inhabitants that make up a community."[159] On the other hand, the ecological character is "focused on natural processes and natural resource production."[160] Consequently, urban commons are essential in mitigating climate change and socioeconomic inequalities.[161]

Regarding the **benefits** of the **human right to adequate food**, recent studies have focused on the potential of community gardens in addressing the lack of *food availability* in food deserts in low-income and Black neighbourhoods[162] by utilizing vacant land.[163] Such initiatives offer benefits not only for individuals but also for the urban environment. Research has explicit results demonstrating that community gardens can enhance physical and economic *access* to fresh products, essential to combat food insecurity among various vulnerable social groups, including students

---

154 Steuri and Vignola (2015, p. 115).

155 Steuri and Vignola, op. cit., p. 55.

156 Guitart et al. (2012, pp. 364–373).

157 Jardim et al. (2024).

158 Foster (2013a, b), op. cit.

159 Guttmann, op. cit., p. 140.

160 Guttmann, loc. cit.

161 Guttmann, op. cit., p. 133 and Colding et al. (2022, pp. 103–114).

162 Gripper (2014) and Krajewski (2021, pp. 51–54).

163 Drake (2014, pp. 133–142) and Beam (2021, pp. 403–408).

and older adults.[164] Additionally, studies have indirectly highlighted the importance of community gardens in promoting food *acceptability* by providing opportunities for education and cultural exchange.[165] Moreover, precise evidence or results can be interpreted as the contribution of community gardens to food *sustainability* in three dimensions. Firstly, they can have positive impacts on biodiversity by supporting local ecosystems.[166] Secondly, they can contribute to supplying local markets.[167] Thirdly, community gardens can enhance equity and justice[168] by providing equal access to nutritious food for marginalized communities.

On the other hand, investigations directly or indirectly presented the barriers, challenges, and negative effects of community gardens on the right to food. Current research on community gardens as a source of food *availability* has precisely highlighted the challenge of securing access to land and natural resources.[169] This issue has become a major obstacle to establishing community gardens, particularly in urban areas, where open space is limited and competition for land is high. Also, studies on community gardens providing food *accessibility* have accurately revealed the challenge of alienation in addressing food insecurity roots.[170] Additionally, community gardens face the challenge of participation,[171] which can impact food acceptability as a side effect. Lack of community involvement and engagement can undermine the potential of community gardens to promote food culture and education, hindering their ability to contribute to food security. Furthermore, food *sustainability* in community gardens has been strictly linked to environmental, economic, and social dimensions. Soil contamination[172] and gentrification[173] are some challenges that can impact the long-term viability of community gardens.

Concerning the **activities** in the garden, "people grow trees and perennials, maintain lawns, and install specific features like benches, gazebos, and brick paths that allow people to spend time there and explore."[174] The gardening can happen directly on soil or inside (suspended) containers (to avoid soil contamination). Ordinarily, the gardens are linked to **agroecology**,

> an integrated approach that simultaneously applies ecological and social concepts and principles to the design and management of food and agricultural systems. It seeks to optimize the interactions between plants, animals, humans and the environment while taking into consideration the social aspects that need to be addressed for a sustainable and fair food system. Agroecology is not an invention. It can be identified in scientific literature since the 1920s, and

---

[164] Tims et al. (2021, pp. 85–101) and Thorman and Dhillon (2021, pp. 643–649).

[165] Heerink et al. (2021, pp. 112–115) and Lloyd et al. (2022).

[166] Chan et al. (2016, pp. 842–860) and Felderhoff et al. (2023).

[167] Chow et al. (2020).

[168] Burt (2021) and Barron (2017).

[169] Glowa et al. (2019, pp. 92–115).

[170] Butterfield (2021, pp. 160–168).

[171] Butterfield (2022).

[172] Wong, op. cit.

[173] Braswell (2018, pp. 809–822).

[174] Guttmann, op. cit., p. 122.

> has found expression in family farmers' practices, in grassroots social movements for sustainability and the public policies of various countries around the world. More recently, agroecology has entered the discourse of international and UN institutions. In guiding countries to transform their food and agricultural systems, to mainstream sustainable agriculture on a large scale, and to achieve Zero Hunger and multiple other SDGs, the following 10 Elements emanated from the FAO regional seminars on agroecology: Diversity; synergies; efficiency; resilience; recycling; co-creation and sharing of knowledge (describing common characteristics of agroecological systems, foundational practices and innovation approaches); Human and social values; culture and food traditions (context features); Responsible governance; circular and solidarity economy (enabling environment). The 10 Elements of Agroecology are interlinked and interdependent.[175]

In community gardens, "food products such as vegetables, fruits, herbs, and occasionally small livestock are produced for home consumption, leisure, health, and educational purposes, or within the context of community development programs."[176] However, not always the production includes food. In some gardens, there are only medicinal or decorative plants.[177] Even so, there is solid recognition of their importance for food security.[178] The products can have personal use, the common benefit of the gardens' members, or be open to society.[179] Within this context, in community gardens there are **urban food sharing activities**.

3.3.1 Urban Food Sharing Activities

Urban Food Sharing means: "*having* a portion [of food] *with* another or others; *giving* a portion [of food] *to* others; *using, occupying or enjoying* food [and food related spaces to include the growing, cooking and/or eating of food] *jointly*; possessing an *interest* in food *in common*; or *telling* someone *about* food."[180] This concept is embraced by the commons considering that **food should be a commons, not commodity**.[181] This is *sociologically* relevant because "food sharing is undertaken for and with others; reshaping relations with both human and non-human entities and tangible and intangible resources."[182] These relationships mean commoning **social practices**. Sharing is a historical social practice that "has been identified as the bedrock of human civilization, a means through which sustenance is secured, labour divided, and social relations solidified within and beyond families."[183] However,

175 FAO (2018, p. 2).

176 FAO (2022), op. cit., p.16.

177 Opitz et al. (2016, pp. 341–358).

178 Magalhães (2021) and Rekow (2015).

179 Ferris et al. (2001, pp. 559–568), Beilin and Hunter (2011, pp. 523–538), and Rosol (2011, pp. 263–270).

180 Oxford English Dictionary (2017, pp. 136–149).

181 United Nations University (2013).

182 Agyeman et al. (2013, pp. 1–32) apud Davies (2019).

183 Davies et al. (2018, p. 18).

urban food sharing "has not been explicitly studied as a mechanism for achieving structural transformations toward sustainability."[184] Thus, regarding social practice,

> sharing is not just what people do; it is a coordinated entity, 'a temporally unfolding and spatially dispersed nexus of doings and sayings'[185] and performance – a process of doing – through which sharing as an entity is perpetuated and potentially reshaped. [...] Food sharing demonstrates routinized ways 'in which bodies are moved, objects are handled, subjects are treated, things are described, and the world is understood. [...] It is a "type" of behaving and understanding that appears at different locals and at different points of time and is carried out by different bodies/ minds',[186] with the performative element of food sharing practice occurring around its enactment. It is only through the performance of food sharing that the interdependencies between elements of food sharing (that is, food sharing as an entity) are sustained or changed. Food sharing is a complex assemblage 'of body-minds, things, knowledge, discourse, and structures carried by agents such as individuals, organizations, and institutions.[187]

The expected consequence of investigating practices is the "examination of broad social and economic processes through the consideration of the actions and meanings associated with food sharing."[188] Consequently, it is possible to observe "cultural rituals and individual habits that determine (in part) what is deemed appropriate to share in different contexts and to the rules and forms of power and control that shape how food sharing takes place."[189] In other words, the individuals, organizations, and institutions also encompass the state and its *legal system* to regulate the social practices done by food sharing initiatives. These initiatives are a comprehensive term encompassing networks spanning informal sharing to profit-driven enterprises across local areas, multiple cities, or countries. They aim to facilitate exchanges of tangible food items and enclose intangible exchanges of knowledge, skills, and experiences.[190] Further than in **community gardens**, they also happen in community kitchens and food banks.[191]

The practices there can be organized in a matrix composed of *sharing elements*—foodstuff (including seeds, plants, compost), food spaces (including sites for shared growing, areas for food redistribution), food skills (including sharing knowledge and experiences about food growing, eating, redistribution or disposal)—through different *sharing modes*—informal, illicit, or unorganized (IIU) activities (such as foraging, gleaning), gifting ("bestowing something voluntarily and without compensation"), bartering ("the exchange of goods or services for other goods or services without using money"), monetary exchange ("the exchange of goods or services for monetary payment, although not necessarily for profit") for profit or not.[192]

---

[184] Davies et al. (2018), loc. cit.

[185] Schatzki (1996, p. 89) apud Davies (2019), op. cit., p. 9.

[186] Reckwitz (2002, p. 250) apud Davies (2019), op. cit., p. 9.

[187] Jones and Murphy (2010, p. 319) apud Davies (2019), op. cit., p. 9.

[188] Davies et al. (2017), pp. 136–149) apud Davies (2019), op. cit., p. 9.

[189] Davies (2019), op. cit, p. 9.

[190] Davies et al. (2018), loc. cit.

[191] Mackenzie and Davies (2019).

[192] Davies et al. (2018), loc. cit.

These activities aim social goals ("prosocial behaviour among friends and family"), environmental goals ("themes emerging of food waste reduction, local produce and small scale agriculture, and improved **human connections with nature**"), economic goals ("recurring themes included the promotion of alternatives to the traditional market economy and reducing inequalities"), health goals ("**increasing access to fresh, healthy or nutritious food**"), and political goals ("goals which seek to change how power and **resources** are distributed").[193]

Given that community gardens are *urban food sharing initiatives*, the urban food sharing typology[194] can serve as a basis for identifying the *urban food sharing activities* in community gardens. The above matrix is a vanguardist and consolidated[195] systematization of urban food sharing. After the adaptations explained in the introductory chapter, it will guide the answer to the central research question.

3.4 Integrating Concepts

Initially, it is important to mention that the **human right to adequate food** has four central and complementary components: food availability, accessibility, acceptability, and sustainability. Food *availability* embraces the freedom of choice regarding production, including self-provision and distribution. This is affected by restricted access to natural resources, such as land and water, and food deserts. The economic and physical food *accessibility* depends on stability over time, which can be irregular due to natural and human-related reasons, such as wars, diseases, and climate change. Food *acceptability* is regarding multiple cultural aspects but guarantees that the food is free of contaminants and residues from industrial or agricultural processes. Food *sustainability*, representing long-term availability and accessibility, is guided by resource use efficiency, inclusive well-being, the people, communities, ecosystems resilience, and responsible and effective governance mechanisms. Everybody is responsible for protecting and promoting the right to food, including the *government, non-governmental organizations, the private sector, and civil society*. These stakeholders have a role in the entire human rights system, given that the human right to food is connected to other human rights. In other words, additional requests can be affected when the right to food is violated. As explored in Chapter 2 and here, the human right to food is being infringed in terms of food and land as commodities. This has a higher impact on vulnerable individuals and communities but also brings issues to the entire (global) society.

Given the resource overexploitation based on capital accumulation of private property, the **commons** are an alternative approach composed of four crucial elements. The *social practices and relations (commoning)*, including establishing *governance*

---

[193] Davies et al. (2018), loc.cit., p. 39.

[194] Davies et al. (2018), loc. cit.

[195] Mackenzie and Davies (2019) loc. cit., Davies et al. (2017; 2018) loc. cit., Davies and Evans (2019), pp. 154–159.

towards sustainability. The other fundamental elements are the *resource* (material or immaterial) to managed and a group of *people* (*commoners*) doing practices, developing the relation, and benefiting from the resource. The government can assist or forbid these practices of civil society and non-governmental agents. This can be related to *legal* reasons. Focusing on the use-value, the commons are important to fight the commodification of goods and empower fragile communities. Food and land are also commons when understanding the city as a commons. Many forms of urban commons exist, such as streets, parks, and *community gardens.*

Moving to the third pillar, **community gardens** are new **urban commons** connected to urban agriculture. Around the world, there are many possibilities of gardens regarding location, design, landowner, agents, spatial division, institutional affiliation, and property regimes. They generally occupy vacant urban land (wasteland, dump ground, unbuilt areas of parks and schools, etc.). The gardens can sometimes be situated in socially and economically vulnerable areas. The gardener *(the commoner)* is an amateur or professional organized in a *group* of neighbours, schools, churches, and Non-Governmental Organisations. They have different socioeconomic and demographic backgrounds. Regarding food, the gardeners realize *commoning* activities, the **urban food sharing** of foodstuff, food spaces, and food skills through different sharing modes, informal, illicit, or unorganized activities, collecting, gifting, bartering, and selling for profit. These activities benefit the *human right to adequate food* guided by social, economic, and *ecological* purposes, varying among gardeners, gardens, cities, and countries.

Considering the above description, the combination of standards reveals a *theoretical* affirmation that **community gardens are urban commons transforming vacant land and food. During this process, the new relation to *resources* embraces people *(commoners)* developing food sharing activities *(commoning)* with social, economic, and environmental dimensions in connection to the human right to adequate food**. To empirically confirm this proposition, the next chapter characterizes the profile of territory, gardeners, and experts related to community gardens in *Berlin* and *Rio de Janeiro*. Later, another chapter analyses the urban food sharing activities connected to *food availability, accessibility, acceptability,* and *sustainability* to produce policy recommendations.

References

Agyeman J et al (2013) Briefing: sharing cities. Friends of the earth september, London, pp 1–32

Almeida D (2024) Após 6 anos, Conab retoma política de estoques públicos de alimentos: Governo comprará 500 mil toneladas de milho para garantir preço mínimo. Agência Brasil. https://agenciabrasil.ebc.com.br/economia/noticia/2023-06/apos-6-anos-conab-retoma-politica-de-estoques-publicos-de-alimentos. Accessed 28 Aug 2024

Angelis M de (2013) Does capital need a commons fix? Ephemera 13(3):603. https://ephemerajournal.org/sites/default/files/2022-01/13-3deangelis.pdf. Accessed 28 Aug 2024

Antonucci F (2020) From Urban Commons to commoning as Social Practice. In: Cultural commons and urban dynamics a multidisciplinary perspective. Springer, Cham. https://www.academia.edu/44343601/From_Urban_Commons_to_commoning_as_Social_Practice_. Accessed 28 Aug 2024

Audate PP et al (2021) The motivations of urban agriculture practitioners in deprived neighborhoods: A comparative study of Montreal and Quito. Urban Forestry & Urban Greening, vol 62. https://www.sciencedirect.com/science/article/abs/pii/S1618866721001965/. Accessed 13 Sept 2024

Bakker K (2007) The "Commons" versus the "Commodity": alter-globalization, anti-privatization and the human right to water in the Global South. Antipode 39(3):430–455. https://doi.org/10.1111/j.1467-8330.2007.00534.x. Accessed 20 Aug 2024

Barron J (2017) Community gardening: cultivating subjectivities, space, and justice. Loc Environ, 22(9). https://www.tandfonline.com/doi/abs/10.1080/13549839.2016.1169518. Accessed 13 May 2024

Bauwens M, Ramos J (2020) Awakening to an ecology of the commons. In: Grear A, Bollier D (eds) The great awakening: new models of life amidst capitalist ruins. Punctum Books, p 124

Beam DR (2021) Vacant lot to community garden conversion and crime in Milwaukee: a difference-in-differences analysis. Inj Prev 27(5):403–408. https://pubmed.ncbi.nlm.nih.gov/32912967/. Accessed 13 May 2024

Beilin R, Hunter A (2011) Co-constructing the sustainable city: How indicators help us "grow" more than just food in community gardens. Loc Environ 16(6):523–538. https://www.tandfonline.com/doi/abs/10.1080/13549839.2011.555393. Accessed 16 May 2024

Berry T (2015) Evening thoughts: reflecting on earth as a sacred community. Counterpoint, Berkeley, p 17

Bertmann F et al (2021) The food bank and food pantries help food insecure participants maintain fruit and vegetable intake during COVID-19. Frontiers in Nutrition, vol 6. https://www.frontiersin.org/articles/10.3389/fnut.2021.673158/full. Accessed 28 Aug 2024

Bollier D (2021) The commoner's catalog for changemaking. Schumarcher Center for New Economics, p 67, Massaschussets. https://www.commonerscatalog.org/books/the-commoners-catalog-for-changemaking?page=69. Accessed 24 Aug 2024

Bollier D, Weston B (2014) Green governance: ecological survival, human rights, and the law of the commons. Cambridge University Press, Cambridge, p 104

Borde A (2006) Vazios urbanos: perspectivas contemporâneas. Tese de doutorado, Prourb, UFRJ, Rio de Janeiro. http://www.prourb.fau.ufrj.br/integrantes/andrea-de-lacerda-pessoa-borde/. Accessed 28 Aug 2024

Braswell TH (2018) Fresh food, new faces: community gardening as ecological gentrification in St. Louis, Missouri. Agricul Hum Val 35(4):809–822. https://link.springer.com/article/10.1007/s10460-018-9875-3005. Accessed 16 May 2024

Breton A, Cassone A, Fraschini A (1998) Decentralization and subsidiarity: toward a theoretical reconciliation. Univ Pennsyl J Int Econ L 19(1):21–51

Burt K (2021) A systematic, mixed studies review of the outcomes of community garden participation related to food justice. Loc Environ 26(1). https://www.tandfonline.com/doi/abs/10.1080/13549839.2020.1861589. Accessed 13 May 2024

Burke B (1998) Hardin revisited: a critical look at perception and the logic of the commons. Proceedings of the National Academy of Sciences of the United States of America 95(21):12185–12190. https://www.jstor.org/stable/46034/. Accessed 28 Aug 2024

Burke B (2001) Hardin revisited: a critical look at perception and the logic of the commons. Hum Ecol 29(4). https://www.jstor.org/stable/4603411. Accessed 28 Aug 2024

Butterfield K (2021) Framing food access: do community gardens inadvertently reproduce inequality? Heal Educ Behav 48(2):160–168. https://pubmed.ncbi.nlm.nih.gov/32806951/. Accessed 16 May 2024

Butterfield K (2022) Modeling community garden participation: how locations and frames shape participant demographics. Agricul Hum Val, vol 10. https://link.springer.com/article/10.1007/s10460-022-10406-2. Accessed 16 May 2024

Chan J et al (2016) Social-ecological refuges: reconnecting in community gardens in Lincoln, Nebraska. J Ethnobiol 16(4):842–860. https://bioone.org/journals/Journal-of-Ethnobiology/volume-36/issue-4/0278-0771-36.4.842/Social-Ecological-Refuges--Reconnecting-In-Community-Gardens-In-Lincoln/10.2993/0278-0771-36.4.842.short. Accessed 13 May 2024

Chow E et al (2020) The socioeconomic and health impacts of community gardens. Pacific Northwest Medical Student Research Journal. https://pnwmsrj.org/meta-analysis/2020/10/the-socioeconomic-and-health-impacts-of-community-gardens/. Accessed 13 May 2024

Circle of Rights (2000) Economic, social and cultural rights activism: a training resource. The Right to Adequate Food. http://hrlibrary.umn.edu/edumat/IHRIP/circle/modules/module12.htm. Accessed 05 July 2024

Clemente JC (2012) Vazios urbanos e imóveis subutilizados no centro histórico tombado da cidade de João Pessoa—PB. Dissertação de mestrado, Programa de pós-graduação em Engenharia Urbana e Ambiental, UFPB, João Pessoa. https://repositorio.ufpb.br/jspui/handle/tede/5472?mode=full. Accessed 28 Aug 2024

Colding J et al (2022) Urban commons and collective action to address climate change. Soc Incl 10(1):103–114. https://www.cogitatiopress.com/socialinclusion/article/view/4862. Accessed 13 Sept 2024

Coriat, B. (2015). Le retour des communs: la crise de l'idéologie propriétaire. Les Liens qui Libèrent: Paris.

Costa AM da, Sampaio LC (2021) Transmutação da natureza jurídica de bens de uso comum em privados, em face da intervenção imobiliária na praia do Paiva do litoral pernambucano: aspectos jurídicos controversos. Revista de Direito da Cidade 12(1):1–36. https://www.e-publicacoes.uerj.br/rdc/article/view/38799. Accessed 28 Aug 2024

Dantas C (2019) Areas of the Amazon that should have 'zero deforestation' lose 6 cities in SP in three decades. G1. https://g1.globo.com/natureza/desafio-natureza/noticia/2019/05/21/areas-da-amazonia-que-deveriam-ter-desmatamento-zero-perdem-6-cidades-de-sp-em-tres-decadas.ghtml. Accessed 19 Aug 2024

Das K, Ramaswami A (2022) Who gardens and how in urban USA: Informing social equity in urban agriculture action plans, vol 6. https://www.frontiersin.org/articles/10.3389/fsufs.2022.923079/full/. Accessed 13 Sept 2024

Davies A et al (2017) Making visible: interrogating the performance of food sharing across 100 urban areas. Geoforum 86:136–149. https://www.sciencedirect.com/science/article/pii/S001671851730266X. Accessed 01 June 2024

Davies A, Evans D (2018) Urban food sharing: emerging geographies of production, consumption and exchange. Geoforum 99:154–159. Available on: https://www.sciencedirect.com/science/article/pii/S0016718518303440?via%3Dihub. Accessed 01 June 2024

Davies A et al (2018a) Fare sharing: interrogating the nexus of ICT, urban food sharing, and sustainability. Food, Culture & Society, p 18. https://www.tandfonline.com/doi/abs/https://doi.org/10.1080/15528014.2018.1427924. Accessed 16 May 2024

Davis A et al (2018b) Communicating goals and impacts of urban food sharing. Urban Agriculture Mag 34:39. https://edepot.wur.nl/468052. Accessed 01 June 2024

Davies A (2019) Urban food sharing. Bristol: Policy Press. Available at: https://library.oapen.org/bitstream/handle/20.500.12657/25248/1/9781447349860.pdfAccessed: 16 May 2024

Davies A, Evans D (2019) 'Urban food sharing: Emerging geographies of production, consumption and exchange', Geoforum, 99, pp. 154–159. Available at: https://www.sciencedirect.com/science/article/pii/S0016718518303440. Accessed: 1 June 2024

Dellenbaugh-Losse M, Zimmermann N, Vries N (2020) The urban commons cookbook: strategies and insights for creating and maintaining urban commons, Berlin, p 9. http://urbancommonscookbook.com/urbancommonscookbook.pdf/. Accessed 28 Aug 2024

Dias J, Rocha S, Neves N (2022) Legal and institutional frameworks for the Right to Food and Nutrition. FIAN Internacional Portugal. https://www.fian.org/files/is/htdocs/wp11102127_GNIAANVR7U/www/files/Module_1_English.pdf. Accessed 05 July 2024

Doswald-Beck L (1986) The right to food. Brit Yearbook Int L 57(1):371–372. https://academic.oup.com/bybil/article-abstract/57/1/371/294342?redirectedFrom=fulltext. Accessed 28 Aug 2024
Drake L (2014) Validating verdancy or vacancy? The relationship of community gardens and vacant lands in the US. Cities 40:133–142. https://www.sciencedirect.com/science/article/abs/pii/S0264275113001042. Accessed 13 May 2024
European Comission (2024) Food safety. https://commission.europa.eu/strategy-and-policy/food-safety_en. Accessed 28 Aug 2024
FAO (2004) Right to food and indigenous peoples, p 1. https://www.fao.org/3/a1603e/a1603e.pdf. Accessed 19 Aug 2024
FAO (2005) Voluntary guidelines: to support the progressive realization of the right to adequate food in the context of national food security. Rome. https://www.fao.org/3/y7937e/y7937e.pdf. Accessed 28 Aug 2024
FAO (2007a) Right to food and HIV/AIDS. https://www.fao.org/3/a1611e/a1611e.pdf. Accessed 28 June 2024
FAO (2007b) Questions and answers. https://www.fao.org/3/i0093e/i0093e.pdf. Accessed 28 June 2024
FAO (2007c) What is the right to food? https://www.fao.org/3/i0094e/i0094e.pdf. Accessed 02 July 2024
FAO (2008) Women and the Right to Food: International Law and State Practice. Rome, p 21. https://www.fao.org/3/ap549e/ap549e.pdf. Accessed 05 July 2024
FAO (2009) The right to adequate food and indigenous peoples: How can the right to food benefit indigenous peoples? p 30. https://www.fao.org/3/ap552e/ap552e.pdf. Accessed 02 July 2024
FAO (2010a) The right to adequate food. Geneva, p 5. https://www.ohchr.org/sites/default/files/Documents/Publications/FactSheet34en.pdf. Accessed 05 July 2024
FAO (2010b) Responsible governance of land tenure: an essential factor for the realization of the right to food. https://www.fao.org/3/AL382E/al382e.pdf. Accessed 07 Feb 2024
FAO (2011) op cit FAO (2009) The Right to Food and Access to Justice: Examples at the national, regional and international levels. Rome. https://www.fao.org/3/k7286e/k7286e.pdf. Accessed 04 July 2024
FAO (2014) Building a common vision for sustainable food and agriculture: Principles and approaches. Rome, https://www.fao.org/3/i3940e/i3940e.pdf. Accessed 28 Aug 2024
FAO (2018) The 10 elements of agroecology: guiding the transition to sustainable food and agricultural systems, p 2. https://www.fao.org/3/i9037en/i9037en.pdf. Accessed 13 Sept 2024
FAO (2020) Intergovernmental Technical Panel on Soils, Global Soil Biodiversity Initiative, Convention on Biological Diversity and European Commission State of knowledge of soil biodiversity: Status, challenges and potentialities. Available at: https://www.fao.org/documents/card/en/c/cb1928en. Accessed: 5 July 2024
FAO (2021) The state of food security and nutrition in the World 2021: Transforming food systems for food security, improved nutrition and affordable healthy diets for all. Rome. https://www.fao.org/3/cb4474en/cb4474en.pdf. Accessed 04 July 2024
FAO (2022) Urban and peri-urban agriculture sourcebook: from production to food systems. Rome, p 16. https://www.fao.org/3/cb9722en/cb9722en.pdf/. Accessed 13 Sept 2024
FAO (2022b) The Right to Food around the Globe. Available at: https://www.fao.org/right-to-food-around-the-globe/countries/en/Accessed: 13 April 2024.
FAO (2023a) Hunger and food insecurity. https://www.fao.org/hunger/en/. Accessed 05 July 2024
FAO (2023b) Protecting health, facilitating trade. Rome. https://www.fao.org/fao-who-codexalimentarius/en/. Accessed 28 Aug 2024
Feeny D et al (1990) The tragedy of the commons: twenty-two years later. Hum Ecol 18(1):1–19. https://www.jstor.org/stable/4602950/. Accessed 28 Aug 2024
Felderhoff J et al (2023) Vegetation complexity and nesting resource availability predict bee diversity and functional traits in community gardens. Ecol Appl 33(2). https://esajournals.onlinelibrary.wiley.com/doi/10.1002/eap.2759. Accessed 13 May 2024

Fernandes E (2021) The city as a common good: a pillar of the right to the city. Global Platform for the Right to the City, Barcelona. https://www.right2city.org/wp-content/uploads/2021/10/Right-to-the-City-Bien-Comun_EN_OK_alta.pdf. Accessed 20 Aug 2024

Ferris J et al (2001) People, land and sustainability: community gardens and the social dimension of sustainable development. Soc Pol 35(5):559–568. https://onlinelibrary.wiley.com/doi/10.1111/1467-9515.t01-1-00253. Accessed 16 May 2024

Flynn A (2018) Conceptualizing the urban commons: the place of business improvement districts in city governance. Working Papers, Allard School of Law, University of British Columbia. https://commons.allard.ubc.ca/cgi/viewcontent.cgi?article=1477&context=fac_pubs. Accessed 28 Aug 2024

Follmann A, Viehoff V (2015) A green garden on red clay: creating a new urban common as a form of political gardening in Cologne, Germany. Glob Platf Right City 20(10):1148–1174. https://www.right2city.org/wp-content/uploads/2021/10/Right-to-the-City-Bien-Comun_EN_OK_alta.pdf_. Accessed 28 Aug 2024

Foster SR (2011) Collective action and the urban commons. Notre Dame L Rev 87(1):94. https://scholarship.law.nd.edu/cgi/viewcontent.cgi?article=1001&context=ndlr/. Accessed 13 Sept 2024

Foster SR (2013a) Collective action and the urban commons. Notre Dame Law Review, p 57. https://scholarship.law.nd.edu/ndlr/vol87/iss1/2/. Accessed 28 Aug 2024

Foster SR (2013b) The city as an ecological space: social capital and urban land use. Notre Dame Law Review, p 528. https://scholarship.law.nd.edu/ndlr/vol82/iss2/1. Accessed 24 Aug 2024

Foster SR (2020), Iaione C. urban commons. https://www.oxfordbibliographies.com/display/document/obo-9780190922481/obo-9780190922481-0015.xml. Accessed 28 Aug 2024

Foster S, Iaione C (2016) The city as a commons. Yale L Pol Rev 34(2). https://ylpr.yale.edu/city-commons. Accessed 28 Aug 2024

Frischmann BM, Marciano A, Ramello GB (2019) Retrospectives: tragedy of the commons after 50 years. J Econ Persp 33(4):211–228. https://www.jstor.org/stable/26796843/. Accessed 28 Aug 2024

Gidwani V (2010) Urban commons, p 43. https://www.academia.edu/30124054/Urban_Commons_2010_. Accessed 28 Aug 2024

Glowa K et al (2019) Agroecologies of displacement: a study of land access, dislocation, and migration in relation to sustainable food production in the Beach Flats Community Garden. Agroecol Sustain Food Syst 43(1):92–115. https://www.tandfonline.com/doi/abs/10.1080/21683565.2018.1515143. Accessed 16 May 2024

Gripper A (2014) Practices of care and relationship-building: a qualitative analysis of urban agriculture's impacts on Black People's agency and wellbeing in Philadelphia. Int J Environ Res Pub Heal 20(6). https://www.mdpi.com/1660-4601/20/6/4831. Accessed 13 May 2024

Guetta M, Bensusan N (2018) Tutela dos conhecimentos tradicionais face à sua diversidade: A emergência dos protocolos comunitários. In: Ungaretti D, Lessa MR, Coutinho DR, Prol FM, Miola IZ, Ferrando T (eds) Propriedades em transformação: abordagens multidisciplinares. Blucher, São Paulo, pp 117–140

Guitart D, Pickering C, Byrne J (2012) Past results and future directions in urban community gardens research. Urb Forest Urb Green 11(4):364–373. https://www.sciencedirect.com/science/article/abs/pii/S1618866712000830. Accessed 13 Sept 2024

Guttmann A (2022) Plateformes de développement urbain, villes de la connaissance et développement durable: l'économie politique des biens communs urbains dans le contexte du changement climatique. Sociology, Université Paris-Nord, Paris XIII, p 186. https://theses.hal.science/tel-04160619. Accessed 04 Oct 2024

Hardin G (1968) The tragedy of the commons. New Ser 162(3859):1243–1248. https://www.jstor.org/stable/1724745. Accessed 28 Aug 2024

Hardt M, Negri A (2000) Empire. Harvard University Press, London, p 302

Hardt M, Negri A (2004) Multitude: war and democracy in the Age of Empire. The Penguin Press, New York, p xii

Heerink S et al (2021) Expanding field education: hope trust community garden. Aotearoa New Zealand Soc Work 33(1):112–115. https://anzswjournal.nz/anzsw/article/view/829. Accessed 13 May 2024
Helfrich S (2012) Common goods don't simply exist–They are created. In: Bollier D, Helfrich S (eds) The wealth of the commons: a world beyond market and state. Leveller Press, Amherst, MA, pp 61–67
Hock D (2000) Nascimento Da Era Caórdica. Editora Cultrix, São Paulo. https://books.google.com.br/books?id=8i-TUQBjtYYC&pg=PA52&lpg=PA52&dq=#v=onepage&q&f=false_. Accessed 28 Aug 2024
Iaione C (2015) Governing the urban commons. Ital J Pub L. https://www.researchgate.net/publication/318393613_GOVERNING_THE_URBAN_COMMONS. Accessed 28 Aug 2024
Iaione C (2016) City as a commons. https://dlc.dlib.indiana.edu/dlc/bitstream/handle/10535/8604/Iaione_prelversion.pdf?sequence=1&isAllowed=yord-Iaione_cityasacommons_EN. Accessed 28 Aug 2024
Jardim F (2018) IPTU progressivo no tempo ou arrecadação de bem vago abandonado? aplicabilidade de instrumentos jurídico-urbanísticos em imóveis ociosos do bairro do Recife. Mestrado em Desenvolvimento Urbano—UFPE, Recife. https://repositorio.ufpe.br/handle/123456789/32193. Accessed 28 Aug 2024
Jardim F, Santos A, Eversberg D, Moura E (2024) How is a community urban garden program related to the law? Analysis of Hortas Cariocas (Rio de Janeiro, Brazil). St. Thomas J L Pub Pol 16(1). https://ir.stthomas.edu/ustjlpp/vol16/iss1/9/. Accessed 13 Sept 2024
Jones A, Murphy J (2010) Practice and economic geography. Geogr Compass 4(4):319
Junge B (2010) Another commons is possible. Focaal J Glob Hist Anthropol 2010(57). https://www.berghahnjournals.com/view/journals/focaal/2010/57/focaal570110.xml. Accessed 28 Aug 2024
Krajewski M (2021) Reflections on the North Central community gardens branch out project. J Agricul Food Syst Commun Dev 10(4):51–54. https://www.foodsystemsjournal.org/index.php/fsj/article/view/1015. Accessed 13 May 2024
Landiva N et al (2012) Human rights: a strategy for the fight against hunger. https://www.fao.org/3/ap560e/ap560e.pdf. Accessed 04 July 2024
Lauriola VM (2013) Indigenous lands, commons, juridical pluralism and sustainability in Brazil: Lessons from the Indigenous lands of Raposa Serra Do Sol. J Latin Am Geograp 12(1):157–85. http://www.jstor.org/stable/24394847. Accessed 3 Oct 2024
Linebaugh P (2008) The Magna Carta manifesto: liberties and commons for all. University of California Press, Berkeley California. http://www.jstor.org/stable/10.1525/j.ctt1pp4q2. Accessed 28 Aug 2024
Lloyd D et al (2022) Learning science locally: Community gardens and our future. Front Educ 7. https://www.frontiersin.org/articles/10.3389/feduc.2022.850016/full#:~:text=The%20wholistic%20nature%20of%20gardening,%E2%80%94knowing%2C%20feeling%2C%20connecting. Accessed 13 May 2024
Lu F (2006) The commons in an Amazonian context. Social analysis: Int J Soc Cult Pract 50(3):187–94. http://www.jstor.org/stable/23182118. Accessed 3 Oct 2024
Mackenzie S, Davies A (2019) Share it: co-designing a sustainability impact assessment framework for urban food sharing initiatives. Environ Impact Assess Rev 79. https://www.sciencedirect.com/science/article/pii/S0195925519301064?via%3Dihub. Accessed 01 June 2024
Magalhães MJ (2021) Hortas comunitárias in the favelas of Rio de Janeiro: how new ideas are adopted and spread across communities. In: Trapani F et al (ed) Advanced studies in efficient environmental design and city planning. Springer International Publishing, Cham. https://link.springer.com/chapter/10.1007/978-3-030-65181-7_21. Accessed 20 May 2024
Mceldowney J (2017) Urban agriculture in Europe: patterns, challenges and policies. https://www.europarl.europa.eu/RegData/etudes/IDAN/2017/614641/EPRS_IDA(2017)614641_EN.pdf/. Accessed 13 Sept 2024
Meretz S (2012) The structural communality of the commons. In: Bollier D, Helfrich S (eds) The wealth of the commons: a world beyond market and state. Levellers, Amherst, pp 28–34

Messina N (2019) A imaginação poética vivida no Jardim Secreto do Poço da Panela: ensaios de devaneio. Dissertação (Mestrado em Desenvolvimento Urbano), Universidade Federal de Pernambuco, Recife. https://repositorio.ufpe.br/handle/123456789/35890. Accessed 19 Aug 2024

Monterroso I, Cronkleton P, Larson A (2019) Commons, indigenoues rights and governance. In: Hudson B, Rosenbloom J, Cole D (eds) Routledge handbook of the study of the commons. Routledge, New York, pp 376–391

Morrom O (2019) Sharing food and risk in Berlin's urban food commons. Geoforum 99:202–212. https://www.sciencedirect.com/science/article/pii/S0016718518302641?via%3Dihub#b0260. Accessed 24 Aug 2024

Muller A et al (2015) Urban commons: moving beyond state and market. Birkhauser, Basel, Switzerland

Nacur E (2022) O regime jurídico dos rios urbanos e a reforma urbanística na cidade capitalista: da exploração socioeconômica à racionalidade ambiental. Dissertação (Mestrado em Direito da Cidade), Universidade do Estado do Rio de Janeiro, Conselho Nacional de Desenvolvimento Científico e Tecnológico

Nascimento B (1985) The concept of Quilombo and black cultural resistance. Afrodiaspora 3(6–7):41–49. Translated by Smith C, Davies A, Gomes B. https://www.hkw.de/en/programme/o-quilombismo/the-concept-of-quilombo-and-black-cultural-resistance. Accessed 29 Sep 2024

Opitz I et al (2016) Contributing to food security in urban areas: differences between urban agriculture and peri-urban agriculture in the global north. Agricul Hum Val 33(2):341–358. https://link.springer.com/article/10.1007/s10460-015-9610-2/. Accessed 13 Sept 2024

Ostrom E (1990) Governing the commons: the evolution of institutions for collective action. Cambridge University Press.

Ostrom E et al (1999) Revisiting the commons: local lessons, global challenges. Science's Compass, vol 284. https://www.laits.utexas.edu/~mbs31415/Ostrom_etal.pdf. Accessed 28 Aug 2024

Oxford English Dictionary (2017) Oxford: Oxford University Press apud Davies A et al (2014) Making visible: interrogating the performance of food sharing across 100 urban areas. Geoforum 86:136–149. https://www.sciencedirect.com/science/article/pii/S001671851730266X. Accessed 16 May 2024

Ponstingel D (2022) The governance of community gardens as commons and its role in the socio-ecological outcomes of gardening in Austin, Texas, USA. Socioecol Pract Res 4(4):355–376. https://www.ncbi.nlm.nih.gov/pmc/articles/PMC9651095/. Accessed 13 Sept 2024

Reckwitz A (2002) Towards a theory of social practice. Sage, London, p 250

Rekow L (2015) Fighting insecurity: experiments in urban agriculture in the favelas of Rio de Janeiro. Field Actions Science Reports, vol 8. https://journals.openedition.org/factsreports/pdf/4009. Accessed 16 May 2024

Relly E (2022) Sob a sombra dos commons: capital social, meio ambiente e imigração alemã no Brasil meridional. Oikos, São Leopoldo, p 17

Rogge N, Theesfeld I (2018) Categorizing urban commons: community gardens in the Rhine-Ruhr Agglomeration, Germany. Int J Comm 12(2):255. https://www.jstor.org/stable/26511528. Accessed 28 Aug 2024

Rosol M (2011) Community gardens in Berlin: A new form of citizen participation. In: Endlicher W (ed) Perspectives in urban ecology: Studies of ecosystems and interactions between humans and nature in the metropolis of Berlin. Springer, Berlin, pp 263–270

Schatzki T (1996) Social practices: a Wittgensteinian approach to human activity and the social. Cambridge University Press, Cambridge, p 89

Sen A (2001) Development as freedom. Oxford University Press, Oxford, New York, p 161

Sepúlvida M et al (2004) Human rights reference handbook. Mundo gráfico, San Jose. https://www.corteidh.or.cr/tablas/23861.pdf. Accessed 28 June 2024

Sinay L et al (2014) Parque Natural Municipal da Paisagem Carioca: ecoturismo e sustentabilidade. Revista Brasileira De Ecoturismo 7(3). https://doi.org/10.34024/rbecotur.2014.v7.6388. Accessed 24 Aug 2024

Sousa C (2010) Do cheio para o vazio: metodologia e estratégia na avaliação de espaços urbanos obsoletos. Mestrado em Arquitetura, Universidade Técnica de Lisboa, Lisboa. https://fenix.tecnico.ulisboa.pt/downloadFile/395142195938/DO%20CHEIO%20PARA%20O%20VAZIO_versao%20final.pdf. Accessed 19 Aug 2024

Steuri B, Vignola G (2015) Towards productive and socio-natural urban landscapes: tapping urban agriculture's potential as a tool for sustainable development. Master's thesis on Resource efficiency in architecture and planning. Hamburg University, p 115. https://repos.hcu-hamburg.de/bitstream/hcu/650/2/2022-06-01_steuri-bettina_vignola-gionatan_masterarbeit.pdf. Accessed 13 Sept 2024

NobelPrize (2024) The Sveriges Riksbank prize in economic sciences in memory of Alfred Nobel 2009. Illustrated Presentation. https://www.nobelprize.org/prizes/economic-sciences/2009/illustrated-information/. Accessed 28 Aug 2024

Thorman A, Dhillon H (2021) No food for thought: documenting the prevalence of food insecurity among medical students at one western university. J Hung Environ Nut 16(5):643–649. https://www.tandfonline.com/doi/abs/10.1080/19320248.2021.1873885. Accessed 13 May 2024

Tims K et al (2021) Gardening for change: community giving gardens and senior food insecurity. J Agricult Food Syst Commun Dev 10(4):85–101. https://www.foodsystemsjournal.org/index.php/fsj/article/view/1018#:~:text=Community%20giving%20gardens%2C%20like%20the,while%20building%20local%20food%20economies. Accessed 13 May 2024

Tzul G (2018) Gobierno Comunal Indígena y Estado Guatemalteco: algunas claves críticas para pensar su tensa relación. Ediciones Bizarras/Instituto Amaq´: Ciudad de Guatemala

United Nations (1948) Universal declaration of human rights. https://www.un.org/en/about-us/universal-declaration-of-human-rights. Accessed 28 Aug 2024

United Nations (1966) General Assembly resolution 2200A. https://www.ohchr.org/en/instruments-mechanisms/instruments/international-covenant-economic-social-and-cultural-rights. Accessed 28 Aug 2024

United Nations (1999) General Comment N°. 12: The Right to Adequate Food (Art. 11 of the Covenant), Committee on economic, social and cultural rights (CESCR). https://www.refworld.org/docid/4538838c11.html. Accessed 28 June 2024

United Nations (2007) United Nations declaration on the rights of indigenous peoples. https://social.desa.un.org/sites/default/files/migrated/19/2018/11/UNDRIP_E_web.pdf. Accessed 28 Aug 2024

United Nations University (2013) Why food should be a commons not a commodity. https://ourworld.unu.edu/en/why-food-should-be-a-commons-not-a-commodity. Accessed 28 Aug 2024

Warde P (2002) Common rights and commons lands in southwest Germany, 1500–1800. In: De Moor M, Taylor L, Warde P (eds) The management of common land in north-west Europe, c. 1500–1850. Brepols, Turnhout, Bélgica, pp 195–224

Wong R, Gable L, Rivera-Nunez Z (2018) Perceived benefits of participation and risks of soil contamination in St. Louis Urban Community Gardens. J Commun Heal 35(4):809–822. https://pubmed.ncbi.nlm.nih.gov/29274067/. Accessed 16 May 2024

Chapter 4
Profile of Investigated Community Gardens and Interviewees in Berlin and Rio de Janeiro

4.1 The Case of Berlin

4.1.1 Overview of Socioeconomic and Urbanistic Relevant Data

Socioeconomic data reveals low food insecurity and poverty in Germany.[1] On the one hand, regarding **poverty**,[2] "17.3 million people were affected in 2022. 14.7% of the population were at risk of poverty, 6.1% were affected by severe material and

[1] Pfeiffer et al. (2017).

[2] "Poverty is a multidimensional problem that encompasses monetary, social, and cultural aspects. In a wealthy country such as the Federal Republic of Germany, being poor means above all: Being indigent or ridden with debt due to a limited capacity to work, a dearth of job opportunities, or low wages; Experiencing a persistent shortage in the possessions perceived as necessary to lead a more or less "normal" life; Being disadvantaged in multiple arenas such as work, housing, leisure, and sport; Being excluded from (good) education and from the (high) cultural and social networks that are necessary for social inclusion; Facing increased existential risks, health deficiencies, and diminished life expectancy; Experiencing a loss of social status and social respect, and by extension frequently losing self-confidence; Experiencing powerlessness or the inability to wield influence in all key spheres of society (the economy, politics, governance, knowledge production, and mass media). It is important to differentiate here between absolute, extreme, or existential poverty on the one hand and relative poverty on the other. Absolute poverty affects people who cannot meet their basic needs: not enough to eat, no safe drinking water, no appropriate (warm) clothing, no housing, and no access to medical care. Those suffering relative poverty, in contrast, are able to meet their basic needs but cannot afford the extras that others consider normal, such as occasionally eating a restaurant meal or going to the movies or the theater. Moreover, people in this situation participate minimally socially, culturally, and politically. In Germany, absolute poverty mainly takes the form of homelessness. The designation of the "unhoused" (*wohnungslos*) refers to those who do not own or rent their own living space and who instead live at shelters or bunk with friends or acquaintances. In contrast, the "unsheltered" (*obdachlos*) are those who live on the streets and, for example, sleep on park benches. The people most at risk of being unhoused or unsheltered

F. Jardim, *Right to Food in Community Gardens*, LITES - Legal Issues in Transdisciplinary Environmental Studies 6,
https://doi.org/10.1007/978-3-032-19612-5_4

social deprivation, and 9.7% were living in a household with very low work intensity."[3] Then, poverty exists, "albeit less spectacular and less visible[4] forms than in the Global South."[5] On the other hand, **"food insecurity** could be an intermittent reality for some 7% of Germany's population. The number of food banks in Germany increased from 480 in 2005 to 916 in 2013, and 60,000 volunteers currently serve food to 1.5 million so-called 'regular customers'."[6] No specific data was identified about poverty and food insecurity in *Berlin*, but an indicator of food insecurity[7] is that 74,000 people monthly have the support of a charity food bank (Berliner Tafel and Berliner Kirchengemeinden Ausgabestellen).[8] Additionally, there is generic information about **food deserts** in Germany, including in *Berlin.*[9] Food affordability is consolidated in Germany. Moreover, quality and safety, as well as sustainability and adaptation, are at good levels. In contrast, food availability calls attention due to a moderate level (Fig. 4.1).[10]

The **COVID-19** incidence was homogenous among the neighborhoods,[11] and official data reports a growing city economy rapidly recovering from the COVID-19 pandemic economic effects.[12] Nevertheless, the "COVID-19 crisis and the effects of inflation have deepened the chasm between rich and poor"[13] and affected the food banks (temporarily closed).[14] In 2023, there is a 3.2% **unemployment** rate in Germany,[15] while in *Berlin,* it is an 8.7% rate.[16] "The social integration of specific vulnerable groups (migrants, disabled, older people at risk of poverty, drug addicts)"[17] is a challenge in *Berlin*. This city has an elevated city development index (Fig. 4.2).

---

and who are truly impoverished are serious drug addicts, "street children"—mostly adolescents—unaccompanied refugee minors, citizens of EU member states with no access to social services, and illegal migrants." Butterwegge (2023).

[3] Germany (2024).

[4] Vonberg.

[5] Butterwegge (2023).

[6] Pfeiffer et al. (2017, pp. 99–109).

[7] Depa et al. (2018, pp. 96–101).

[8] Tafel.

[9] Reimer (2020).

[10] The Economist Impact (2022).

[11] Berlin.

[12] Berlin (2023).

[13] Butterwegge (2023).

[14] Simmet and Stroebele-Benschop (2023, pp. 356–371).

[15] Germany (2023).

[16] Berlin.

[17] Kramer (2013, p. 35).

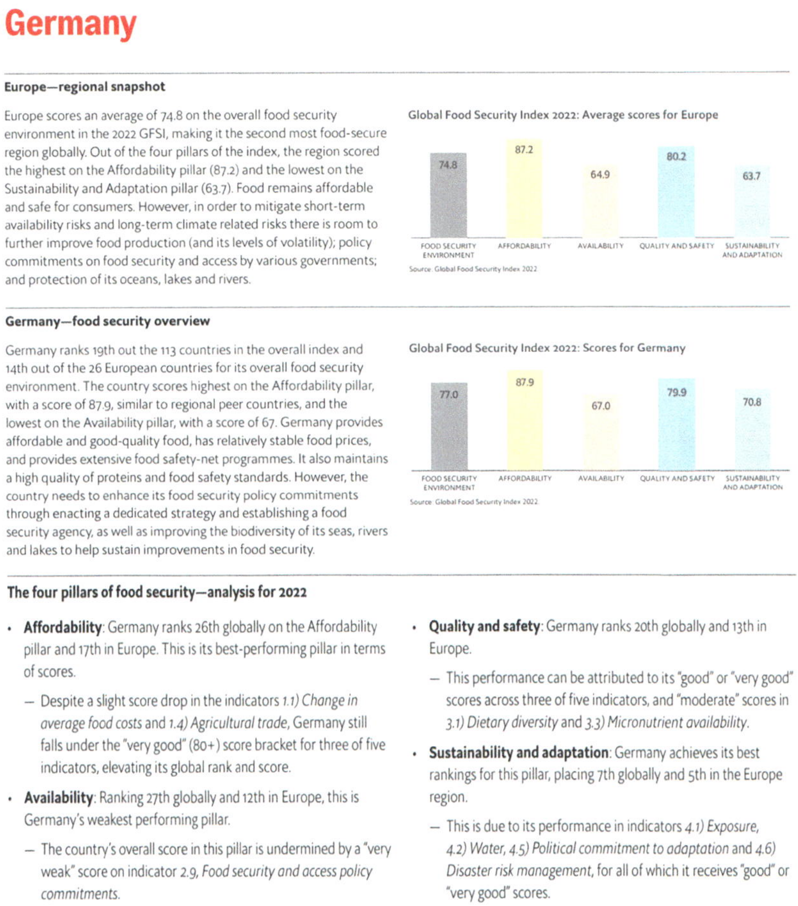

Germany

Europe—regional snapshot

Europe scores an average of 74.8 on the overall food security environment in the 2022 GFSI, making it the second most food-secure region globally. Out of the four pillars of the index, the region scored the highest on the Affordability pillar (87.2) and the lowest on the Sustainability and Adaptation pillar (63.7). Food remains affordable and safe for consumers. However, in order to mitigate short-term availability risks and long-term climate related risks there is room to further improve food production (and its levels of volatility); policy commitments on food security and access by various governments; and protection of its oceans, lakes and rivers.

Germany—food security overview

Germany ranks 19th out the 113 countries in the overall index and 14th out of the 26 European countries for its overall food security environment. The country scores highest on the Affordability pillar, with a score of 87.9, similar to regional peer countries, and the lowest on the Availability pillar, with a score of 67. Germany provides affordable and good-quality food, has relatively stable food prices, and provides extensive food safety-net programmes. It also maintains a high quality of proteins and food safety standards. However, the country needs to enhance its food security policy commitments through enacting a dedicated strategy and establishing a food security agency, as well as improving the biodiversity of its seas, rivers and lakes to help sustain improvements in food security.

The four pillars of food security—analysis for 2022

- **Affordability**: Germany ranks 26th globally on the Affordability pillar and 17th in Europe. This is its best-performing pillar in terms of scores.
  - Despite a slight score drop in the indicators *1.1) Change in average food costs* and *1.4) Agricultural trade*, Germany still falls under the "very good" (80+) score bracket for three of five indicators, elevating its global rank and score.
- **Availability**: Ranking 27th globally and 12th in Europe, this is Germany's weakest performing pillar.
  - The country's overall score in this pillar is undermined by a "very weak" score on indicator 2.9, *Food security and access policy commitments*.
- **Quality and safety**: Germany ranks 20th globally and 13th in Europe.
  - This performance can be attributed to its "good" or "very good" scores across three of five indicators, and "moderate" scores in *3.1) Dietary diversity* and *3.3) Micronutrient availability*.
- **Sustainability and adaptation**: Germany achieves its best rankings for this pillar, placing 7th globally and 5th in the Europe region.
  - This is due to its performance in indicators *4.1) Exposure, 4.2) Water, 4.5) Political commitment to adaptation* and *4.6) Disaster risk management*, for all of which it receives "good" or "very good" scores.

Fig. 4.1 Global Food Security Index 2022: Germany (parts 1 and 2). *Source* The Economist (2022)

Nonetheless, there are regional disparities (Fig. 4.3),[18] including Neukölln, one of the poorest areas of Germany.[19] This neighborhood had the stigma of a slum, and it is currently under gentrification.[20]

Regarding **vacant land**, during World War II, many buildings, especially in the eastern inner-city districts, were damaged and left unrepaired. After the fall of the Berlin Wall in November 1989, the public housing policy neglected the old stock,

[18] "Areas in which social disadvantages are concentrated to an above-average extent require a special urban development policy focus and are identified MSS [Social city development monitoring] as "areas in need of special attention". They are defined as areas with very low social status or low social status with negative dynamics at the same time. In total, this group includes 56 of the 536 planning areas considered (10 percent)." Berlin (2021).

[19] Council of Europe.

[20] Soederberg (2017, pp. 478–495).

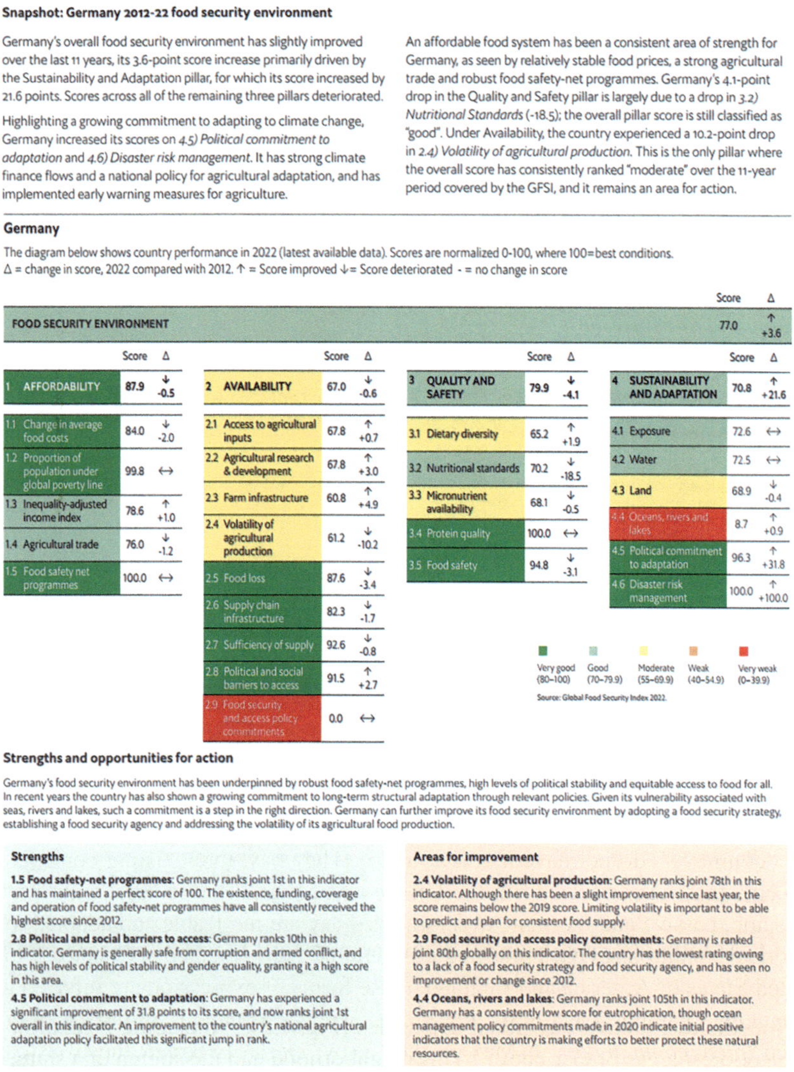

Snapshot: Germany 2012-22 food security environment

Germany's overall food security environment has slightly improved over the last 11 years, its 3.6-point score increase primarily driven by the Sustainability and Adaptation pillar, for which its score increased by 21.6 points. Scores across all of the remaining three pillars deteriorated.

Highlighting a growing commitment to adapting to climate change, Germany increased its scores on *4.5) Political commitment to adaptation* and *4.6) Disaster risk management*. It has strong climate finance flows and a national policy for agricultural adaptation, and has implemented early warning measures for agriculture.

An affordable food system has been a consistent area of strength for Germany, as seen by relatively stable food prices, a strong agricultural trade and robust food safety-net programmes. Germany's 4.1-point drop in the Quality and Safety pillar is largely due to a drop in *3.2) Nutritional Standards* (-18.5); the overall pillar score is still classified as "good". Under Availability, the country experienced a 10.2-point drop in *2.4) Volatility of agricultural production*. This is the only pillar where the overall score has consistently ranked "moderate" over the 11-year period covered by the GFSI, and it remains an area for action.

Germany

The diagram below shows country performance in 2022 (latest available data). Scores are normalized 0-100, where 100=best conditions.
Δ = change in score, 2022 compared with 2012. ↑ = Score improved ↓= Score deteriorated - = no change in score

	Score	Δ
FOOD SECURITY ENVIRONMENT	77.0	↑ +3.6

	Score	Δ
1 AFFORDABILITY	87.9	↓ -0.5
1.1 Change in average food costs	84.0	↓ -2.0
1.2 Proportion of population under global poverty line	99.8	↔
1.3 Inequality-adjusted income index	78.6	↑ +1.0
1.4 Agricultural trade	76.0	↓ -1.2
1.5 Food safety net programmes	100.0	↔

	Score	Δ
2 AVAILABILITY	67.0	↓ -0.6
2.1 Access to agricultural inputs	67.8	↑ +0.7
2.2 Agricultural research & development	67.8	↑ +3.0
2.3 Farm infrastructure	60.8	↑ +4.9
2.4 Volatility of agricultural production	61.2	↓ -10.2
2.5 Food loss	87.6	↓ -3.4
2.6 Supply chain infrastructure	82.3	↓ -1.7
2.7 Sufficiency of supply	92.6	↓ -0.8
2.8 Political and social barriers to access	91.5	↑ +2.7
2.9 Food security and access policy commitments	0.0	↔

	Score	Δ
3 QUALITY AND SAFETY	79.9	↓ -4.1
3.1 Dietary diversity	65.2	↑ +1.9
3.2 Nutritional standards	70.2	↓ -18.5
3.3 Micronutrient availability	68.1	↓ -0.5
3.4 Protein quality	100.0	↔
3.5 Food safety	94.8	↓ -3.1

	Score	Δ
4 SUSTAINABILITY AND ADAPTATION	70.8	↑ +21.6
4.1 Exposure	72.6	↔
4.2 Water	72.5	↔
4.3 Land	68.9	↓ -0.4
4.4 Oceans, rivers and lakes	8.7	↑ +0.9
4.5 Political commitment to adaptation	96.3	↑ +31.8
4.6 Disaster risk management	100.0	↑ +100.0

Very good (80–100) Good (70–79.9) Moderate (55–69.9) Weak (40–54.9) Very weak (0–39.9)

Source: Global Food Security Index 2022.

Strengths and opportunities for action

Germany's food security environment has been underpinned by robust food safety-net programmes, high levels of political stability and equitable access to food for all. In recent years the country has also shown a growing commitment to long-term structural adaptation through relevant policies. Given its vulnerability associated with seas, rivers and lakes, such a commitment is a step in the right direction. Germany can further improve its food security environment by adopting a food security strategy, establishing a food security agency and addressing the volatility of its agricultural food production.

Strengths

1.5 Food safety-net programmes: Germany ranks joint 1st in this indicator and has maintained a perfect score of 100. The existence, funding, coverage and operation of food safety-net programmes have all consistently received the highest score since 2012.

2.8 Political and social barriers to access: Germany ranks 10th in this indicator. Germany is generally safe from corruption and armed conflict, and has high levels of political stability and gender equality, granting it a high score in this area.

4.5 Political commitment to adaptation: Germany has experienced a significant improvement of 31.8 points to its score, and now ranks joint 1st overall in this indicator. An improvement to the country's national agricultural adaptation policy facilitated this significant jump in rank.

Areas for improvement

2.4 Volatility of agricultural production: Germany ranks joint 78th in this indicator. Although there has been a slight improvement since last year, the score remains below the 2019 score. Limiting volatility is important to be able to predict and plan for consistent food supply.

2.9 Food security and access policy commitments: Germany is ranked joint 80th globally on this indicator. The country has the lowest rating owing to a lack of a food security strategy and food security agency, and has seen no improvement or change since 2012.

4.4 Oceans, rivers and lakes: Germany ranks joint 105th in this indicator. Germany has a consistently low score for eutrophication, though ocean management policy commitments made in 2020 indicate initial positive indicators that the country is making efforts to better protect these natural resources.

Fig. 4.1 (continued)

and planned construction projects failed, leading to empty lots. Moreover, there was a complex process for the restitution of dispossessed properties in former East Berlin, so they remained unused and in disrepair for years. Furthermore, economic changes led to the closure of industries in both East and West Berlin, leaving behind empty industrial spaces. In the 1990s and 2000s, the construction of office buildings

Fig. 4.2 City development index Berlin 2020. *Source* City Development Index (2020)

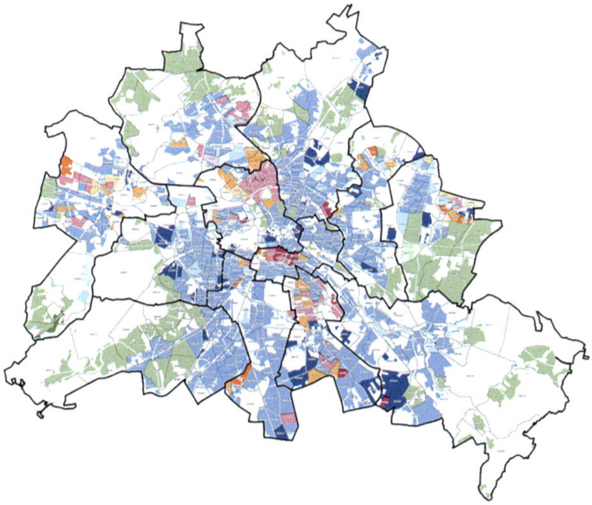

Fig. 4.3 Report monitoring social urban development Berlin 2021. *Source* Berlin (2021)

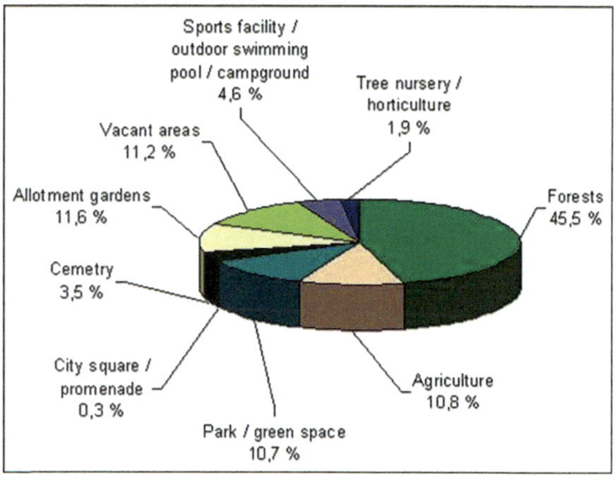

Fig. 4.4 Inventory of green and open spaces of Berlin 2000. *Source* Berlin (2000)

generated a surplus of vacant office space.[21] However, the vacant land scenario is decreasing. There were 11.2% vacant areas in 2010 (Fig. 4.4).[22]

Recently, the concept was updated to "**fallow area,**"[23] and it is part of different neighborhoods (Fig. 4.5).

According to the Inventory of Green and Open Spaces of Berlin (2020a, b),[24] **agriculture** happens in the **outskirts** of the city (illustrated by the Fig. 4.6), and **urban agriculture** has as visible important expressions the allotment gardens.

> **Areas used for agricultural purposes**, which account for almost 9 % of the inventory of open space, are found particularly in the northeastern area (Pankow and Weißensee). Other agricultural areas are located on the remaining outskirts. **Allotment gardens**, which account for some 8 % of the open space inventory, are found almost exclusively outside the City Rail Circle Line, albeit still in the vicinity of the city center in some cases. Often, they are located near canals, rivers, and railway lines. The currently unused fallow areas are distributed throughout the entire urban area, particularly along railway lines and bodies of water. They account for some 9 % of the total open space. The few remaining **Tree nurseries and horticultural areas** are found predominantly on the outskirts, while areas of the categories.[25]

[21] Mariko (2017, pp. 1–16).

[22] Berlin (2020a, b).

[23] "A Fallow area is an area that is not in use or maintained at the time of recording, on which variegated stands of vegetation can often develop undisturbed, which is, however, subject to great pressure of use and change. A distinction is made between a Fallow area free of vegetation on the one hand, which includes mostly excavations, soil or rubble dumps, or demolition areas, where no vegetation has yet taken root, due to the fact that their utilisation has only recently been abandoned. In some cases, the site conditions ensure that no vegetation will enter the area for some time. These may be brownfields where little vegetation grows due to the very high degree of imperviousness, or else sand dunes and beaches, on which spontaneous growth of vegetation occurs only very slowly, due to a lack of nutrients, or due to regular disturbances." Berlin (2020a, b), op. cit.

[24] Berlin (2020a, b), op. cit.

[25] Berlin (2020a, b), op. cit.

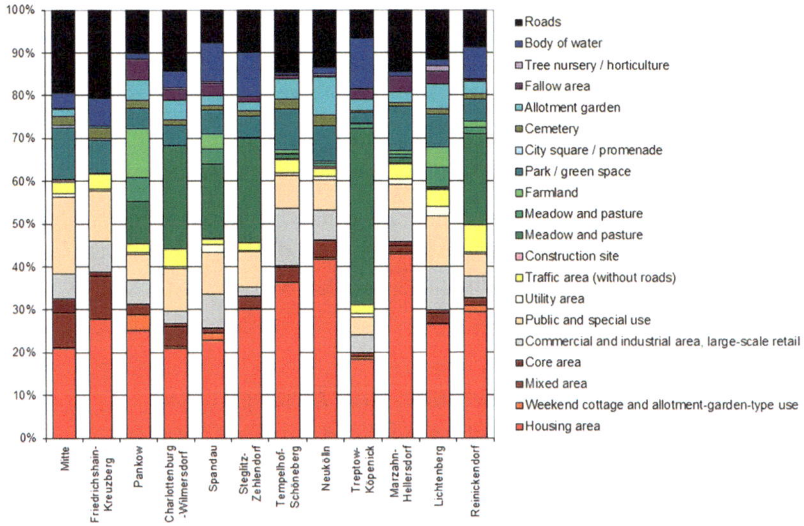

Fig. 4.5 Area shares of uses in the total area of Berlin's boroughs (%) 2020. *Source* Berlin (2020a, b)

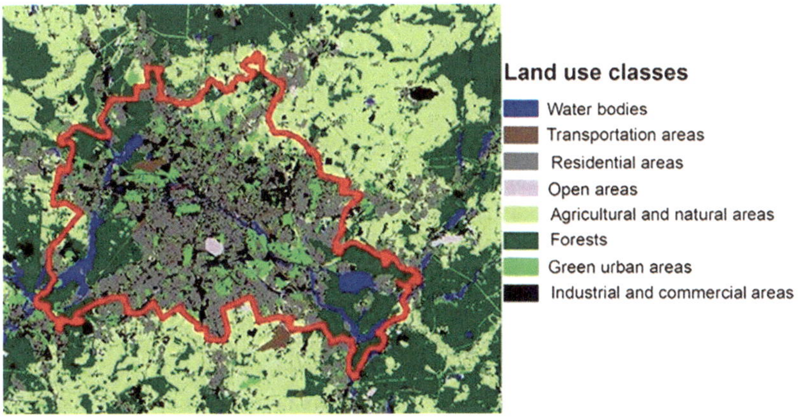

Fig. 4.6 Land use map of Berlin and its surrounding. *Source* Hamid and Sahar (2017, p. 2271). *Note* The red line is the boundary of Berlin

In addition, the number of **community gardens** in *Berlin* is also interesting (more than 200), despite the unclear precise official data about them—probably due the gardens' continuous dinamic of creation, moving, and closing during the years. The government program for community gardens (Berliner Gemeinschaftsgarten-Programm) is part of the Berlin Senate Department for Mobility, Transport, Climate Protection, and the Environment. The concept of community gardens adopted by the city government is that:

> In Germany today, many community gardens are about joint design, participation, and an active commitment to the environment. In contrast to allotment gardens, community gardens are collectively managed gardens that usually occupy a smaller area of land shared by all gardeners and are managed according to the criteria of organic farming. In almost all cases, community gardens are run by an open, regular plenary session or an elected board. Many community gardens pursue socially integrative goals and, in addition to gardening in the narrower sense, are also committed to passing on environmental knowledge.[26]

Urban agriculture is under pressure for other uses, such as housing and leisure,[27] especially considering the reduction of available land (fallow area) in the last years due to the construction of new buildings.[28] This has been raising the dispute for land.

4.1.2 Territorial, Socioeconomic, and Demographic Information of Investigated Community Gardens

There were sixteen community gardens investigated in *Berlin*: Moritzplatz, Prinzessinnengarten, Allmende-Kontor, Mathematik, Informatik, Naturwissenschaft und Technik (M.I.N.T.) Grünes Klassenzimmer, Elisabeet, Bürger*innen-Garten (Citizens Garden), Freie Universität Berlin (Free University of Berlin), Peace of Land, Rübezahl, Stadtteilgarten Schillerkiez, Stadtacker Berlin, Klunkergarten, Himmelbeet (in two different addresses due a forced moving), Frieda Süd, Möhrchenpark, Kiez-Garten. There was also an interview and questionnaires with a representative from the Senate of Berlin. The total representation of field visits on the city level can be observed in Fig. 4.7.

These gardens were former **vacant land** with various past uses (store, part of a cemetery, side area of a train station, side area of a riding hall linked to a university, porcelain factory, closed airport, mall rooftop, sports area, and public square, former flower market). They only became community gardens after **2009**. The land was mostly owned by the State but managed by civil society through voluntary associations. Some gardens had fees for maintenance or renting plant beds. A security deposit was required to access the land for more than half of the gardens. A few gardens experienced stressful situations such as forced or voluntary moves (Tables 4.1, 4.2).

Interviewees mentioned 36 different garden products, with container-based cultivation being common. Plots are mostly collectively shared, with varying numbers of people in the core team (7–30) and gardeners (10–300).

There were 20 participants *(commoners)* in interviews and questionnaires, nine *gardeners* and 11 *experts*, as organized in Table 4.3.

The participants' average age was 33, and most were female. They were well-educated (undergraduate and graduate) and mostly had no religious or political affiliations, although some expressed interest in left-wing, socialist, or green political

[26] Berlin.

[27] Deutscher Städtetag (2021, p. 5).

[28] Berlin (2020a, b). op. cit.

parties. The average monthly household income was 891 Euros (around 992 United States Dollars). In terms of origin, Germans were the prevalent nationality. However, there were also some participants from other countries (United Kingdom, France, Luxembourg, Belgium, Italy, Brazil, and the United States of America), including those with dual citizenship, and very few were born and raised in *Berlin*.

Most of them lived in apartments, and about half of them had access to a green area. Their food diet was mostly vegetarian, with little reliance on meat. The group comprised people who received some income from the garden (hired as professionals or volunteers with symbolic financial support); a major part were volunteers without financial support.

On average, they were gardening for 4.4 years, with less than half of the interviewees being involved with the garden since its foundation (including the move to a new address). For half of the interviewees, the garden where the interview took place was their first contact with community gardening. They consumed products from the garden, although their diet was not solely dependent on it as they mostly bought food from supermarkets. The products were sold to non-profits to contribute to the project's maintenance in a few cases. They lived about 3 km from the garden, with more than half of them preferring bicycle as a mode of transportation.

The monthly hours spent in the garden variated greatly between seasons. Less than half of the interviewees mentioned the relation of food production to ancestral

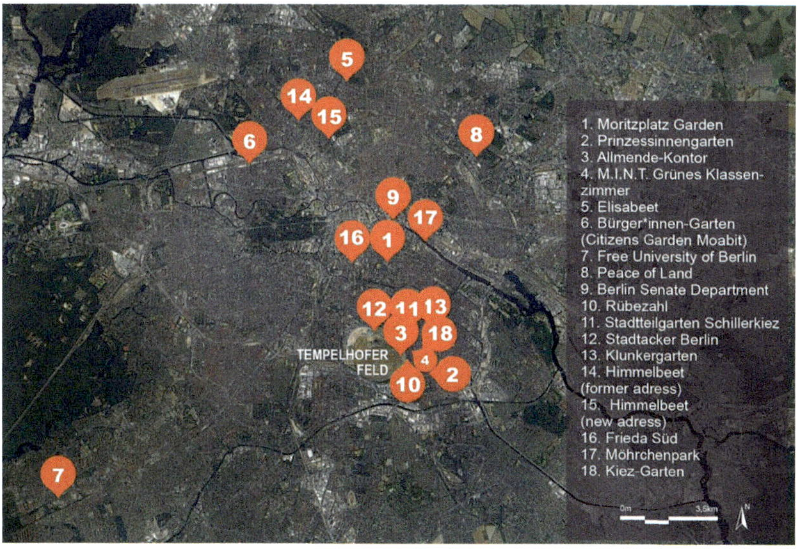

Fig. 4.7 Investigated community gardens in Berlin. *Source* Jardim (2024)[29]

[29] Collaboration with Jéssica Lucena. Google Earth Data Basis. Illustrator Software.

Table 4.1 Investigated community gardens in Berlin (part 1)

ID	Garden	Address	Interview	Previous use of the area	Starting year	Lend tenure stress	Type of cultivation	Type of plot
1	Moritzplatz	Prinzenstraße 35–38, 10,969	BERG9	Store	2009	2019 (voluntary move)	Container-based cultivation Ground-based cultivation	Individual or closed group Collective (mostly)
2	Prinzessinnengarten	Hermannstraße 99–105, 12,051	BERG1 BERG2 BERG3 BERG4 BERE1 BERE2 BERE5 BERE9 BERE10	Part of a cemetery	2018	No register	Container-based cultivation Ground-based cultivation	Collective
3	Allmende-Kontor	Tempelhofer Feld	BERG8 BERE4 BERE6	Airport	2011	No register	Container-based cultivation	Individual or closed group (mostly) Collective
4	M.I.N.T. Grünes Klassenzimmer	Tempelhofer Feld	BERG7	Airport	2012	No register	Container-based cultivation	Collective
5	Elisabeet	Wollankstraße 66, 13,359 Berlin	BERE7 BERE8	Part of a cemetery	2020	No register	Ground-based cultivation	Collective
6	Bürger*innen-Garten (Citizens Garden)	Siemensstraße 27, 10,551 Berlin	BERG6	Side area of a train station	2012	No register	Ground-based cultivation Container-based cultivation	Individual or closed group

(continued)

Table 4.1 (continued)

ID	Garden	Address	Interview	Previous use of the area	Starting year	Lend tenure stress	Type of cultivation	Type of plot
7	Freie Universität Berlin (Free University of Berlin)	Bibliothek, Oertzenweg 19B, 14,163	BERG5	Side area of a riding hall	Less than ten years ago	No register	Container-based cultivation	Individual or closed group
8	Peace of Land	Am Weingarten 14, 10,407 Berlin	BERE11	Porcelain Manufactory	2016	2022 (forced move)	Container-based cultivation Ground-based cultivation Forest gardening	Individual or closed group
9	Senate Department	Am Köllnischen Park 3, 10,179	BERE3					
10	Rübezahl	Tempelhofer Feld	No	Airport	2010	No register	Container-based cultivation	No information
11	Stadtteilgarten Schillerkiez	Tempelhofer Feld	No	Airport	2010	No register	Container-based cultivation	No information
12	Stadtacker Berlin	Tempelhofer Feld	No	Airport	2011	No register	Container-based cultivation	No information
13	Klunkergarten	Karl-Marx-Straße 66, 12,043	No	Mall rooftop	2016	No register	Container-based cultivation	No information
14	Himmelbeet	Gartenstraße/ Ecke, Grenzstraße, 13,355	No	Sports area (former address) and public square (new address)	Foundation in 2012. New address in 2022	2022 (forced move)	Ground-based cultivation (former address) Container-based cultivation (former and new address)	Individual or closed group (former and new address) Collective (former address)

(continued)

Table 4.1 (continued)

ID	Garden	Address	Interview	Previous use of the area	Starting year	Lend tenure stress	Type of cultivation	Type of plot
15	Frieda Süd	Friedrichstraße 19, 10,969	No	Flower market	2021	No register	Container-based cultivation	Collective (mostly)
16	Möhrchenpark	Holzmarktstraße 33, 10,243	No	No information	2013	No register	Container-based cultivation	No information
17	Kiez-Garten	Briesestraße S/N, 12,053 Berlin	BERE9 BERE10	Square	2022	No register	Container-based cultivation	No information

Source Jardim (2024)

Table 4.2 Investigated community gardens in Berlin (part 2)

ID	Garden	Land property		Land possession			Fee to do gardening	Number of involved people
				Type of representant	Representant	Fee to use the space		
1	Moritzplatz	State	Public land	Common grounds e.V	Voluntary association	Yes	No fee	Around ten co-organizers
2	Prinzessinnengarten	Private (church)	Evangelische Friedhofsverband Berlin Stadtmitte	Nomadisch Grün gGmbH	Non-profit company	No information	No fee	Around 30 hired people
3	Allmende-Kontor	State	Public land	Allmende Kontor e.V	Voluntary association	Yes	Annual fee for plant bed of 30–60 euros, and membership fee of 12 euros	Around 300 gardeners
4	M.I.N.T. Grünes Klassenzimmer	State	Public land	Familie e.V	Voluntary association	Yes	Annual fee of 50 euros for costs, plus 15 euros for membership	Thirty parents vinculated, including the seven parents co-organizing. Around 60 children from the school
5	Elisabeet	Private (church)	Evangelische Friedhofsverband Berlin Stadtmitte	Himmelbeet gGmbH	Non-profit company	No information	No fee	Around ten co-organizers
6	Bürger*innen-Garten (Citizens Garden)	State	Public land	KUNSTrePUBLIK e.V	Voluntary association	No information	Annual fee of 70 euros	No information

(continued)

Table 4.2 (continued)

ID	Garden	Land property		Land possession			Fee to do gardening	Number of involved people
				Type of representant	Representant	Fee to use the space		
7	Freie Universität Berlin (Free University of Berlin)	State	Public land	Veterinary students and professors	Voluntary association	No	No fee	Around 20 gardeners
8	Peace of Land	State	Not identified	Peace of Land e.V	Voluntary association	No information	Monthly contribution of 5 euros for costs, and annual membership fee of 30 euros	Around 10–15 coorganizers
9	Senate Department							
10	Rübezahl	State	Public land	Gemeinschaftsgarten Rübezahl e.V	Voluntary association	No information	No information	No information
11	Stadtteilgarten Schillerkiez	State	Public land	Verein Teilhabe e.V	Voluntary association	No information	No information	No information
12	Stadtacker Berlin	State	Public land	Albatros gGmbH	Non-profit company	No information	No information	No information
13	Klunkergarten	Private (mall)	Neukölln Arcaden	Horstwirtschaft eV	Voluntary association	No information	No information	No information

(continued)

Table 4.2 (continued)

ID	Garden	Land property		Land possession			Fee to do gardening	Number of involved people
				Type of representant	Representant	Fee to use the space		
14	Himmelbeet	State	Public land (former and new address)	Himmelbeet gGmbH	Non-profit company	Yes	From 50 euros (collective) to 150 euros (individual) to rent a plant bed in the former address	No information
15	Frieda Süd	State	Public land	Bauhütte Kreuzberg e.V	Voluntary association	No information	No information	No information
16	Möhrchenpark	Private (cooperative)	Möhrchenpark e.V	Mörchenpark e.V	Voluntary association	No information	Annual fee of 25 euros for membership	No information
17	Kiez-Garten	State	Degewo Aktiengesellschaft (Degewo)	Degewo Aktiengesellschaft	State house company	No	No fee	No information

Source Jardim (2024)

Table 4.3 Interviews and questionnaires participants in Berlin (2021–2022)

Category	Stakeholder	Connection to community garden	Quantity	
Gardener	Civil society	Non-professional, non-researchers, and non-public agents	9	
Expert	Civil society	Professional	6	11
		Researcher	4	
	Public sector	Public Agent	1	
Total				20

Source Jardim (2024)

practices and knowledge. For the future, they mostly had positive expectations of the community gardening activity growth but also desired more governmental support and changes in the society's mentalities and practices.

Most of the interviewees did gardening activities (watering, planting, harvesting, caring for graves, offering information, selling products, cleaning the material from the last season and not want green, preparing compost, filling the water tanks, pruning, maintaining plant beds, painting), and social activities (talking to neighbors, talking to gardeners, meeting friends, making new friends, neighborhood, enjoy the community, community care, meet new people). The administrative activities (moderating events, organizing events, coordinating volunteers, supporting other gardens, checking contracts and finances) were shared between *gardeners* and *experts*.

When observing the internal distribution of *gardeners* and *experts* in *Berlin*, it was possible to note that they shared **similarities** in terms of age, gender and nationality distribution, absence of religious or political affiliations, food diet mostly without meat, proximity from home to the garden, mobility options to reach the garden, and mentions of food production about ancestral practices and knowledge. Moreover, the *gardeners* and *experts* were doing gardening, administrative and social activities. However, one notable **difference** is that, among the *gardeners*, there were "gender-diverse" interviewees, but the same could not be seen among the *experts*. In addition, *experts* had a monthly household income of around 1,057 Euros (approximately 1.176 United States Dollars), while *gardeners* had a revenue of about 742 Euros (about 826 United States Dollars). The gap between them was 315 Euros (approximately 350 United States Dollars). Also, more *gardeners* missed green areas in their apartments. The core team (co-leaders, co-organizers) had more *experts* than *gardeners*, and only a few interviewees rented a plant bed.

4.2 The Case of Rio de Janeiro

4.2.1 Overview of Socioeconomic and Urbanistic Relevant Data

Regarding 2022, **socioeconomic data** indicates that in Brazil, the **extreme poverty** (under 208,73 Reais per monthly income, around 38 United States Dollars) rate was 6,4%, while the **poverty** rate was 33% (under 665,02 Reais per monthly income, around 122 United States Dollars).[30] The city economy is growing.[31] However, in 2021, Rio de Janeiro State had around 1.2 million people in **extreme poverty** and 2.8 million people in **poverty**.[32] In 2023, the **unemployment** rate in Brazil was 8%,[33] and in the city of *Rio de Janeiro,* it was 9.3%.[34]

Food insecurity in Brazil is moderate. More precisely, food affordability, availability, sustainability, and adaptation are moderate, while food quality and safety have very good levels (Fig. 4.8).[35] However, the **COVID-19 pandemic** raised the food insecurity levels (Fig. 4.9).[36]

The **COVID-19** incidence in the city of *Rio de Janeiro* was higher in low-development neighborhoods.[37] There are **food deserts** in *Rio de Janeiro* city. In low-income areas, health food establishments sell fresh and mixed foods. The same is true for unhealthy food establishments selling ultra-processed foods. However, even richer areas can face problems of lack of access to healthy food establishments.[38] The access to street fairs of organic food is restricted (Fig. 4.10).

The city of *Rio de Janeiro* has a low **city development** index (Fig. 4.11), and within it, there are many development disparities (Fig. 4.12), especially considering that "the territorial and socioeconomic structure of the city presents characteristics very specific, with the existence of poorer regions within more developed areas of the city."[39]

The Census 2010 informed that 19,28% of 2,352,594 houses were part of **Favelas and Urban Communities** (low-income areas) (Fig. 4.13).[40]

The city **population** is around 6.7 million people. 1,4 million residents in Favelas and Urban Communities, and around 65% of them were registered as **Black and**

[30] IJSN (2023).

[31] Rio de Janeiro (2013).

[32] IBGE (2022a, b).

[33] IBGE.

[34] Rio de Janeiro (2023).

[35] The Economist (2022).

[36] Vigisan (2021).

[37] Miranda (2010).

[38] Brasil. pp. 20–25.

[39] Miranda, op. cit., p. 14.

[40] ArcGIS Web Application.

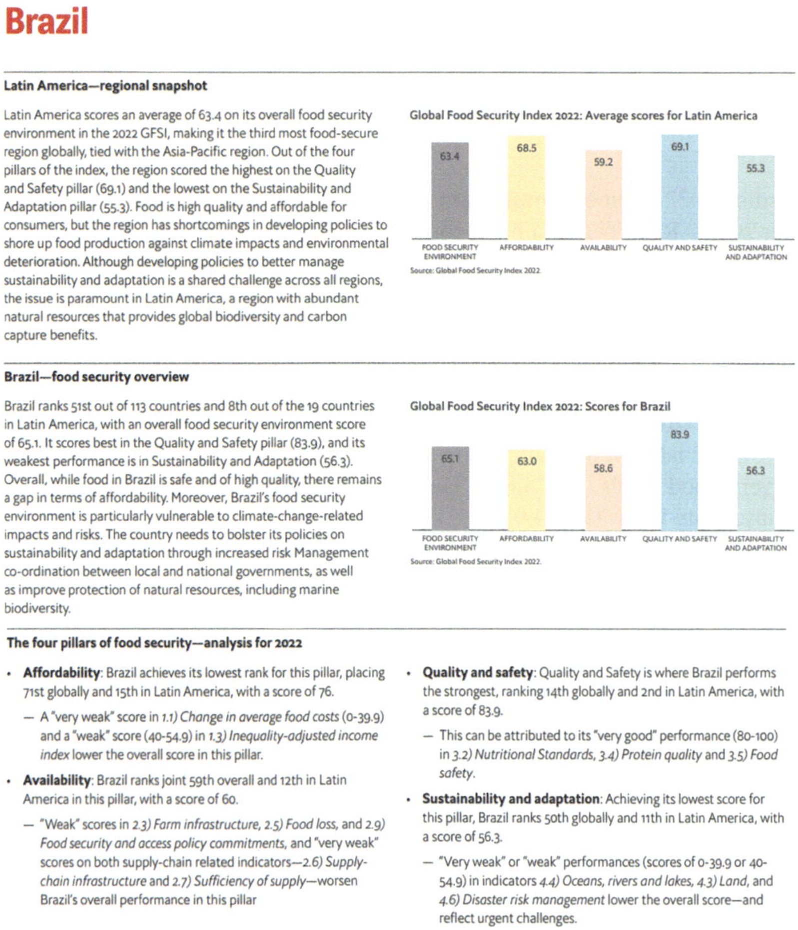

Brazil

Latin America—regional snapshot

Latin America scores an average of 63.4 on its overall food security environment in the 2022 GFSI, making it the third most food-secure region globally, tied with the Asia-Pacific region. Out of the four pillars of the index, the region scored the highest on the Quality and Safety pillar (69.1) and the lowest on the Sustainability and Adaptation pillar (55.3). Food is high quality and affordable for consumers, but the region has shortcomings in developing policies to shore up food production against climate impacts and environmental deterioration. Although developing policies to better manage sustainability and adaptation is a shared challenge across all regions, the issue is paramount in Latin America, a region with abundant natural resources that provides global biodiversity and carbon capture benefits.

Global Food Security Index 2022: Average scores for Latin America

Brazil—food security overview

Brazil ranks 51st out of 113 countries and 8th out of the 19 countries in Latin America, with an overall food security environment score of 65.1. It scores best in the Quality and Safety pillar (83.9), and its weakest performance is in Sustainability and Adaptation (56.3). Overall, while food in Brazil is safe and of high quality, there remains a gap in terms of affordability. Moreover, Brazil's food security environment is particularly vulnerable to climate-change-related impacts and risks. The country needs to bolster its policies on sustainability and adaptation through increased risk Management co-ordination between local and national governments, as well as improve protection of natural resources, including marine biodiversity.

Global Food Security Index 2022: Scores for Brazil

The four pillars of food security—analysis for 2022

- **Affordability**: Brazil achieves its lowest rank for this pillar, placing 71st globally and 15th in Latin America, with a score of 76.
  - A "very weak" score in *1.1) Change in average food costs* (0-39.9) and a "weak" score (40-54.9) in *1.3) Inequality-adjusted income index* lower the overall score in this pillar.
- **Availability**: Brazil ranks joint 59th overall and 12th in Latin America in this pillar, with a score of 60.
  - "Weak" scores in *2.3) Farm infrastructure, 2.5) Food loss*, and *2.9) Food security and access policy commitments*, and "very weak" scores on both supply-chain related indicators—*2.6) Supply-chain infrastructure* and *2.7) Sufficiency of supply*—worsen Brazil's overall performance in this pillar
- **Quality and safety**: Quality and Safety is where Brazil performs the strongest, ranking 14th globally and 2nd in Latin America, with a score of 83.9.
  - This can be attributed to its "very good" performance (80-100) in *3.2) Nutritional Standards, 3.4) Protein quality* and *3.5) Food safety*.
- **Sustainability and adaptation**: Achieving its lowest score for this pillar, Brazil ranks 50th globally and 11th in Latin America, with a score of 56.3.
  - "Very weak" or "weak" performances (scores of 0-39.9 or 40-54.9) in indicators *4.4) Oceans, rivers and lakes, 4.3) Land*, and *4.6) Disaster risk management* lower the overall score—and reflect urgent challenges.

Fig. 4.8 Global Food Security Index 2022: Brazil (parts 1 and 2). *Source* The Economist (2022)

Brown people.[41] The city has violence (Fig. 4.14) and illegal housing constructions (Fig. 4.15).

Concerning **vacancy** of housing units, there is a rising level in the city of *Rio de Janeiro*.[42] From 2010 (193,682 vacant properties) to 2022 (388,345 from a total of 2,920,302), the rate grew by 100,5%. "Experts point to reasons such as high prices, pandemic, migration due to violence and growth in the number of housing units."[43] There are strong correlations between abandoned establishments and protected properties (historical and cultural value) and socioeconomic factors, such as income, rental

[41] IBGE (2010).

[42] IBGE.

[43] Grinberg et al. (2023).

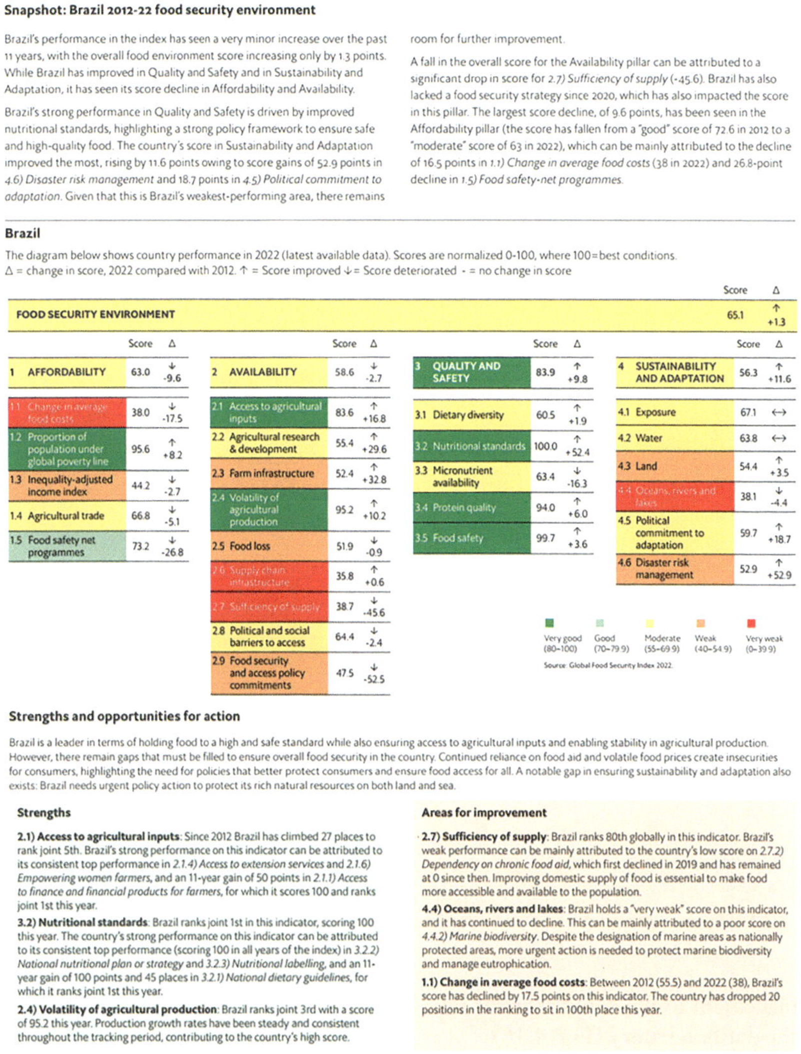

Snapshot: Brazil 2012-22 food security environment

Brazil's performance in the index has seen a very minor increase over the past 11 years, with the overall food environment score increasing only by 1.3 points. While Brazil has improved in Quality and Safety and in Sustainability and Adaptation, it has seen its score decline in Affordability and Availability.

Brazil's strong performance in Quality and Safety is driven by improved nutritional standards, highlighting a strong policy framework to ensure safe and high-quality food. The country's score in Sustainability and Adaptation improved the most, rising by 11.6 points owing to score gains of 52.9 points in *4.6) Disaster risk management* and 18.7 points in *4.5) Political commitment to adaptation*. Given that this is Brazil's weakest-performing area, there remains room for further improvement.

A fall in the overall score for the Availability pillar can be attributed to a significant drop in score for *2.7) Sufficiency of supply* (-45.6). Brazil has also lacked a food security strategy since 2020, which has also impacted the score in this pillar. The largest score decline, of 9.6 points, has been seen in the Affordability pillar (the score has fallen from a "good" score of 72.6 in 2012 to a "moderate" score of 63 in 2022), which can be mainly attributed to the decline of 16.5 points in *1.1) Change in average food costs* (38 in 2022) and 26.8-point decline in *1.5) Food safety-net programmes*.

Brazil

The diagram below shows country performance in 2022 (latest available data). Scores are normalized 0-100, where 100=best conditions.
Δ = change in score, 2022 compared with 2012. ↑ = Score improved ↓= Score deteriorated - = no change in score

	Score	Δ
FOOD SECURITY ENVIRONMENT	65.1	↑ +1.3

	Score	Δ
1 AFFORDABILITY	63.0	↓ -9.6
1.1 Change in average food costs	38.0	↓ -17.5
1.2 Proportion of population under global poverty line	95.6	↑ +8.2
1.3 Inequality-adjusted income index	44.2	↓ -2.7
1.4 Agricultural trade	66.8	↓ -5.1
1.5 Food safety net programmes	73.2	↓ -26.8

	Score	Δ
2 AVAILABILITY	58.6	↓ -2.7
2.1 Access to agricultural inputs	83.6	↑ +16.8
2.2 Agricultural research & development	55.4	↑ +29.6
2.3 Farm infrastructure	52.4	↑ +32.8
2.4 Volatility of agricultural production	95.2	↑ +10.2
2.5 Food loss	51.9	↓ -0.9
2.6 Supply chain infrastructure	35.8	↑ +0.6
2.7 Sufficiency of supply	38.7	↓ -45.6
2.8 Political and social barriers to access	64.4	↓ -2.4
2.9 Food security and access policy commitments	47.5	↓ -52.5

	Score	Δ
3 QUALITY AND SAFETY	83.9	↑ +9.8
3.1 Dietary diversity	60.5	↑ +1.9
3.2 Nutritional standards	100.0	↑ +52.4
3.3 Micronutrient availability	63.4	↓ -16.3
3.4 Protein quality	94.0	↑ +6.0
3.5 Food safety	99.7	↑ +3.6

	Score	Δ
4 SUSTAINABILITY AND ADAPTATION	56.3	↑ +11.6
4.1 Exposure	67.1	↔
4.2 Water	63.8	↔
4.3 Land	54.4	↑ +3.5
4.4 Oceans, rivers and lakes	38.1	↓ -4.4
4.5 Political commitment to adaptation	59.7	↑ +18.7
4.6 Disaster risk management	52.9	↑ +52.9

Very good (80–100) Good (70–79.9) Moderate (55–69.9) Weak (40–54.9) Very weak (0–39.9)

Source: Global Food Security Index 2022.

Strengths and opportunities for action

Brazil is a leader in terms of holding food to a high and safe standard while also ensuring access to agricultural inputs and enabling stability in agricultural production. However, there remain gaps that must be filled to ensure overall food security in the country. Continued reliance on food aid and volatile food prices create insecurities for consumers, highlighting the need for policies that better protect consumers and ensure food access for all. A notable gap in ensuring sustainability and adaptation also exists: Brazil needs urgent policy action to protect its rich natural resources on both land and sea.

Strengths

2.1) Access to agricultural inputs: Since 2012 Brazil has climbed 27 places to rank joint 5th. Brazil's strong performance on this indicator can be attributed to its consistent top performance in *2.1.4) Access to extension services* and *2.1.6) Empowering women farmers*, and an 11-year gain of 50 points in *2.1.1) Access to finance and financial products for farmers*, for which it scores 100 and ranks joint 1st this year.

3.2) Nutritional standards: Brazil ranks joint 1st in this indicator, scoring 100 this year. The country's strong performance on this indicator can be attributed to its consistent top performance (scoring 100 in all years of the index) in *3.2.2) National nutritional plan or strategy* and *3.2.3) Nutritional labelling*, and an 11-year gain of 100 points and 45 places in *3.2.1) National dietary guidelines*, for which it ranks joint 1st this year.

2.4) Volatility of agricultural production: Brazil ranks joint 3rd with a score of 95.2 this year. Production growth rates have been steady and consistent throughout the tracking period, contributing to the country's high score.

Areas for improvement

2.7) Sufficiency of supply: Brazil ranks 80th globally in this indicator. Brazil's weak performance can be mainly attributed to the country's low score on *2.7.2) Dependency on chronic food aid*, which first declined in 2019 and has remained at 0 since then. Improving domestic supply of food is essential to make food more accessible and available to the population.

4.4) Oceans, rivers and lakes: Brazil holds a "very weak" score on this indicator, and it has continued to decline. This can be mainly attributed to a poor score on *4.4.2) Marine biodiversity*. Despite the designation of marine areas as nationally protected areas, more urgent action is needed to protect marine biodiversity and manage eutrophication.

1.1) Change in average food costs: Between 2012 (55.5) and 2022 (38), Brazil's score has declined by 17.5 points on this indicator. The country has dropped 20 positions in the ranking to sit in 100th place this year.

Fig. 4.8 (continued)

value, and distance to the center.[44] For instance, in the city center, the city hall identified 60 vacant properties, prioritizing 40 of them for future actions.[45] In summary, the phenomenon represents the "reminiscences of large urban interventions, restrictive legislation regarding uses or works on land, overlapping of powers and interests and

[44] Monteiro (2020).

[45] Rio de Janeiro.

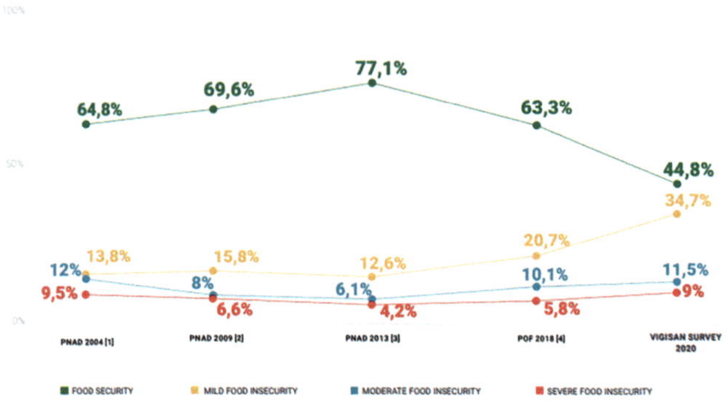

Fig. 4.9 Food insecurity in Brazil. *Source* Rede Penssan (2021, p. 9)

Fig. 4.10 Organic street fairs in Rio de Janeiro. *Source* IDEC

displacement to the south zone of investments."[46] The city has vacant land spread on the entire territory (Fig. 4.16).

Agriculture happens in the **outskirts** of the city, focusing on the western zone[47] (Fig. 4.17), and **urban agriculture** has as important expressions the traditional and family farming.

In addition, there are **community gardens.** The city hall program (Hortas Cariocas, Environmental Secretariat) has 56 gardens in low-income neighborhoods and schools (Fig. 4.18).

Moreover, the city has around 45 other initiatives mapped by the civil society (Fig. 4.19).

---

[46] Neves (2019), Neves, op. cit., p. 14.

[47] Lima et al. (2019).

Fig. 4.11 City development index Rio de Janeiro 2020. *Source* City Development Index (2020)

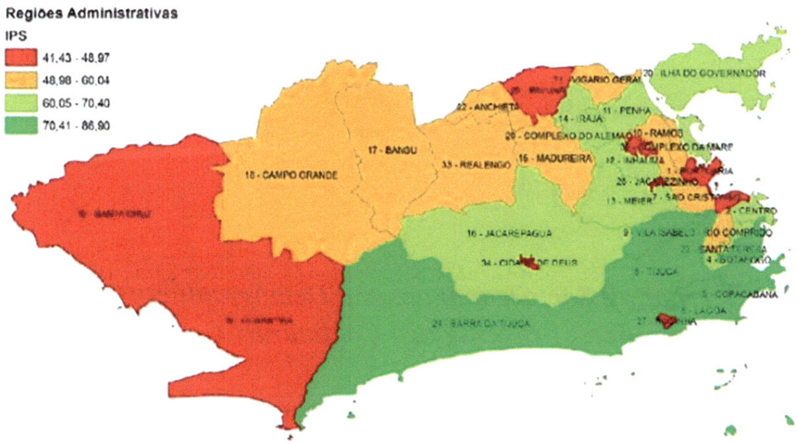

Fig. 4.12 Social Progress Index (IPS) of Rio de Janeiro. *Source* Rio de Janeiro (2019)

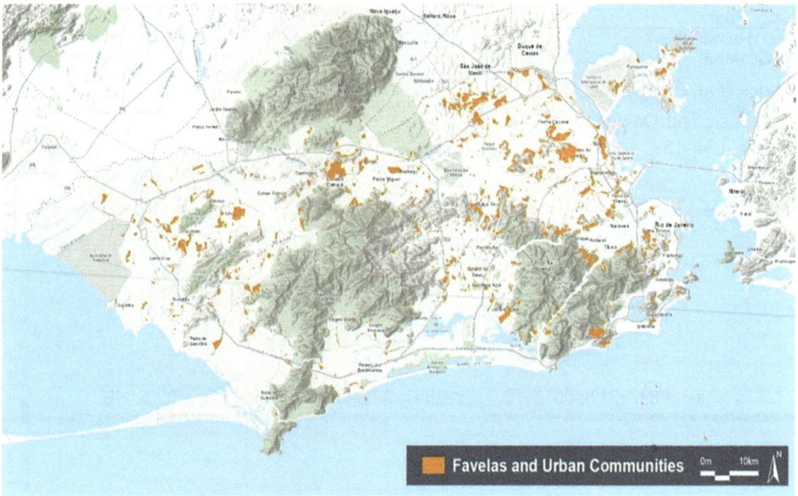

Fig. 4.13 Favelas and Urban Communities in Rio de Janeiro. *Source* Jardim (2024)

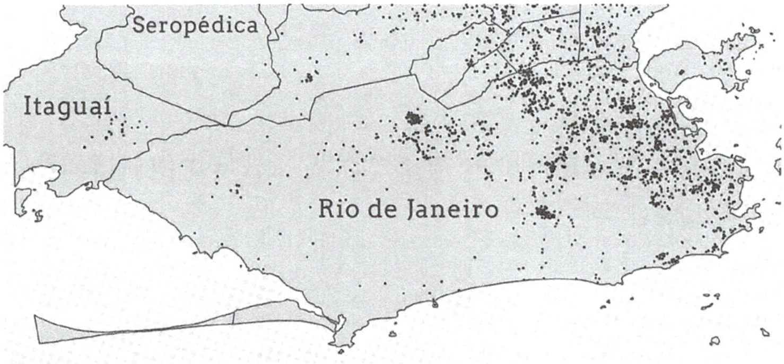

Fig. 4.14 Registered shootings 2019 in Rio de Janeiro. *Source* Casa Fluminense (2020, p. 27); Fogo Cruzado (2019)

4.2.2 Territorial, Socioeconomic, and Demographic Information of Investigated Community Gardens

There were 12 community gardens investigated in *Rio de Janeiro*: Horta Carioca Morro do São Carlos, Horta Carioca Morro da Formiga, Horta Carioca Morro do Borel, Horta Carioca Nação Rubro Negra, Horta Carioca Comunidade Palmeirinha (Madureira's Park), Horta Carioca Jardim Sulacap, Horta Carioca Dirce Teixeira (Jardim do Anil), Horta Carioca Escola Joaquim Fontes (Cidade de Deus), Horta Carioca do Morro do Salgueiro, Federal University of Rio de Janeiro, Quilombo Dona Bilina, Quilombo das Caboclas. In addition, there was an interview with a

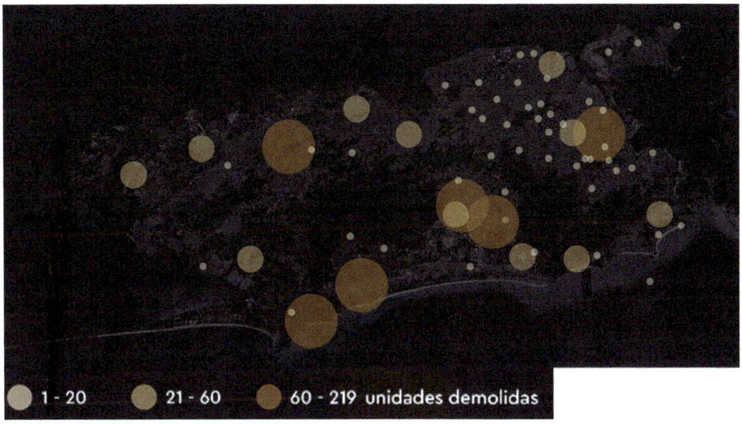

Fig. 4.15 Illegal constructions demolished by Rio de Janeiro city hall 2021–2023. The different circles represent three scales of demolished unities. *Source* Rio de Janeiro (2021–2023)

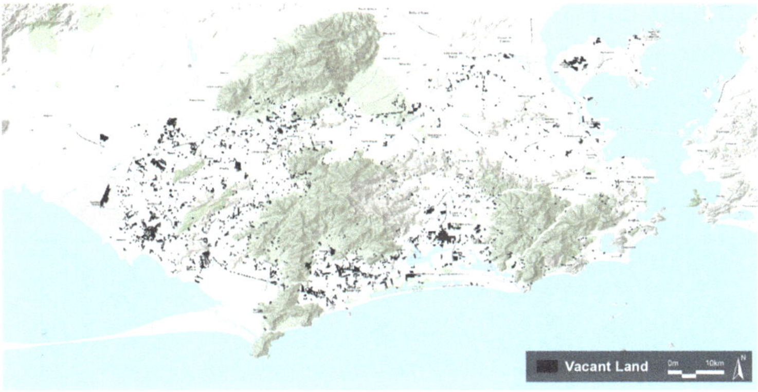

Fig. 4.16 Vacant land in Rio de Janeiro. *Source* Rio de Janeiro (2019)

representative from the city hall and from Advice and Services for Alternative Agriculture Projects (Assessoria e Serviços a Projetos em Agricultura Alternativa, AS-TPA). The total representation on the city level can be observed in the following Fig. 4.20.

In general, before **2006**, these territories were **vacant land** with different former usages (dumping ground in a demolished prison area, wasteland in a public space, a place in a public school and university, a green area threatened by illegal housing construction or under energy transmission line, abandoned private house, a private popular museum). The state mostly owned the land they occupied, but the civil society almost completely handled the possession. There was no fee to do the gardening activity or access the land (security deposit) (Tables 4.4, 4.5).

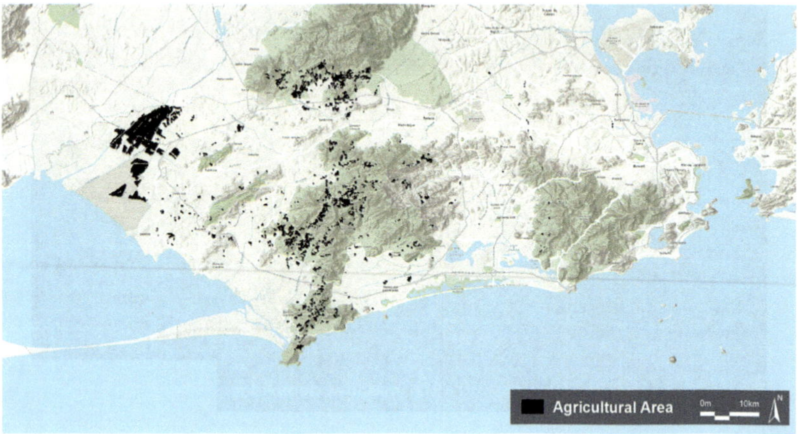

Fig. 4.17 Agricultural area in Rio de Janeiro. *Source* Rio de Janeiro (2019)

Fig. 4.18 Hortas Cariocas and other public food initiatives in Rio de Janeiro. Blue: Community kitchens. Green: Community gardens (Hortas Cariocas program). Red: Popular restaurants. *Source* Rio de Janeiro

Since the foundation, less than half of the gardens have suffered from a stress situation. This can be exemplified when a garden was voluntarily and permanently closed, a garden was voluntarily closed and recreated in another place, a garden was threatened to be closed by criminal agents (militia/drug dealers), and a garden lost part of the territory for illegal agents. Additionally, more than half of the gardens

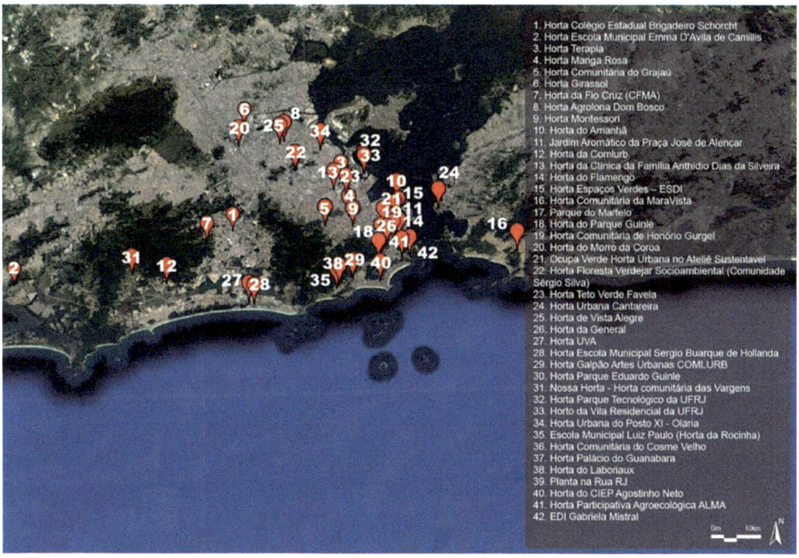

Fig. 4.19 Community gardens collaborative mapping in Rio de Janeiro. *Source* Rio de Janeiro (2019) [Adapted version in collaboration with Jéssica Lucena. Basis Land use Map. Illustrator Software. *Source* https://www.data.rio/datasets/PCRJ::uso-do-solo-2019/about]

had a stress situation related to all gardens, such as unsure maintenance of public funding in Hortas Cariocas.

The participants cited 66 different garden products. All these products mostly came from ground-based cultivation directly on (regenerated) soil. All plots were collectively cultivated. There was no case of a rented plant bed. The number of people in the core team varied between 1–5, while the regular gardeners varied between 1–10. Just a few pieces of information were available online about these gardens.

There were 20 participants *(commoners)* in interviews and questionnaires: 11 *gardeners* and nine *experts*. This is organised in Table 4.6.

The median age of participants was approximately 52 years old. Among them, there was a slight gender imbalance. There were a few more participants who self-registered as men. No interviewee registered as gender-diverse. Mostly had high- or medium-level (finished high school) education. According to the ethnic-racial self-identification, there was a balance (the same amount) of answers to "Black or Brown" and "White." However, there was an underrepresentation of "Indigenous." The few cases of political affiliations were linked to left-wing parties. Regarding nationality, the group was almost entirely composed of Brazilians born and raised in Rio de Janeiro. Most were living in houses, while a few lived in apartments. A small number of interviewees were living in slums. Almost all participants reported having green areas at home. Regarding their food diet, half of the participants ate meat regularly (omnivorous or pescatarian), a few did not eat it (vegan or vegetarian) and avoided it (flexitarian). From the whole group, more than half of the participants received income related to community gardens through the Hortas Cariocas program or by offering technical assistance to urban agriculture. The core team (co-leaders, co-organizers) had more gardeners than experts. No gardener or expert from the core team had certified education or professional skills directly related to agriculture or gardening. There were no plant bed tenants nor fee payments for land access.

Their medium community gardening experience time was approximately eight years. A significant part of co-founded gardens. For most gardeners, the garden where they work was the first contact with community gardening. The experts mostly did not work with a specific community garden. They all ate products from the garden, but their diet did not depend exclusively on the garden. The whole group often bought food in supermarkets but preferred buying from street fairs. Most interviewees mentioned exchanging products, seeds, cutting, and knowledge with gardeners and experts from the same garden. All interviewees reported that the outcomes of the garden were gifted, mostly for poor neighbors, visitors, and schools (students, teachers, workers, and parents of students). A few interviewees expressed that their garden sold part of the products, but by symbolic prices such as 2 Reais (in United States dollars, 37 cents) for any product to reinvest in the project (seeds, materials) and increase the financial support from Hortas Cariocas. Many interviewees (14/20) complained about the lack of biodiversity or physical and economic access (food

Fig. 4.20 Investigated community gardens in Rio de Janeiro. *Source* Jardim (2024)[48]

[48] Collaboration with Jéssica Lucena. Google Earth Data Basis. Illustrator Software.

Table 4.4 Investigated community gardens in Rio de Janeiro (part 1)

ID	Garden	Address	Interview	Previous use of the area	Starting year	Lend tenure stress	Type of cultivation	Type of plot
1	Horta Carioca Morro do São Carlos	Laurindo Rabêlo, 57, Estácio - Rio de Janeiro, 20,250–150	RIOG8	Dumping ground in a demolished prison area side to social housing area (Minha Casa Minha Vida)	2010	Generic	Ground-based cultivation	Collective
2	Horta Carioca Morro da Formiga	Paulino Nogueira S/N, Tijuca, 20,530–100	RIOG1	Green area under energy transmission line	2006	Generic	Ground-based cultivation	Collective
3	Horta Carioca Morro do Borel	Not identified	RIOG3	Wasteland in public area	2012	Criminality	Ground-based cultivation	Collective
4	Horta Carioca Nação Rubro Negra	Praça Nossa Sra. Auxiliadora, S/N - Leblon, 22,441–050	RIOG7	Vacant area in a public school	2017	No register	Ground-based cultivation	Collective
5	Horta Carioca Comunidade Palmirinha (Madureira's Park)	Américo Rocha, 1602 - Mal. Hermes, 21,555–300	RIOE10	Vacant land in public area. The park was a former wasteland	2012	No register	Ground-based cultivation	Collective
6	Horta Carioca Jardim Sulacap	Avenida Carlos Pontes S/N - Jardim Sulacap, 21,741–340	RIOG5	Wasteland in public area	2016	Generic	Ground-based cultivation	Collective
7	Horta Carioca Dirce Teixeira (Jardim do Anil)	Estrada Curipos, 746 - Jacarepaguá, 22,753–330	RIOG4	Green area threatened by illegal housing construction	2006	Generic	Ground-based cultivation Aquaponics	Collective
8	Horta Carioca Escola Joaquim Fontes (Cidade de Deus)	João Mafra, 85 - Cidade de Deus, 22,775–690	RIOG2	Vacant area in a public school	2022	Generic	Ground-based cultivation	Collective

(continued)

Table 4.4 (continued)

ID	Garden	Address	Interview	Previous use of the area	Starting year	Lend tenure stress	Type of cultivation	Type of plot
9	Horta Carioca do Morro do Salgueiro	Morro do Salgueiro S/N, Tijuca, 20,510–050	RIOG6	Vacant land of abandoned private house	2019	Generic	Ground-based cultivation	Collective
10	Federal University of Rio de Janeiro (UFRJ)	Avenida Carlos Chagas Filho, 20 - Cidade Universitária da UFRJ, 21,941–599	RIOE3	Vacant land in public university area	2018	No register	Ground-based cultivation	Collective
11	Quilombo Dona Bilina	Campo Grande 23,017–390	RIOG10	Vacant area in a private popular museum	2020	No register	Ground-based cultivation	Collective
12	Quilombo das Caboclas	Estrada dos Caboclos	RIOE6	Vacant land in public area	2014	Two times, fire (racism, gender, and micro-political motivation)	Ground-based cultivation	Collective
13	Children's garden	Praça Saenz Peña, S/N - Tijuca, 20,520–090	RIOG9	Vacant land in public area	2014–2015	Closed	Ground-based cultivation	Collective

Source Jardim (2024)
Note Many experts were not linked to one specific garden. They were connected to multiple gardens because their personal will or professional activities (RIOE1, RIOE3, and RIOE7), their agenda as public agent (RIOE2, and RIOE8), researcher (RIOE4, and RIOE5), and technical support (RIOE9)

Table 4.5 Investigated community gardens in Rio de Janeiro (part 2)

ID	Garden	Land property		Land possession			Fee to do gardening	Funding	Number of involved people
				Type of representanT	Representant	Fee to use the space			
1	Horta Carioca Morro do São Carlos	State	City government	Neighbourhood association	Voluntary association	No	No	City hall	Around ten co-organizers
2	Horta Carioca Morro da Formiga	State	City government	Neighbourhood association	Voluntary association	No	No	City hall	Around three co-organizers
3	Horta Carioca Morro do Borel	State	City government	Neighbourhood association	Voluntary association	No	No	City hall	Usually one organizer
4	Horta Carioca Nação Rubro Negra	State	City government	Public school	Voluntary association	No	No	City hall	Usually two co-organizers
5	Horta Carioca Comunidade Palmeirinha (Madureira's Park)	State	City government	Neighbourhood association	Voluntary association	No	No	City hall	Not identified
6	Horta Carioca Jardim Sulacap	State	City government	Neighbourhood association	Voluntary association	No	No	City hall	Not identified
7	Horta Carioca Dirce Teixeira	State	City government	Neighbourhood association	Voluntary association	No	No	City hall	Not identified
8	Horta Carioca Escola Joaquim Fontes	State	City government	Public school	Voluntary association	No	No	City hall	Not identified

(continued)

Table 4.5 (continued)

ID	Garden	Land property		Land possession			Fee to do gardening	Funding	Number of involved people
				Type of representanT	Representant	Fee to use the space			
9	Horta Carioca do Morro do Salgueiro	State	City government	Neighbourhood association	Voluntary association	No	No	City hall	Not identified
10	Federal University of Rio de Janeiro	State	Federal government	University project registered by a professor of undergraduation on Nourishment	Voluntary association	No	No	Professors Association	Not identified
11	Quilombo Dona Bilina	Private land	Museum and house	Eco museum Quilombo Dona Bilina	Non-profit company	No	No	Self-funding	Around ten people on the core team
12	Quilombo das Caboclas	Private land	Not identified	Neighbourhood association	Voluntary association	No	No	Self-funding	Around five people on the core team
13	Children's garden	State	City government	Vivenciando Montessori Planta na Rua RJ	Voluntary association	No	No	Self-funding	Around one people on the core team

Source Jardim (2024)

Table 4.6 Interviews and questionnaires participants in Rio de Janeiro (2022–2023)

Category	Stakeholder	Connection to community garden	Quantity	
Gardener	Civil society	Non-professional, non-researchers, and non-public agents	11	
Expert	Civil society	Professional	3	9
		Researcher	3	
	Public sector	Public Agent	3	
Total				20

Source Jardim (2024)

segregation) to organic food in supermarkets or street fairs for themselves or other people.

The participants lived around 1 km from the garden. Their most used mobility option to go to the garden was by feet. There were just a few answers to other possibilities (public transport, by bike, and by car). The monthly hours spent in the garden did not fluctuate between seasons. More than half of the participants mentioned the relation of food production to ancestors' practices and knowledge, especially ancestors that migrated from other areas of Brazil (States of Minas Gerais, Rio Grande do Sul, Ceará, Paraíba) or during early childhood in other countries, Germany and Portugal.

Most of the *gardeners* did gardening activities (watering, planting, harvesting, care of graves, offering information, selling products, cleaning the material from the last season and not wanted green, preparing compost, filling water tanks, pruning, beds maintenance, painting), and social activities (talking to neighbors, talking to gardeners, meeting friends, making new friends, enjoying the community, community caring, meeting new people), while the *experts* were focusing on social, and administrative activities. This included coordinating gardeners, mediating conflicts among gardeners, requesting material for the city hall (Hortas Cariocas), soliciting donations, and crowdfunding (other gardens not from Hortas Cariocas).

Between *Rio de Janeiro*'s *gardeners* and *experts*, there were **similarities** in age, distribution of gender and nationality, no political affiliation, food diet with meat, distance from home to garden, mobility options to go to the garden, and number of mentions of the food production's relation to practices and knowledge of ancestors, and destination of products (self-consume, and donation). Furthermore, *gardeners* and *experts* did social activities. However, the **difference** was that *experts* (medium of approximately 46 years old) were younger than *gardeners* (medium of roughly 58 years old); *expert* was a group composed of people with high levels of education, while *gardeners* had more people with medium education. Additionally, there were more *experts* without religion than *gardeners*. About ethnic-racial profiles, *experts* were mostly composed of people who self-declared "White." At the same time, *gardeners* were mostly reported to be "Black and Brown" people; it was the only group with an Indigenous representative. In addition, *experts* had a monthly household income of around 10,760 Reais (approximately 1,967 United States Dollars), while *gardeners* had a gain of roughly 3,250 Reais (about 594 United States Dollars). The gap between them was 7,510 Reais (approximately 1,373 United States Dollars), so the *gardeners* earned almost four times less than the *experts*. Almost exclusively, the *gardeners* reported complementing their monthly income (from retirement pension or another job) with the garden income. Finally, *gardeners* were focused on gardening, while *experts* centered on administrative activities.

4.3 Brief Discussion of (Side) Results

The results match the literature review regarding the occupation of urban vacant land (unused, underutilized, and unbuilt soil) by community gardens without specific spatial configuration (size and design), highlighting social, economic and environmentally vulnerable areas in *Rio de Janeiro*.[49] Moreover, the results also identified people related to community garden has socioeconomic status that varies greatly from local to local, even within the same country,[50] despite the differences being less expressive in *Berlin*.

In addition, the results indicated the same possibilities for motivation as those already identified by previous studies,[51] the ones benefiting socialization and environmental purposes in *Berlin*, while in *Rio de Janeiro* there is a special contribution to food security and ecological regeneration/preservation. Despite that, in *both cities* the data reveals the **connection human-nature, the sense of belonging to a group, and the altruistic motivations** related to urban commons.

An important contribution to previous research is that more than gardening and social activities,[52] administrative activities are also crucial elements of community gardens. The unexpected result was regarding community gardens in cemeteries in *Berlin* (Prinzessinnengarten and Elisabeet).

Given the above information, this research offers valuable **insights** to support more research and public policies based on the diverse universe of community gardens in *Berlin* and *Rio de Janeiro*, focusing on socioeconomic, demographic, and legal dynamics, practices, and the profiles of participants.

---

[49] Foster (2011, p. 94).

[50] Wong et al. (2018, pp. 604–610), Das and Ramaswami (2022), Mceldowney (2017), Audate et al. (2021).

[51] Steuri and Vignola (2022, p. 55).

[52] Guttmann (2022, p. 122).

References

ArcGIS Web Application. https://dadosgeociencias.ibge.gov.br/portal/apps/webappviewer/index.html?id=67c70e701c624c63a6f1754a8b8bce4a/. Accessed 09 Oct 2024

Audate P et al (2021) The motivations of urban agriculture practitioners in deprived neighborhoods: a comparative study of Montreal and Quito. Urban Forestry & Urban Greening, vol 62. https://www.sciencedirect.com/science/article/abs/pii/S1618866721001965?via%3Dihub. Accessed 04 Oct 2024

Berlin (2000) Government. Land use. https://www.berlin.de/umweltatlas/en/land-use/actual-land-use/2000/map-description/. Accessed 09 Oct 2024

Berlin (2020a) Environmental atlas. Actual use of built-up areas: inventory of green and open spaces. https://www.berlin.de/umweltatlas/en/land-use/actual-land-use/2020/map-description/. Accessed 09 Oct 2024

Berlin (2020b) Government. Land use. https://www.berlin.de/umweltatlas/nutzung/flaechennutzung/2020/kartenbeschreibung/. Accessed 09 Oct 2024

Berlin (2021) Government. Senatsverwaltung für Stadtentwicklung, Bauen und Wohnen. Bericht Monitoring Soziale Stadtentwicklung Berlin. https://www.berlin.de/sen/sbw/stadtdaten/stadtwissen/monitoring-soziale-stadtentwicklung/bericht-2021/. Accessed 09 Oct 2024

Berlin (2023) Government. Senatsverwaltung für Wirtschaft, Energie und Betriebe. Abteilung Wirtschaft. Wirtschaftsleistung. https://www.berlin.de/sen/wirtschaft/konjunktur-und-statistik/wirtschaftsdaten/wirtschaftsleistung/. Accessed 09 Oct 2024

Berlin (2024) Government. Landesamtfür Gesundheit und Soziales. COVID-19 in Berlin, Verteilung in den Bezirken. https://www.berlin.de/lageso/gesundheit/infektionskrankheiten/corona/tabelle-bezirke/. Accessed 09 Oct 2024

Berlin. Government. Unemployment rate in Berlin falls to 8.7 percent. https://www.berlin.de/en/news/7478082-5559700-umeployment-rate-falls-8-percent.en.html/. Accessed 09 Oct 2024

Berlin. Government. Berliner Gemeinschaftsgärten. Plattform Produktives Stadtgrün. Was sind Gemeinschaftsgärten? https://www.berlin.de/gemeinschaftsgaertnern/gemeinschaftsgaerten/was-sind-gemeinschaftsgaerten/artikel.879236.php/. Accessed 09 Oct 2024

Brasil (2019) Estudo Técnico Mapeamento Desertos Alimentares. Caisan, Alimentos, pp 20–25. https://www.scribd.com/document/606102207/Estudo-tecnico-mapeamento-desertos-alimentares/. Accessed 09 Oct 2024

Butterwegge C (2023) Poverty and Homelessness in Germany after the COVID-19 Pandemic. Europe Now. https://www.europenowjournal.org/2023/07/07/poverty-and-homelessness-in-germany-after-the-covid-19-pandemic/. Accessed 09 Oct 2024

Casa Fluminense (2020) Mapa da desigualdade 2020 Região Metropolitana do Rio de Janeiro, p 27

City Development Index (2020) Rio de Janeiro. https://cdindex.net/world/map/Rio%20de%20Janeiro. Accessed 09 Oct 2024

Council Of Europe (2010) Berlin Neukölln, Germany—Intercultural City—Intercultural cities programme. https://www.coe.int/en/web/interculturalcities/berlin-neukolln/. Accessed 09 Oct 2024

Das K, Ramaswami A (2022) Who gardens and how in urban USA: informing social equity in urban agriculture action plans. Frontiers in Sustainable Food Systems, vol 6. https://www.frontiersin.org/articles/ https://doi.org/10.3389/fsufs.2022.923079/full. Accessed 09 Oct 2024

Depa J, Gyngell F, Müller A, Eleraky L, Hilzendegen C, Stroebele-Benschop N (2018) Prevalence of food insecurity among food bank users in Germany and its association with population characteristics. Prev Med Rep 9:96–101. https://doi.org/10.1016/j.pmedr.2018.01.005

Deutscher Städtetag (2021) Urbane Landwirtschaft Positionspapier des Deutschen Städtetages. Deutscher Städtetag Berlin und Köln, p 5. https://www.staedtetag.de/files/dst/docs/Publikationen/Positionspapiere/2021/positionspapier-urbane-landwirtschaft-2021.pdf/. Accessed 09 Oct 2024

Fogo Cruzado (2019) https://www.casafluminense.org.br/wp-content/uploads/2020/07/mapa-da-desigualdade-2020-final_compressed.pdf. Accessed 09 Oct 2024

Foster SR (2011) Collective action and the urban commons. Notre Dame Law Rev 87(1):94. https://scholarship.law.nd.edu/cgi/viewcontent.cgi?article=1001&context=ndlr/. Accessed 13 Sept 2024
Germany (2023) Federal Statistical Office. Employment up slightly in August 2023. https://www.destatis.de/EN/Themes/Labour/Labour-Market/Unemployment/_node.html/. Accessed 09 Oct 2024
Germany (2024) Federal Statistics Office. Just over one-fifth of Germany's population at risk of poverty or social exclusion. https://www.destatis.de/EN/Press/2023/05/PE23_190_63.html#:~:text=Just%20over%2017.3%20million%20people%20in%20Germany%20were,the%20survey%20on%20income%20and%20living%20conditions%20%28EU-SILC%29. Accessed 09 Oct 2024
Grinberg F, Castro M, Schmidt S (2023) Novo Censo: moradias vagas duplicam em 12 anos e chegam a um milhão no Estado do Rio. https://oglobo.globo.com/rio/noticia/2023/07/07/novo-censo-moradias-vagas-duplicam-em-12-anos-e-chegam-a-um-milhao-no-estado-do-rio.ghtml. Accessed 09 Oct 2024
Guttmann A (2022) Plateformes de développement urbain, villes de la connaissance et développement durable: l'économie politique des biens communs urbains dans le contexte du changement climatique. Sociology. Université Paris-Nord, Paris XIII, p 122. https://theses.hal.science/tel-04160619. Accessed 04 Oct 2024
Hamid T, Sahar S (2017) High-resolution air temperature mapping in urban areas: A review on different modelling techniques. Therm Sci 21(6):2271. https://doi.org/10.2298/TSCI150922094T
IBGE (2010) Universo Aglomerados subnormais, Rio de Janeiro. https://cidades.ibge.gov.br/brasil/rj/rio-de-janeiro/pesquisa/23/25359. Accessed 09 Oct 2024
IBGE (2022a) Síntese de Indicadores Sociais: Uma análise das condições de vida da população brasileira 2022. Rio de Janeiro. https://biblioteca.ibge.gov.br/visualizacao/livros/liv101979.pdf/. Accessed 09 Oct 2024
IBGE (2022b) Censo demográfico. https://www.ibge.gov.br/estatisticas/sociais/habitacao/22827-censo-demografico-2022.html?edicao=37225&t=resultados. Accessed 09 Oct 2024
IBGE (2024) Desemprego: O que é desemprego. https://www.ibge.gov.br/explica/desemprego.php/. Accessed 09 Oct 2024
IDEC. Mapa de Feiras Orgânicas. https://feirasorganicas.org.br/. Accessed 09 Oct 2024
IJSN (2023) Análise Especial: Pobreza e miséria nos estados brasileiros 2022. https://ijsn.es.gov.br/Media/IJSN/PublicacoesAnexos/sumarios/IJSN_Especial_Pobreza_Estados_Brasileiros_2022.pdf/. Accessed 09 Oct 2024
Kramer E (2013) Economic, social and territorial situation of Berlin, Germany, p 35. https://www.europarl.europa.eu/RegData/etudes/note/join/2013/495864/IPOL-REGI_NT(2013)495864_EN.pdf. Accessed 09 Oct 2024
Lima C et al (2019) A rede carioca de agricultura urbana e o direito à cidade. Embrapa. https://www.embrapa.br/busca-de-publicacoes/-/publicacao/1122603/a-rede-carioca-de-agricultura-urbana-e-o-direito-a-cidade. Accessed 09 Oct 2024
Mariko I (2017) Temporary use of vacant urban spaces in Berlin: three case studies in the former Eastern Inner-city District Friedrichshain. Geogr Rev Jpn Ser B 91(1):1–16. https://www.jstage.jst.go.jp/article/geogrevjapanb/91/1/91_910101/_pdf/-char/en. Accessed 09 Oct 2024
Mceldowney J (2017) Urban agriculture in Europe: patterns, challenges and policies. https://www.europarl.europa.eu/RegData/etudes/IDAN/2017/614641/EPRS_IDA(2017)614641_EN.pdf. Accessed 04 Oct 2024
Miranda P et al (2010). Aspectos socioeconômicos da Covid-19: o que dizem os dados do município do Rio de Janeiro?. https://www.ipea.gov.br/portal/images/stories/PDFs/nota_tecnica/200731_nt_diset_n_72.pdf. Accessed 09 Oct 2024
Monteiro M dos S (2020) Reocupação de vazios urbanos como estratégia para cidades (mais) sustentáveis: um olhar sobre a cidade do Rio de Janeiro. Dissertação em Gestão para Competitividade. FGV. http://bibliotecadigital.fgv.br:80/dspace/handle/10438/29162. Accessed 09 Oct 2024

Neves L (2019) Vazios urbanos na área central do Rio de Janeiro preservação e reabilitação urbana. Universidade Federal do Rio de Janeiro (UFRJ). Revista Impulso. https://antigo.mdr.gov.br/images/stories/ArquivosSNPU/Biblioteca/ReabilitacaoAreasUrbanas/Biblioteca_Vazios_Urbanos_Area_Central_RJ.pdf. Accessed 09 Oct 2024

Penssan R (2021) Food insecurity and COVID-19 in Brazil, p 9. https://olheparaafome.com.br/VIGISAN_AF_National_Survey_of_Food_Insecurity.pdf. Accessed 09 Oct 2024

Pfeiffer S, Ritter T, Oestreicher E (2017) Food insecurity and poverty in Germany. In: Sustainable nutrition in a changing world. Biesalski HK et al (eds) Springer, Cham, pp 99–109. https://link.springer.com/chapter/ https://doi.org/10.1007/978-3-319-55942-1_7/. Accessed 09 Oct 2024

Reimer B (2020) Food deserts across Germany. Arcgis. https://storymaps.arcgis.com/stories/2a7e27f1e4564c4e846f12cf45a746b6/print. Accessed 09 Oct 2024

Rio de Janeiro (2013) Prefeitura. Indicador municipal mostra que economia do Rio cresceu 2,4% no primeiro trimestre deste ano. Prefeitura da Cidade do Rio de Janeiro. https://prefeitura.rio/desenvolvimento-economico-inovacao-simplificacao/indicador-municipal-mostra-que-economia-do-rio-cresceu-24-no-primeiro-trimestre-deste-ano/. Accessed 09 Oct 2024

Rio de Janeiro (2023) Prefeitura. Cidade do Rio tem a menor taxa de desemprego em seis anos. Prefeitura da Cidade do Rio de Janeiro. https://prefeitura.rio/desenvolvimento-economico-inovacao-simplificacao/cidade-do-rio-tem-a-menor-taxa-de-desemprego-em-seis-anos/. Accessed 09 Oct 2024

Rio de Janeiro (2024) Prefeitura. Instituto Rio Patrimônio da Humanidade. Projeto Vazios Urbanos, Rio de Janeiro. http://www.rio.rj.gov.br/dlstatic/10112/5333332/4139324/24VaziosUrbanosIRPH082014.pdf. Accessed 09 Oct 2024

Simmet A, Stroebele-Benschop N (2023) Food bank operations during the COVID-19 pandemic in Germany. J Hunger Environ Nutr 18(3):356–371. https://www.tandfonline.com/ https://doi.org/10.1080/19320248.2021.1943590. Accessed 09 Oct 2024

Soederberg S (2017) Governing stigmatised space: the case of the 'slums' of Berlin-Neukölln. New Polit Econ 22(5):478–495. https://www.tandfonline.com/ https://doi.org/10.1080/13563467.2017.1240671. Accessed 09 Oct 2024

Steuri B, Vignola G (2022) Towards productive and socio-natural urban landscapes: tapping urban agriculture's potential as a tool for sustainable development, p 55. https://repos.hcu-hamburg.de/bitstream/hcu/650/2/2022-06-01_steuri-bettina_vignola-gionatan_masterarbeit.pdf. Accessed 09 Oct 2024

Tafel. Die berliner tafel feiert ihren 30. Geburtstag. Berline tafel. https://www.berliner-tafel.de/. Accessed 09 Oct 2024

The Economist (2022) Global Food Security Index, Brazil. https://impact.economist.com/sustainability/project/food-security-index/explore-countries/brazil. Accessed 09 Oct 2024.

The Economist Impact (2022) The Global Food Security Index. https://impact.economist.com/sustainability/project/food-security-index/reports/Economist_Impact_GFSI_2022_Germany_country_report_Sep_2022.pdf/. Accessed 09 Oct 2024

VIGISAN (2021) National survey of food insecurity in the context of the Covid-19 pandemic in Brazil. https://olheparaafome.com.br/VIGISAN_AF_National_Survey_of_Food_Insecurity.pdf/. Accessed 09 Oct 2024

Vonberg J. Germany's hidden hunger: on the breadline in Europe's richest country. https://www.cnn.com/interactive/2017/09/world/germany-food-bank-cnnphotos/. Accessed 09 Oct 2024

Wong R et al (2018) Perceived benefits of participation and risks of soil contamination in St. Louis urban community gardens. J Community Health 43(3):604–610. https://link.springer.com/article/ https://doi.org/10.1007/s10900-017-0459-8. Accessed 13 Sept 2024

Chapter 5
The Human Right to Food in Community Gardens of Berlin and Rio de Janeiro

5.1 Food Availability

The theoretical framework and the empirical evidence indicate that urban food sharing activities in the investigated community gardens of *Berlin* and *Rio de Janeiro* have a relation to food availability. This can be observed when considering that physical availability means fulfillment of nutritional requirements of individuals based on demand, allowing for the freedom of choice in production (including self-sufficiency) and distribution (being accessible for purchase in markets and stores).

In this sense, a **common** activity in *both cities* is **transforming vacant land into (public) open spaces for growing on a not-for-profit basis, including the offer of acquiring food in exchange for labor.** This mostly depends on the governmental structure and city regulation, but *both cities* also have gardens in private areas. For instance, this is institutionally organized in *Rio de Janeiro's* city hall as Agroecology and Organic Production Management. At the same time, *Berlin's* government has an Editorial Platform called Productive Urban Green—Community Gardening. This raises a **common** point between these cities: the territorial conflicts before establishing a community garden. Even so, these problems are related to **different** agents and (il)legal relations that can hinder the successful establishment and maintenance of community gardens.

Initially, interviewees reported that community gardens in *Berlin* faced challenges in navigating complex bureaucratic administrative processes and regulations related to land use or permissions. Even when the land access was authorized, there were complicated and restrictive rules. Also, there was a lack of guidance from public authorities and the core team for newcomers about how to get involved, what is expected of them, how the garden operates, etc., and missing participation in the city hall's decisions affecting the garden was more often mentioned in *Berlin*. The **motivation** can be related to the insufficient number of employees on the city hall and the garden's core team considering the number of gardens and *gardeners*, including the ones doing the activity in a temporary or non-associated form. Also, an *expert*

F. Jardim, *Right to Food in Community Gardens*, LITES - Legal Issues in Transdisciplinary Environmental Studies 6,
https://doi.org/10.1007/978-3-032-19612-5_5

mentioned the pandemic as a barrier to popular participation.[1] Other reasons affecting participation can be the lack of available digital information on many gardens and the language barriers (half of the interviewed *gardeners* were not Germans) impeding effective communication and collaboration among community garden participants or between the garden and local authorities.

For the interviewees, a singular case of opening a growing space in *Berlin* was extremely relevant. It is the referendum about the new land use for Tempelhofer Feld. The airport closed in 2008, where five of the investigated community gardens in this study are situated. The citizens claimed to access the area and organized demonstrations. As a result, there were conflicts with the police in 2009.[2] According to the interviewees and the literature, the reason for the dispute on land use can be found in urban land commodification.[3] "The gardens are very vulnerable to neoliberal policies because voluntary practices are seen as temporary."[4] In this sense, a *gardener* pointed out that with temporary land use contracts, after contributing to the co-production of a better neighborhood and the rise of the land value,[5] obstacles such as increased land mortgage for a new contract already caused a garden's forced moving.[6] In the case of Tempelhofer Feld, the area is central, wide, and equipped with infrastructure, a possible "gold mine."

This inspired the imagination of transforming the urban land from the perspective of the real estate market,[7] resulting in political conflicts. Despite the citizen's choice in the referendum of 2014, in 2019, the Free Democratic Party (FDP), Social Democratic Party of Germany (SPD), and Christian Democratic Union of Germany (CDU) planned a new referendum to approve a peripheral development that has been repeatedly discussed against the background of the lack of housing in the city. The idea was to build 12,000 apartments for moderate development combined "with social housing."[8] The coalition partners Left and the Green, and the Alternative for Germany (AfD) were against the housing plan, arguing that "the approval comes from the real estate and business sectors."[9] Some interviewees realized the above project would face the risk of elevating the area's gentrification.[10]

Moreover, community gardens may be vulnerable to exploitation by entities looking to appear environmentally conscious (greenwashing) without genuinely supporting the garden's mission.

---

[1] BERE3. Doctoral dissertation study. [Interview to Felipe Jardim]. Berlin/Rio de Janeiro, 2024.

[2] Freundeskreis Videoclips.

[3] Maricato (1997), Harvey (1980).

[4] BERE4. Doctoral dissertation study. [Interview to Felipe Jardim]. Berlin/Rio de Janeiro, 2024.

[5] Braswell (2018, pp. 809–822), Steuri and Vignola (2022, p. 77).

[6] BERG7. Doctoral dissertation study. [Interview to Felipe Jardim]. Berlin/Rio de Janeiro, 2024.

[7] Berarcurb (2016).

[8] Kiesel Von (2020), Der Tagesspiegel Online (2019).

[9] Kiesel Von (2019).

[10] BERG1, BERG7, BERG9, BERE4. Doctoral dissertation study. [Interview to Felipe Jardim]. Berlin/Rio de Janeiro, 2024.

> These practices [community gardens] are related to gentrification, but there is also something else: greenwashing use in the image. But even though these green infrastructures are also sometimes transformed into sports areas, etc., there is enormous and increasing pressure on the ground in Berlin. This has been happening since the fall of the wall.[11]

Even so, the public housing company of *Berlin*, Dewego, has been responsible for opening a few community gardens inside communal areas of its social housing buildings, such as in Kiez-Garten. This was in partnership with residents and technical support of Prinzessinnengarten.

> A corporate housing company owns this place. They thought that together, with a social part of the administration, it would be nice to have a community garden here, and they made a call. We applied for that call, and today, it was the first time we announced to the neighbors that there would be a community garden here. Then, our job is to help them if they want it, to have it, to run it, to imagine it, and to build a community garden. Our job is to help give that garden birth, but today was the first time people knew about it. There was not a community here beforehand. Who said we want a garden? So, we will check what people want. They might not need a garden if they want to have a place to play with their children. This is a beautiful place for a garden. I think it could work. And I think there are enough people who are kind of interested. I think it is not an easy place here. We found some needles in the morning. There was someone sleeping in the bushes. [...] The people who are supposed to run the community garden need to feel a sense of ownership before the garden, which I think we can only really do by letting them decide and not having an idea already and then trying to bring it to the people. Just really giving our experience, not deciding what is going to happen.[12]

During the inauguration day of Kiez-Garten (2022), it was possible to observe the participatory panel for decision-making. An expert created the categories because of her experience in Prinzessinnengarten and other gardens. They were just an example of the possibilities that the garden could offer. Any person could pin on the board as many red dots as they wished. So far, the garden did not have a proper name because it was going to be decided collectively during the event. They also voted for other possibilities for the garden, such as culture offers, relaxing areas, and a hotel for bees.[13] This reveals the **social co-production of the space** of urban commons.

In *Berlin*, as a barrier to creating food growing spaces, interviewees also reported episodes of prejudice regarding urban agriculture and racism from district managers (responsible for green areas) against community garden initiatives and gardeners in general. For instance, in one of the cases, a district manager was "from a right-wing political party that tried to keep us out by bureaucracy reasons."[14] This represents legal ways to create discriminatory obstacles to opening a growing space. One of the **motivations** can be based on the number of non-German gardeners using the space as a social activity, as registered by the sociodemographic questionnaire of this research and in the literature.[15]

---

[11] BERE4. Doctoral dissertation study. [Interview to Felipe Jardim]. Berlin/Rio de Janeiro, 2024.

[12] BERE10. Doctoral dissertation study. [Interview to Felipe Jardim]. Berlin/Rio de Janeiro, 2024.

[13] BERE9. Doctoral dissertation study. [Interview to Felipe Jardim]. Berlin/Rio de Janeiro, 2024.

[14] This topic was mentioned by two experts, but who mentioned it will be not identified, as requested by them.

[15] FAO (2022, p. 16).

Moving to the topic of starting public growing space in *Rio de Janeiro* by the local government (Hortas Cariocas), it is important to mention the initiation of a garden project occurs when an individual or a group submits a formal request to the Environment Secretariat at City Hall. After conducting a thorough feasibility assessment, if the project is granted approval, a specific budget is created to provide financial support to gardeners, which includes appointing a leader for each garden and acquiring the necessary materials and tools. Once the grant recipients are selected and the required equipment is procured, the actual implementation of the garden project commences. This phase involves the allocation of funds and continuous technical supervision.[16]

Consequently, the lack of participation in decisions was not a relevant problem for the participants. The motivation is probably because the Hortas Cariocas gardens depended on the neighbors' request, a strategy of permanence, and local acceptance of the garden. In the garden, the gardeners have the freedom to decide many food growing issues (what, when, and where to plant, etc.) horizontally and democratically,[17] as illustrated by a gardener: "Even though the other gardeners have more time here, we always work in harmony, right? If something is wrong, I hold a meeting, and we get together and discuss the garden. 'What do you think could be done?' everyone gives a suggestion, and we choose the best one, right? [...] Everyone suggests something, everyone should give their opinion."[18] This is a demonstration of the democratic process during the governance of commons.

Nonetheless, *gardeners* did not feel they participated in the choice of the Agroecology and Organic Production Management administrator, a position held by a person appointed by a politician and, consequently, vulnerable to political pressure. The politicians also influence whether a garden (land access) is open according to financial and electoral interests,[19] but the same influence does not apply to a garden closure.

Regarding the guidance for newcomers, the gardens in private areas are in quilombos, where knowledge sharing is part of their tradition. At Hortas Cariocas, newcomers are taught by a leader in each garden. Even so, some *experts* reported Hortas Cariocas' limited human and financial resources to support all gardens. Concerning language, only two foreigners were interviewed in *Rio de Janeiro*, one from Portugal and one from Germany, but the latter had lived in Brazil for decades and was fluent in Portuguese. Therefore, unlike the scenario in Berlin, the language barrier is not listed as an issue related to the public authorities or core team.

Furthermore, a clear **difference** between *both cities'* growing spaces is the location, the surrounding urban infrastructure of the former vacant area, and the landowner. In *Berlin*, the gardens are usually central, in areas with easy access via paved streets, availability of different modes of public transport, electric lighting,

---

[16] Jardim et al. (2023).

[17] RIOE8. Doctoral dissertation study. [Interview to Felipe Jardim]. Berlin/Rio de Janeiro, 2024.

[18] RIOG4. Doctoral dissertation study. [Interview to Felipe Jardim]. Berlin/Rio de Janeiro, 2024.

[19] RIOE8. Doctoral dissertation study. [Interview to Felipe Jardim]. Berlin/Rio de Janeiro, 2024.

sewage system, and afforestation. Flat, well-defined quadrilateral terrains of public parks and plazas or private cemeteries exist.

Rio de Janeiro's gardens are more on the city's outskirts, usually improvised in public green areas close to the Tijuca Forest, plazas, and schools, without the previously mentioned urban infrastructure. There is a variation of flat and inclined terrains due to the local geography where most of the slums are situated as alternative solutions for the housing crisis, and the plots have quadrilateral and triangular designs, given the occupation of vacant land, wherever it is.

One more **divergence** regarding spaces for growing is that in *Berlin,* there are some cases of gardener's membership fees to use a plot (from 15 to 150 euros, and some plots for individual or collective rent. In the opposite direction, in *Rio de Janeiro,* there is no fee in any case and no plots for rent. The possible **explanation** for this difference is the funding. In *Berlin*, one of the state's requirements to allow land access in some cases was a deposit, as identified by interviewees of Moritzplatz, Allmende-Kontor, M.I.N.T. Grünes Klassenzimmer, and Himmelbeet (in this last case, 60,000 euros[20]). Also, many gardens have no funding source other than association fees, plot fees, events, or, in rare cases, a store or restaurant. In *Rio de Janeiro*, the funding comes from public resources (city hall for Hortas Cariocas) and self-funding (such as selling products on a non-profit basis for the other gardens, donations, and institutional funds).

Sharing for free, selling on a non-profit basis, and swapping foodstuff "liberated," foraged, or gleaned is a common activity in *both cities.* In *Berlin*, this can be noticed in the interviews' citation: "When do you need, you can come here and collect food. Everybody is welcome."[21] Another gardener shares this: "If someone is hungry and plants grow, they can eat. It is their right to go there and get their potatoes out of the soil."[22] In *Rio de Janeiro*, food gifting is one of the purposes of the Hortas Cariocas program,[23] and the sense of exchanging foodstuff and skills between gardeners from the same garden or between different gardens was registered by the questionnaires of almost all participants.

The **reason** for the similar foodstuff sharing, including seeds, soil, water, tools, etc., can be theoretically linked to the nature of community gardens as urban commons, especially to its founding principles (sharing, collaboration, civic engagement, inclusion, equity, and social justice). In addition, urban commons pay attention to sustainability, particularly for the most vulnerable populations. A clear proof of that is a garden's name in *Berlin*, the Allmende-Kontor, a commons office, where "a **commons** are an ancient novelty, a jointly managed public space, a 'gift to all.'"[24] In light of that, a *gardener* stated that

> Here are concepts of common use, which is an idea that still needs to be even more integrated into what we call sustainability, but I think that the basis of Allmende-Kontor, and it is even in

[20] BERE7. Doctoral dissertation study. [Interview to Felipe Jardim]. Berlin/Rio de Janeiro, 2024.

[21] BERG3. Doctoral dissertation study. [Interview to Felipe Jardim]. Berlin/Rio de Janeiro, 2024.

[22] BERG6. Doctoral dissertation study. [Interview to Felipe Jardim]. Berlin/Rio de Janeiro, 2024.

[23] Rio de Janeiro.

[24] Allmende-Kontor.

the name of this garden, comes from inspiration from use common spaces, non-privatization of resources and collective care. So, in that sense, I think this garden is well connected with the idea that only a life where things are shared and not privatized is sustainable.[25]

A *gardener* in *Rio de Janeiro* also expressed this view:

There are a lot of people who come here and say, "I do not understand this garden. What do you mean by 'we can take it'?" So, I reply: "It is simple: we can take it!" Also, sometimes those already planting and coming weekly to care for the garden say, "But the person did not even plant anything, and can they take it away?" So, I answer, "Yes, they can take it. The word 'community' comes from what is common, so it is okay if they take it today and come to plant another day. No problem."[26]

Besides that, the empirical investigation's participants demonstrated shared concerns about the urban crises. The **distinction** is that in *Berlin*, this is more related to **environmental issues**, such as climate change, land grabbing, pollution, deforestation, lack of green areas, and **socialization concerns** (the garden as social space to overcome the self-isolation, even before the pandemic), while in *Rio de Janeiro* the focus is on the **fight against food insecurity**. For instance, some *gardeners* who recently moved to *Berlin* from others declared that they use the garden as a potential place to make new friends.[27] Regarding environmental concerns, another gardener in *Berlin* stated that

we can produce food here very locally, which is one aspect of battling climate change and also for climate justice. We can experiment here with plants that have a bigger potential to change the systems, the exploitative systems that we are in so far because normal agriculture with annual plants is really exporting the ground, and it is going to lead to more and more land-grabbing everywhere, and taking lands from people in other parts of the world just to produce food for us here in the industrialized countries, which is really fucked up, like, how many spaces we are using.[28]

An important interview citation from a *gardener* on social vulnerability in *Rio de Janeiro* exists:

Human beings have the right to eat – as the president [Lula] says, "at least three times a day" –. Without food, what do you do? You do not do anything! You do not work, develop, think, study, love, play, smile! How will a hungry person produce? And without quality food, it is very difficult too. And what else does Brazil have? It is called the world's great granary... It is the world's greatest poison granary! And it is a country where people still go hungry and go hungry in big cities, for example, Rio de Janeiro. I think it is unbelievable! When you think about human rights, the first thing that comes to mind is food. Then come the other means: right to health, right to school, right to leisure, right to education, right to security... so if you think about human rights, you start to think about which ones we all have, following our Constitution, we have many rights, equal according to the Constitution, we are all equal before the law... when in fact this is not true! But I think the minimum is the right to food. It is for you to stand up, for you to think and do other things. A hungry individual is unable to do

[25] BERG8. Doctoral dissertation study. [Interview to Felipe Jardim]. Berlin/Rio de Janeiro, 2024.

[26] RIOG10. Doctoral dissertation study. [Interview to Felipe Jardim]. Berlin/Rio de Janeiro, 2024.

[27] BERG2; BERG3. Doctoral dissertation study. [Interview to Felipe Jardim]. Berlin/Rio de Janeiro, 2024.

[28] BERG1. Doctoral dissertation study. [Interview to Felipe Jardim]. Berlin/Rio de Janeiro, 2024.

> anything else, including primary things. He only thinks about food. I think when you think about food and quality food, which are two different things, I think we need to review this urgently so that no one goes hungry anymore. It is absurd that you are eating and thinking that there might be someone next to you who is hungry, and you are doing nothing. I cannot accept it![29]

An *expert* can illustrate the same view:

> I am a person who has always had a bad feeling seeing people starving on the street. So this was also an awakening of trying to improve in some way what I can help to improve because as I am already a government employee, I earn the same thing practically stamping paper and being the manager of a program like this, you know? So, it was more of a life choice, of changes in quality of life too, of cool things to do, and I made this decision to really change this outlook, you know? It is more of a look. Food also changes something, right?[30]

However, it is important to highlight that interviewees in *Rio de Janeiro* also pay attention to **income generation** and **environmental issues**, pillars of Hortas Cariocas.[31] Representing this last view, a *gardener* stated that "Community agriculture is the manifestation of the community in the fight for its fundamental rights, for better reframing of the environment, fight against the aggressive environment that has been built in cities with the unbridled advancement of construction and land occupation, without proper public administration."[32] This is a clear illustration of the **regenerative character of urban commons**.

One possible cause for these different central concerns is that *Berlin* has higher city development than *Rio de Janeiro*.[33] In addition, *Germany* has fewer inequalities than *Brazil*.[34] Illustrating that the prevalence of moderate or severe food insecurity in the population levels (2020–2022) in *Germany* (3.5%, representing 3.2 million people) is much lower than in *Brazil* (32.80%, representing 70.3 million people),[35] where the number of daily explicit historical emergence for basic needs (aggravated

[29] RIOG10. Doctoral dissertation study. [Interview to Felipe Jardim]. Berlin/Rio de Janeiro, 2024.

[30] RIOE8. Doctoral dissertation study. [Interview to Felipe Jardim]. Berlin/Rio de Janeiro, 2024.

[31] Rio de Janeiro.

[32] RIOG8. Doctoral dissertation study. [Interview to Felipe Jardim]. Berlin/Rio de Janeiro, 2024.

[33] "The City Development Index is based on three main domains (i.e., social, economic, and cultural) and their sub-dimensions. These three domains correspond to the three main structures upon which all cities throughout history have been built and that ensure the continuity of a city's social reality. In addition, these three basic domains also have their own dimensions. Ideally, urban development basically depends on the harmony among these three elements and the balanced distribution of their measurable sub-indicators." City Index. The index includes 55 cities (2020). By this system, *Berlin*'s score is 57.21, occupying the 9th position. *Rio de Janeiro's* score is 37.65, on the 45th position. The best score is of Prague (61.9), while the worst is Lagos (26.4).

[34] On the Poverty and Inequality Platform from the World Bank, "the Gini index measures the extent to which the distribution of income or consumption among individuals or households within an economy deviates from a perfectly equal distribution. A Gini index of 0 represents perfect equality, while an index of 100 implies perfect inequality." Concerning the last available data, Germany's index is 31.72% (2019), and Brazil's index is 52.92% (2021). World Bank.

[35] Global Alliance for Food Security.

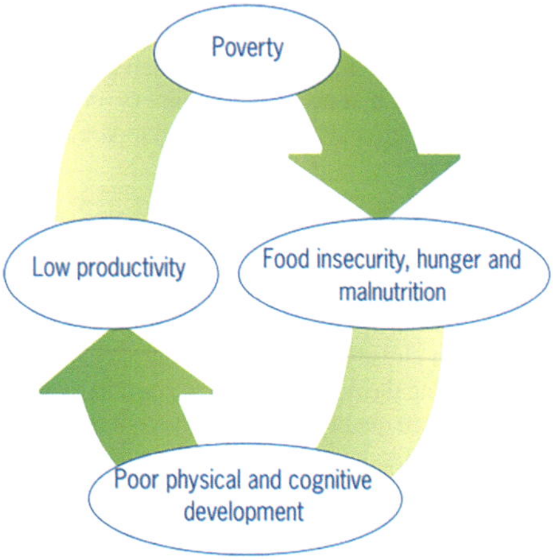

Fig. 5.1 Food insecurity, malnutrition, and poverty are interrelated. *Source* FAO (2008, p. 3)[39]

by the COVID-19 pandemic) can be seen on the streets of cities, like in *Rio de Janeiro*.[36]

Moreover, another possible **reason** is that the investigated *gardeners* in *Berlin* had a higher level of formal education than *gardeners* in *Rio de Janeiro*. In addition, the median income difference between *gardeners* and *experts* in *Berlin* was much lower than in *Rio de Janeiro*,[37] where, almost exclusively, the *experts* had access to a high level of education. With lower education and a lower income, many of the *gardeners* from *Rio de Janeiro* depended on the community garden's income to **supplement their central income** to pay their household bills, including a few retired interviewees. In this sense, when a garden offers paid work, as it happens in Hortas Cariocas, there is a potential way to tackle poverty and, consequently, part of the violations of the human right to food (a cycle observed on Fig. 5.1).[38]

Also, the concern about food insecurity can be related to food apartheid[40] (Chapter 2, Sect. 2.2), given that a significant number of interviews (14/20) in *Rio de Janeiro* expressed the lack of biodiversity in the supermarkets and the absence of street fairs of organic products in their neighborhood or surrounds. Participants in *Berlin* did not notice this.

In addition, to provide more food availability in *Rio de Janeiro*, *gardeners* and *experts* were doing urban food sharing activities to benefit people in social, economic, and environmental vulnerability. For instance,

---

[36] Lopes and Brêtas (2022), Hora do Povo (2021).

[37] The *experts* also had a higher monthly household income, with an average around 315 Euros (around 350 United States Dollars) more than *gardeners*. In *Rio de Janeiro*, the *experts* had an income more than 3 times higher than *gardeners*.

[38] FAO (2010, p. 5).

[39] FAO (2008).

[40] GCAP UCR.

> community urban agriculture is more for donation. If you know that someone is in need and you make a donation... this has no price! No price! Young wives of men in jail have 2 or 3 kids but no conditions to care for the family. So, we are who take care of them. I send some food straight to house a specific person that I know that is in need. The person does not need to come here to the garden to collect food.[41]

Consequently, another **contrast** between cities is what is done with the products. In *Berlin,* the products are mostly for self-consumption since eating organic products brings a great deal of satisfaction: "For me, it is a great pleasure to be there and be able to collect something that I will take home and eat. It makes a lot of difference and is a kind of prize. Even though I still do not depend on it to feed me, it is like a reward for my work. Eating organic and harvesting, planting, sowing by myself, this whole process."[42] In another case, many interviewees in *Rio de Janeiro* also expressed the pleasure of eating fresh and healthy self-produced food and having contact with nature. However, the main reason was to feed the local community (gardeners, neighbours, students, health units) by gifting or selling food for symbolic prices. This resulted in good feelings. For instance, a *gardener* in *Rio de Janeiro* reinforced that sense: "I eat organic products without pesticides; it helps with my diet, and what I like most is donating. I like to donate. This gives me joy!".[43]

Literature can also explain the multiple ways in which one can be connected to food growing. Previous studies reported an "environmentalism of the poor," (as noticed on the final part of 2.4 topic) finding solutions to daily problems in nature,[44] while rich people would use nature for individual hedonistic purposes when using community gardening "as a trend—created and lived out solely by hip and bohemian citizens."[45]

Another possible urban sharing activity for the destination of products is the **establishment of a garden restaurant or café**. However, the **difference** is that in *Rio de Janeiro,* these spaces were registered only in association with the kitchens of public schools (Hortas Cariocas) as food nutrition and culture. There was no aim to generate income, even on a non-profit basis, like in some cases in *Berlin*. The gardens' restaurants/cafés in *Berlin* are not only to support the funding for materials but also have the **purpose** of bringing/attracting more people to contribute to the garden, guaranteeing the payment of workers. For instance, in 2008, the Moritzplatz garden in *Berlin* was not economically sustainable by selling vegetables, so the solution was to incorporate a restaurant.[46] Nevertheless, it was seen as a "business mindset,"[47] running away from common sense and uninviting people. A possible **logic** for this contrast is that most studied gardens in *Rio de Janeiro* were from Hortas Cariocas, and this public policy does not aim to offer prepared meals in a

---

[41] RIOG1. Doctoral dissertation study. [Interview to Felipe Jardim]. Berlin/Rio de Janeiro, 2024.

[42] BERE5. Doctoral dissertation study. [Interview to Felipe Jardim]. Berlin/Rio de Janeiro, 2024.

[43] RIOG5. Doctoral dissertation study. [Interview to Felipe Jardim]. Berlin/Rio de Janeiro, 2024.

[44] Martinez-Alier (2014, pp. 239–241).

[45] Steuri and Vignola (2022, p. 115).

[46] BERE10. Doctoral dissertation study. [Interview to Felipe Jardim]. Berlin/Rio de Janeiro, 2024.

[47] BERG9. Doctoral dissertation study. [Interview to Felipe Jardim]. Berlin/Rio de Janeiro, 2024.

restaurant or café for guests. These structures are not easy to find in *Berlin*, except in Prinzessinnengarten, Peace of Land (closed), Klunkergarten, Himmelbeet (closed), Frieda Süd, and Möhrchenpark. A restaurant or café requires electric, hydraulic, and sanitary installations and authorizations, many hours of work, and money to cover the costs of maintenance and payment of workers; it could also become a source of income for the garden.[48]

Finally, food availability can also happen through **learning and practicing nutrition, how to co-produce food, identifying places where gleaning or foraging might occur, and swapping seeds.** In *both cities*, this includes knowledge regarding medicinal and wild food. For example, in *Berlin,* there was in Piece of Land the Wilderness & Survival School Walk on the Wildside, while Prizessinnengarten still offered the Wild Kitchen, where people "discover–admire–feel–smell–taste"[49] herbs and berries collected on the garden, harvesting or preparing them on a camping stove. Nonetheless, unlike *Rio de Janeiro*, *Berlin* has more specific events, courses, and workshops. A possible **reason** for that is that the gardens offer environmental education and transformation in *Berlin*, and there is more space for events (parties, courses, workshops, etc.), reinforcing the social and educational benefits of community gardens.[50]

In addition, the events with voluntary monetary contributions can support the projects. In another sense, many gardens from Hortas Cariocas in *Rio de Janeiro* have no proper structure for events. They are in areas of difficult access (sometimes controlled by criminality and no public transport in the neighbourhood), which is unattractive for visitors. Furthermore, even when an event happens, the learning and practicing are usually for free, such as the organic and native seeds exchange meetings.

Closing this section, it is relevant to discuss that several reports have shown that food availability can be connected to community gardens in *both cities* by **providing (public) open spaces for growing food**. What is ordinary among these scenarios is the utilization of vacant land as a strategic approach, primarily not centered on food-related purposes but rather aimed at transforming or preventing the creation of wastelands and dumpsites[51] and on social justice and environmental sustainability.[52] However, in *Rio de Janeiro*, there was an additional concern about curtailing drug-related activities, including sales, purchases, and consumption, and preventing further housing construction.[53]

In conclusion, as indicated in the literature, the physical **food accessibility** varies across *both cities*. In *Berlin*, gardens serve as a symbolic addition to people's daily food intake over time.[54] Conversely, in *Rio de Janeiro*, several studies explicitly

---

[48] Karge (2015).

[49] Prinzessinnengarten.

[50] Gobster et al. (2004, pp. 149–151), Karge (2015), op. cit., Steuri and Vignola, op. cit.

[51] Magalhães (2021), Véron (2023).

[52] Rekow (2015).

[53] Magalhães, op. cit.

[54] Halder (2017, p. 169) et seq., Steuri and Vignola, op. cit.

analyse how community gardens contribute to alleviating, though not completely resolving, food insecurity issues stemming from the absence of markets and street fairs and the economic constraints Black communities face (food apartheid).[55]

The results presented here are coincident with that, except for the findings about *Rio de Janeiro* focused on food-related goals. This contrast can be **explained** in the sense that most of the gardens investigated in *Rio de Janeiro* are part of Hortas Cariocas, where food security is one of the central pillars. Out of this public policy, the garden at Quilombo Dona Bilina exemplifies a garden's creation due to the food insecurity related to the COVID-19 pandemic, a scenario just recently added to the literature. Even so, a note of caution is due here since it is possible that these results may not be generalizable to a broader range of community gardens in *Rio de Janeiro,* given this study's limitations in collecting empirical data.

Moreover, the results here presented expand the literature through the deeper investigation of food availability in *Berlin* and *Rio de Janeiro* by transforming vacant land into (public) open spaces for growing on a non-profit basis, including the offer of acquiring food in exchange for labor; establishment of a gardens' restaurant or café; and learning and practicing nutrition, how to co-produce food, identifying places where gleaning or foraging might occur, and swapping seeds.

5.2 Food Accessibility

Further analysis shows a relation between urban food sharing activities in the investigated community gardens of *Berlin* and *Rio de Janeiro* and food **accessibility**. This concept encompasses consistent economic and physical accessibility over time without compromising the fulfillment of human rights, basic needs, or resources for future generations, the non-nutritional values associated with food and food consumption, and providing adequate information about the nature of available food supplies.

The concept can be noticed in *both cities* when economic savings happen on **self-produced foodstuff**, **sharing it for free, buying it for a symbolic price, or acquiring it by swapping.** The **contrast** is that these savings are unimportant in *Berlin* because of the "irrelevant"[56] amount of production (gardens with educational purposes), weather conditions, soil limitations, food insecurity levels, etc. For instance, an *expert* pointed out that "people come here, and they get two cucumbers, and yeah, they are not going to buy those two cucumbers at the supermarket. Ok. That is good, but it is only two cucumbers; it is not what will make things change. It would be an illusion to think that unless it is a massive scale."[57] Complementing this, another *expert* expressed his view on the urban agriculture types.

[55] Zanotto (2016), Siniscalchi (2020, p. 241) et seq., Lima (2019, p. 119) et seq.

[56] Prinzessinnengarten Kollektiv Berlin.

[57] BERE7. Doctoral dissertation study. [Interview to Felipe Jardim]. Berlin/Rio de Janeiro, 2024.

> I guess, basically, worldwide, there are two different types of urban gardening that one can distinguish. One is actually really for food production, and this is basically happening in areas where there are people with financial problems. Would be really poorer countries. But there are also examples, for example, from Detroit, the United States. Still, in the United States, there are people who need fresh products, especially as the price structure for vegetables is crazy in the United States. It is cheaper to buy meat, which is weird. The other type of gardening, which I would count in the Prinzessinnengarten, is basically for social and pedagogic aspects, I would say so. It is people. When I learn something about vegetable production, we want to know something about old varieties of vegetables. Up to now, roughly 80 to 90% of the existing types are already extinct. It is basically hybrids that are grown nowadays, especially in the cities; many people are not really connected to food production and are looking for a space to come together with other people to do something meaningful.[58]

It is interesting to note that the above citation dialogue with the literature review regarding the central role of urban agriculture in the Global North and Global South. The North emphasizes the positive impacts on social connections, health, emotional well-being, and education, while in the South, it has a crucial role in meeting food security and nutritional requirements.

In *Rio de Janeiro*, savings were mentioned by many participants because even the symbolic financial contribution matters for people in economic vulnerability. In this sense, a *gardener* stated, "By producing food, you are saving money to buy bread, vegetables, or anything else."[59] Furthermore, receiving organic food as a donation or buying it as a symbolic price is relevant given its representation of another relation to the food system than the agro-industrial system, a **social-ecological transformation**. For instance, a *gardener* pointed out that.

> Look how this organic food is different from everything industrially produced, with pesticides, preservatives, chemical preservatives... that the person has money, goes into the supermarket, goes to the shelf and picks it up... then buys it, which comes by the bag, by the kilo, he pays, he knows it is food. However, food also kills and causes him illness.[60]

This **contrast** between cities can be associated with the income issue discussed in the food availability section and the nature of community gardens as urban commons. What can be added is that the problems of the COVID-19 pandemic have brought more social inequalities and vulnerability to *Brazil*,[61] including *Rio de Janeiro*, affecting the purchasing power of many people and the lives of low-income communities.[62] At the same time, most of the interviewees in *Berlin* said that the pandemic affected only their social life, and one of the city hall program's concerns is to activate community gardens as a strategy to access shared areas, which is connected to freedom. This has a special role "in times of crisis like the COVID-19 pandemic."[63]

---

[58] BERE1. Doctoral dissertation study. [Interview to Felipe Jardim]. Berlin/Rio de Janeiro, 2024.

[59] RIOG10. Doctoral dissertation study. [Interview to Felipe Jardim]. Berlin/Rio de Janeiro, 2024.

[60] RIOG7. Doctoral dissertation study. [Interview to Felipe Jardim]. Berlin/Rio de Janeiro, 2024.

[61] Regueira (2021).

[62] Agência Brasil (2020).

[63] Berlin.

As a result, the food insecurity levels in *Rio de Janeiro* increased,[64] and *Brazil* returned to the FAO hunger map (2022). Tackling this problem, during most of the COVID-19 pandemic, 100% of the production of Hortas Cariocas was gifted, despite the program guideline of 50% of output for donation and 50% for sale, except in schools, where 100% of the food is donated.[65] For instance, there was a total of 22 tons of food donated between April and December 2020. Later, still on the effects of the pandemic, during the initial half of 2022, the gardens yielded approximately 35 tons of produce. Specifically, the gardens generated 107,000 seedlings and 7.2 tons of food in June 2022. Out of this total, 3.1 tons were sold, and 4.1 tons were donated.[66] Around 50,000 families are involved with the program.[67]

Additionally, the garden of Quilombo Dona Bilina was created to supplement the diet of hungry people during the pandemic because the donated food was only industrialized.[68] Also, the Quilombo das Caboclas community organization was essential to survive the pandemic,[69] as observed in the following interview extract from an *expert:* "I think I grew a lot during the pandemic. I saw a lot. It affected the poorest and Black families cruelly… we have the right to life, life with food, and the garden provides that."[70]

In another economic sense, community gardens can provide job opportunities *in both cities*. The **difference** is that in *Berlin,* there were more forms of generating income (volunteering with financial subsidies and hiring professionals) to develop administrative activities, and *experts* occupied these paid work positions. For instance, an *expert* affirmed that "producing food is not the main goal. It is not contributing too much to my diet; it is my work."[71] In *Rio de Janeiro*, the only registered option to volunteer in gardening activities with financial subsidy was in Hortas Cariocas, a position occupied by *gardeners*. The *experts* were paid not because of the garden but given other reasons (e.g., be a professor at university, a public agent from city hall, or a technical assistant from a Non-Governmental Organization).

The possible **explanation** for this divergence is that the most interviewed *gardeners* in *Rio de Janeiro* were from Hortas Cariocas, which has as one of the principles to provide remunerated opportunities for people in social vulnerability but without employment ties.[72] The subsidy is worth 500 Reais (around 92 United States dollars) for 180 gardeners,[73] 630 Reais (around 115 United State Dollars) for 56 garden managers (responsible for each garden, who are in direct contact with the program management), and 1,000 Reais (around 182 United State Dollars) for the

---

[64] Oliveira and Galdo (2022).

[65] Rio de Janeiro.

[66] Rio de Janeiro.

[67] Centro de Inteligência em Orgânicos (2022).

[68] RIOG10. Doctoral dissertation study. [Interview to Felipe Jardim]. Berlin/Rio de Janeiro, 2024.

[69] RIOE6. Doctoral dissertation study. [Interview to Felipe Jardim]. Berlin/Rio de Janeiro, 2024.

[70] RIOG9. Doctoral dissertation study. [Interview to Felipe Jardim]. Berlin/Rio de Janeiro, 2024.

[71] BERE7. Doctoral dissertation study. [Interview to Felipe Jardim]. Berlin/Rio de Janeiro, 2024.

[72] Instituto Escolhas (2022).

[73] Rio de Janeiro (2020).

five community integrators (who carry out mobilization work and dissemination of practices between multiple gardens).

This study indicates the same findings regarding the economic relevance (even symbolic, in *Rio de Janeiro*) or not (in *Berlin*) of the **self-produced foodstuff, sharing it for free, buying it for a symbolic price, or acquiring it by swapping.**

Additionally, the findings presented in this study contribute to the existing literature by conducting a more in-depth examination of food economic accessibility in *Berlin* and *Rio de Janeiro* by exploring the community gardens as a source of **income generation opportunities through gardening, social, administrative work, and vegetable sales.** However, caution must be applied with a small sample size, as the findings might be limited. The reason is that *both cities* face funding problems and have gardens based on voluntary actions, such as at Freie Universität *Berlin* and in Quilombo Dona Bilina in *Rio de Janeiro.*

5.3 Food Acceptability

Turning now to the experimental evidence on the relation of urban food sharing activities in community gardens in *Berlin* and *Rio de Janeiro* to food **acceptability**, it is important to mention that this key component of the right to food entails activities promoting food devoid of harmful substances, and meeting specific dietary requirements based on factors like age, living circumstances, health, occupation, gender, and more. Furthermore, it should be devoid of contaminant residues from industrial or agricultural practices, such as pesticides, fertilizers, hormones, or veterinary drugs, while aligning with cultural consumption norms.

Following that, in *both cities*, there was **agroecological food production (regarding no use of artificial chemicals, fertilizers, pesticides, etc.)**. This rule was usually written and exposed on boards or orally transmitted between the commoners, gardeners, and experts. All interviewees were strongly against the industrial agri-food system (intensive and exploratory monoculture, using artificial products, genetically modified seeds, related to land grabbing etc.). The **reason** for that can be found in the principles of urban commons focusing on sustainability and the agroecological way to produce food in community gardens, in contrast to conventional agriculture. This can be illustrated in *Berlin* by an *expert*'s interview extract:

> I guess this place has a role in sustainability. First, because it's about growing food locally, you must use plants in this area. If you are able to produce enough food to sustain an entire community, that would mean that it would cut down transportation, and yeah, that is also an organic garden, so there is no chemical pesticide or fertilizers. They try to reuse all the plant waste as, for example, composts. It's a kind of circular production of vegetables.[74]

In *Rio de Janeiro*, the Hortas Cariocas slogan announces the agroecological practices (chemical-free). This was reaffirmed by **all** interviewees related to the program.

[74] BERE8. Doctoral dissertation study. [Interview to Felipe Jardim]. Berlin/Rio de Janeiro, 2024.

They are informed to use traditional knowledge and natural pesticides (e.g., plants and oils that keep plagues away).

Furthermore, *both cities* had examples of urban food sharing activity based on **knowledge transfer about food culture.** A possible **explanation** is the proposal of food as a common resource, not a commodity.[75] For example, a *gardener* in *Berlin* stated that the garden "is a place to relax after work, to put my hand on the earth and cultivate the land, whatever it is, pruning, watering, planting is a time for me of destress, in short, of energy discharge, energy recharge, so I come alone with pleasure too, to be thinking."[76] Other *gardener* expressed that "everybody needs a connection with nature somehow, even if are you living in the city. [...] Find a place where you can have a bit of peace when the city is loud and moving all the time. It is good to be able to slow down."[77]

Additionally, by studying the empirical data, it is possible to observe that the participants are doing the resumption of a familiar tradition done in the countryside during their childhood. For example, in *Berlin*:

> I did gardening when I was a kid. My grandmother grew plants and vegetables for us to eat, so I am very used to having fruits from my garden. There is some knowledge that I remember from early childhood, for example, composting and the names of plants that you can use and which ones you should avoid.[78]

In *Berlin*, the knowledge transfer has interesting examples of food culture, such as in Café Ukraine, in Frieda Süd garden, where language meetings and workshops have a key role for immigrants (beekeeping, language café) that goes beyond food: "Every Saturday afternoon, people from all over the world, with and without a migration biography, meet in the language café on the premises of the Kreuzberg workshop. They cook together, play games, and talk to each other and learn German: easily accessible, sociable and open."[79] Another interesting offer is the meeting place for the Narcotics Anonymus, a community where drugs have become a major problem. There are sessions in English, Farsi, Russian and Polish. The group also offers special interest meetings for men, women, and people from the LGBTQ* community.

In *Rio de Janeiro*, the familiar food culture can be illustrated by a *gardener*:

> The garden belonged to my great-grandmother, and this garden was not a community garden; it was a family garden. [...] So, in a family way, we always produced: my father was a farmer, we worked at the fair as teenagers, I always weeded, I always planted, I always liked to plant, I always liked to eat the things I plant, but I could not imagine one day doing a community garden. There were about 5 or 6 plant beds for the family that we produced. It was me, the children, sometimes a nephew, sometimes a neighbor. Before the pandemic, we never thought about gardening; everybody, together with the community, I never did. But it is a very good experience![80]

---

[75] Gordillo and Jerónimo (2013, p. 4).

[76] BERG8. Doctoral dissertation study. [Interview to Felipe Jardim]. Berlin/Rio de Janeiro, 2024.

[77] BERG2. Doctoral dissertation study. [Interview to Felipe Jardim]. Berlin/Rio de Janeiro, 2024.

[78] BERG7. Doctoral dissertation study. [Interview to Felipe Jardim]. Berlin/Rio de Janeiro, 2024.

[79] Bauhütte Kreuzberg.

[80] RIOG10. Doctoral dissertation study. [Interview to Felipe Jardim]. Berlin/Rio de Janeiro, 2024.

Further than nutrition, food culture was a special topic cited by another *gardener*:

> Community urban agriculture does not guarantee your complete nutrition, but it expands your concept of what food is, and it adds knowledge about food and nutrition that gives you more autonomy to manage your access to food. So, I think it goes beyond what you physically eat and the product you are going to eat. I think that the garden is part of human rights.[81]

Given that food culture relates to ethnic background,[82] among other factors, the **difference** between *Berlin* and *Rio de Janeiro* is that in *Berlin,* the general profile of *gardeners* and *experts* was composed of White people.[83] In *Rio de Janeiro,* there was a strong influence of Black culture (e.g., Quilombo Dona Bilina and Quilombo das Caboclas) and some participation of Indigenous culture. Still, these ethnicities were almost exclusively among *gardeners.* Most *experts* in *Rio de Janeiro* declared themselves as White people. The possible **explanation** for the dissimilarity can be found in each country's historical and ethnic construction.

In conclusion, prior studies have noted evidence of food acceptability in community gardens in both cities. In *Berlin,* this connection revolved around disseminating information and education about food culture, focusing on imparting knowledge about food preparation and consumption, especially for children.[84] It also encouraged the preservation of culinary traditions and allowed individuals to cultivate plants native to their countries or cities of origin.[85] *Rio de Janeiro*'s cultural linkage centered on ancestral wisdom concerning medicinal plants.[86]

This study found evidence reinforcing the literature on the **knowledge transfer about food culture.** The surprising finding was to identify the elements of the literature of *Berlin* in *Rio de Janeiro* and vice versa. On the one hand, this means the citations in *Berlin* to ancestral wisdom on plants and growing techniques. On the other hand, there was evidence of food education for children and adults in *Rio de Janeiro.* The results also expanded the literature on ethnical and migratory backgrounds and relevant factors to differentiate food cultures. On behalf of that, the case of *Berlin* was more associated with a German and White background, despite many migrants from other parts of Europe. Even so, there is space for more diversity.[87] The case of *Rio de Janeiro* had a mixed ethnical background, with a strong Black influence among *gardeners.*

Nonetheless, it is important to consider the possible bias in these responses. The reason is the limitation of the data collection. For instance, there was no ethnic

---

[81] RIOG9. Doctoral dissertation study. [Interview to Felipe Jardim]. Berlin/Rio de Janeiro, 2024.

[82] Butterfield (2021, pp. 160–168).

[83] The racial identification was not a data collected by the questionnaire in *Berlin.* Even so, the lack of people non-European and non-White was noticed during the field visits, photos published by gardens on social media, and by the interviewees. For example, BERE9 stated that "most of the team is German and White." Indeed, an estimate from United Nations is around one million people with "African roots" in Germany, more than 1% of the population. United Nations (2017).

[84] Gobster et al., op. cit.

[85] Karge, op. cit.

[86] Silva et al. (2014).

[87] Butterfield, op. cit.

identification in the *Berlin* questionnaires; in this city, there are community gardens focused on migrants' integration (Intercultural Gardens), but not visited. Also, in *Rio de Janeiro,* there are community gardens not included in the empirical investigation but with a White ethnic background. Further than that, the investigated gardens in *Rio de Janeiro* were inside or close to low-income communities and quilombos, areas mostly composed of Black people.[88]

Furthermore, the results presented here enlarge the existing literature in *Berlin* and *Rio de Janeiro* by researching food acceptability also being realized through a common activity of **agroecological food production (regarding no use of artificial chemicals, fertilizers, pesticides, etc.)**. This is a positive finding that can be generally applied to community gardens because of their link to sustainable food production respecting nature.

5.4 Food Sustainability

The final part of the analysis indicates a relationship between the investigated urban food sharing activities in *Berlin* and *Rio de Janeiro* community gardens and economic, social, and environmental food **sustainability** (long-term food availability and accessibility). The efficiency in resource utilization guides sustainable agriculture, proactive efforts to preserve, safeguard, and enrich natural resources, protection and enhancement of rural livelihoods, equity, and social well-being, strengthening the resilience of individuals, communities, and ecosystems, and responsible and effective governance mechanisms.

In *both cities*, the **sharing of the excess foodstuff** avoids food waste, representing better efficiency in resource utilization. The **difference** between them is that in *Berlin,* excess of products is not a regular fact due to conditions already discussed on food availability, especially in recreative or experimental individual plots, where there is not much space for growing food. In *Rio de Janeiro,* the foodstuff "excess" is easily absorbed because of an already mentioned high demand and favorable food growing conditions. For example, in the gardens within a school, children can bring home fresh food.

In **common** among the investigated cities, there is also long-term food availability and accessibility by **gifting and swapping foodstuff.** These activities are an alternative to foodstuff commodification and support maintaining local food traditions. The **deviation** is that in *Berlin,* the gardens have less interconnection than in *Rio de Janeiro.* Illustrating this, *Berlin*'s participants almost did not register for food or seed swapping. Even so, it is possible to affirm that the exchange breaks a garden's isolation of skills in courses or workshops or supports common causes with other gardens, such as those related to climate justice or against closing a garden, which are not daily activities.

[88] Zenker (2008).

In **contrast**, in *Rio de Janeiro*, almost all participants registered food exchanging foodstuff and food skills between gardens. One possibility to **explain** this difference is that most of the studied gardens are under the same management and goals of Hortas Cariocas. Then, getting in touch with other gardens directly or using the support of an integrator agent is easier. This is useful to overcome daily difficulties, such as the delay of the city hall in providing material or finding a solution for plagues, so the solution can be found in solidarity and sharing. For instance, when there is a problem with an insect in a garden, this person learns how other gardens are dealing with that to share the knowledge as a common resource. In many cases, the request for help or the offer of overproduction happens through social media (WhatsApp group). For instance, they also share discoveries to improve the irrigation system or soil quality.[89] This also occurs among gardens unrelated to the city hall within the different networks for daily activities and common interests, such as legal creations and bureaucratic problems. The local examples are the Carioca Network of Urban Agriculture (Rede Carioca de Agricultura Urbana, or Rede CAU),[90] West Zone Solidarity Network (Teia de Solidariedade da Zona Oeste),[91] and Advice and Services for Alternative Agriculture Projects (AS-PTA—Assessoria e Serviços a Projetos em Agricultura Alternativa).[92]

Moreover, in *both cities,* there is the **provision of (public) spaces for growing by the transformation of vacant land**, which is a crucial sustainability tool from three points of view: economy, society, and environment.

Concerning *social sustainability,* there is the case of community building and a sense of belonging.[93] This is crucial for integrating new residents in *Berlin*, especially during the COVID-19 pandemic. For example, a gardener reported, "I spend significantly more time in the garden, and I felt very connected to the place because it was the only place I could meet up with people. We could be outside and have a distance between each other. The pandemic affected my relationship with the garden, but of course, the relationship to everything in my life."[94] The sense of connection to the resource and belonging to the common land across neighborhoods was noticed by an *expert* in *Rio de Janeiro*:

> Many women in the agroecology movement did not understand why we would plant in gardens from other neighborhoods. "Wow, what are we going to do?" they asked, and I answered, "We are going to plant like we plant in our region." Then, we started to provoke the agroecology movement by looking at this issue. Why do we think we do not have any relation to the other neighborhood? Why do we think that the people in the favela face the police in one way, and we face it in another way? Why do we think there are different issues? And that is the question, right? They are Black and poor women, too; our land is the same land they plant. The soil color is black here and there. The mother who suffers from a shooting and sees her son on the ground bloody, killed by the police is the same mother who

[89] RIOE8. Doctoral dissertation study. [Interview to Felipe Jardim]. Berlin/Rio de Janeiro, 2024.

[90] Rede Carioca de Agricultura Urbana.

[91] Wikifavelas (2023).

[92] AS-PTA.

[93] Gobster et al., op. cit., Karge, op. cit., Steuri et al., op. cit.

[94] BERG9. Doctoral dissertation study. [Interview to Felipe Jardim]. Berlin/Rio de Janeiro, 2024.

suffers here with the son who also suffers violence from the police. It is the same mother, it is the same soil, it is the same people. And then, we start to encourage the agroecology movement to think about urban agriculture in a much broader way from the perspective of Black women.[95]

The above citation is also notable and relevant for being a surprising result related to **gender empowerment**. In Quilombo das Caboclas, there are only female gardeners, and they created a network to prevent and report violence against women.

An *expert* in *Rio de Janeiro* illustrated another example of social sharing of the same goal:

I see political empowerment as a huge advantage of the garden for people to see themselves a little more represented and to be able to see things that bring effective changes. [...]. It greatly strengthens individuals and collectives in the territories. I think it is the beginning of a process. Once, we started a vegetable garden, agroforestry, in a square in Campo Grande, and many people arrived to get involved. The plants also did not cause confusion between political parties; different people sometimes got together and started a relationship based on that common goal of building something.[96]

In *both cities,* there is a dispute against the commodification of resources. This includes the food,[97] as illustrated by a *gardener* in *Berlin*: "Everything that we grow is communal. So, nobody has their private vegetable or something. Buy, yeah, if one goes to these regular days, like, on Mondays, there is a raised bed day, and wherever there is something to harvest, usually it gets shared between the people working."[98] There is also the view that community gardens are common land, as exposed by an *expert* in *Berlin*:

He [the district manager of parks] refused to speak about community gardens in public parks. He said, "This is privatization of land. I will not do it. Never ever this will happen to me." So, in the end, he was posted somewhere else, but only last year or this year. I think, and now there is a new manager, which is completely different. He is more open to it, of course. He has some limits to his action also, but he is now saying, "OK, yeah, a community garden can be part of the public park on public green land because this is a benefit or the people want it, they go there, they enjoy it. That is what the public green should be for." Of course, we have to speak about rules like opening times, do you have to pay for things there, or these questions about the public infrastructure, but he is open to doing something, so a change of person sometimes changes a lot.[99]

Additionally, community gardens are fighting the privatization of public space (commodification):[100]

Urban community gardens create new green places and access to urban nature; they enable participation in urban design. They encourage self-organization and healthy eating and promote communication and cooperation between gardeners, the administration, research,

---

95 RIOE6. Doctoral dissertation study. [Interview to Felipe Jardim]. Berlin/Rio de Janeiro, 2024.

96 RIOE7. Doctoral dissertation study. [Interview to Felipe Jardim]. Berlin/Rio de Janeiro, 2024.

97 Gordillo and Jeróimo (2013, p. 4).

98 BERG1. Doctoral dissertation study. [Interview to Felipe Jardim]. Berlin/Rio de Janeiro, 2024.

99 BERE3. Doctoral dissertation study. [Interview to Felipe Jardim]. Berlin/Rio de Janeiro, 2024.

100 Colding et al. (2013, pp. 1039–1051).

> and politics. Urban community gardens are outdoor neighborhood centers and can be shelters for people in need. They are a counter-argument to the increasing privatization of public space. The gardens preserve values for the city that are difficult to measure in monetary terms. So they are hardly competitive when it comes to inner-city areas. Too many gardens are threatened, and creating new community gardens can be difficult.[101]

Furthermore, from the long-term perspective, gardens in *both cities* had to deal with the social barrier of acceptance of the garden's value, which is representatively broken by vandalism, stolen materials, and irregular waste disposal.

On *economic sustainability*, there is the case of savings to maintain the area, and the place becomes an area to generate income and work. For instance, in *Berlin*, the Evangelische Friedhofsverband Berlin Stadtmitte (EVFBS) is the landowner of a 7.5-hectare cemetery, the New St. Jacobi Friedhofs. With a decreasing number of funerals and religious affiliations (resulting in less income from taxes or donations and fewer human resources) in the last decades, the cemetery was closed in 2016. Maintaining the area clean and safe was difficult, so the space was open for different uses, such as the Prinzessinengarten.[102] A similar process happened with Elisabeet Garden, located in St.-Elisabeth-Friedhof II, owned by the Evangelische Friedhofsverband Berlin Stadtmitte.

In *Rio de Janeiro,* work opportunities were already debated on the topic of food accessibility. However, it is important to consider that the long-term economic perspective of Hortas Cariocas depends on public funding and monetary compensation due to damages to nature.[103] Moreover, the political administration is crucial due to the lack of legal guarantees specific to Hortas Cariocas.[104] In addition to the city hall payment, the extra income for selling vegetables depends not only on nature but also on seeds, clean water accessibility, soil health, tools, etc.

Regarding *environmental sustainability*, there is the case of preserving or creating green areas, environmental education, resource regeneration (compost for soil), and attention to waste (water).[105] This was observed by Allmende-Kontor, *Berlin*, during daily care of water and by experiments. From 2017 to 2021, the "Water Management Experiment" was carried out in the garden by the Working group Brandenburg-Berlin Water Management (Arbeitsgemeinschaft Brandenburgische-Berliner Wasserver) and Humboldt University.[106] There were also experiments with soybeans and beekeeping.[107]

In *Rio de Janeiro*, one of the program's pillars of Hortas Cariocas is preventing deforestation by avoiding the illegal and unsafe occupation of green areas as housing alternatives for low-income families. Following the same logic, an *expert* stated that one of the garden's areas "had rubble, a lot of rubbish, hundreds of stolen burnt-out

---

[101] Allmende-Kontor (2023).

[102] Prinzessinnengarten.

[103] Instituto Escolhas (2022).

[104] Jardim et al. (2023).

[105] Colding et al., op. cit., Steuri et al., op. cit.

[106] Allmende-Kontor (2023), op. cit.

[107] Davies et al. (2019, pp. 8–20).

cars lying around. The city council collected all that material, and we cleaned the space and transformed it there."[108]

According to a *gardener*, there is a mentality change with community gardens.

> Changes are happening. The colonialist process that took place in the country involved more than 500 years of destruction of forests. Gardens are part of raising people's awareness about this aggression that the environment has been suffering. I believe we can work to raise people's awareness to better observe nature and the environment in which they live.[109]

Finally, it is important to note that these three dimensions of sustainability are not excluding each other. Given this, as an *expert* in *Berlin* exposed that

> These small green dots in the city are important for climate change adaptation. We are facing heavy, heavy rain and hot summers in Berlin. For that we need places where water can be stored and, for example, in the garden soil and we also need small places where it is where you cool down the neighborhood, so this is, for example, the contribution of gardens and there is more effect, of course, for the social sustainability. It brings people together. It makes people more resilient against personal crises and so on to have these local networks. So, economic sustainability can create or be part of local economic networks. There are community gardens that are having, like, yeah, we are part of the local economic circles, and even though there is not a big production of food.[110]

One of the **contrasts** of providing (public) spaces for growing by transforming vacant land in *Berlin* and *Rio de Janeiro* is the long-term maintenance of the gardens. In *Berlin*, there is the threat of conflicting interests on land use, such as the ones resulting in the forced move of Himmelbeet and Peace of Land. Attending political interests, the gardens gave space for future sportive installations.

Rio de Janeiro had multiple registries on territorial disputes with criminal agents (militia/drug dealers), resulting in the garden's temporary or permanent closing and loss of territory. The **reason** would be that with the gardens, people can have an opportunity to be far from drugs, earn some money, and change their lives, as pointed out by a *gardener:*

> Homeless people also need to work. If you need it, we put it to work. Instead of being on the street doing something bad, the person is doing something good, right? The person is working, helping people, leaving marginalization, earning that money, being away from drugs, etc… So I think these gardens are changing people.[111]

An *expert* in *Rio de Janeiro* also noticed the sense of a relation between garden and peace: "Sometimes some residents have the initiative and the desire to put a vegetable garden there to, let's say, ease these tensions, urban violence."[112] This was noticed by the literature[113] and reported by the media[114] on Hortas Cariocas of Manguinhos.

---

[108] RIOE10. Doctoral dissertation study. [Interview to Felipe Jardim]. Berlin/Rio de Janeiro, 2024.

[109] RIOG8. Doctoral dissertation study. [Interview to Felipe Jardim]. Berlin/Rio de Janeiro, 2024.

[110] BERE3. Doctoral dissertation study. [Interview to Felipe Jardim]. Berlin/Rio de Janeiro, 2024.

[111] RIOG4. Doctoral dissertation study. [Interview to Felipe Jardim]. Berlin/Rio de Janeiro, 2024.

[112] RIOE8. Doctoral dissertation study. [Interview to Felipe Jardim]. Berlin/Rio de Janeiro, 2024.

[113] Magalhães, op. cit., Rekow (2015), op. cit., Rekow (2016), op. cit.

[114] Lichterbeck (2021).

According to the news from 2022, the garden was a starting point for police interventions against drug dealers. Then, the criminals decided to build houses as a barrier to mobility and use concrete on the soil to promote parties. With the size of four football camps, the urban garden is famous for being the biggest in Latin America. It is responsible for supporting 800 families and producing around 3 tons of food annually, but the criminal action has already reduced 20% of the production.[115]

As mentioned in the literature review, **food sustainability** (long-term *food availability* and *accessibility*) can be identified in community gardens of *both cities*. Nevertheless, the emphasis in *Berlin* was on the *social*[116] and *environmental*[117] *sustainability* dimensions. In *Berlin*, the sustainable upkeep of a food cultivation site faced jeopardy when the state, often as the landowner, developed new interests in land use, typically for recreational purposes, leading to impending threats and compulsory relocations.[118] In *Rio de Janeiro*, previous studies present the importance of *social, economic, and environmental sustainability* dimensions as food security and a peaceful approach to facing risks due to criminality.[119]

This research indicates similar results in *both cities* by **sharing the excess foodstuff, gifting or swapping foodstuff, and providing (public) spaces for growing by transforming vacant land.** The unexpected findings were in *Berlin* the relation to many citations to job opportunities as contributing to *economic sustainability*, and in *Rio de Janeiro*, the *social sustainability* by gender empowerment in the case of Quilombo das Caboclas. However, given the limited sample, these findings cannot be extrapolated to all gardens.

5.5 Chapter Resume

Given the amount of information presented and discussed in this chapter, this section presents a resume to the answer to the research question[120] in four parts:

a. The **similar** community gardens' urban food sharing activities related to **food availability** in *Berlin* and *Rio de Janeiro* are (a) transforming vacant land in (public) open spaces for growing on a not-for-profit basis, including the offer of acquiring food in exchange for labor; (b) establishment of a gardens' restaurant or café; and (c) learning and practicing nutrition, how to co-produce food, identifying places where gleaning or foraging might occur, and swapping seeds.

---

[115] G1.

[116] Colding et al. (2013, pp. 1039–1051).

[117] Gobster et al., op. cit.

[118] Davies et al. (2019, pp. 8–20).

[119] Rekow (2015), op. cit., Rekow (2016), op. cit.

[120] How do notions of right to food connect to food sharing activities in community gardens in Berlin and Rio de Janeiro, and, within and between cities, how to explain these connections' similarities and differences?.

From the above result, it is important to note that *both cities* have community gardens as public policy (*Gemeinschaftsgarten-Programm* in *Berlin* and *Hortas Cariocas* in *Rio de Janeiro*) institutionally situated in the Environmental office. Also, they faced territorial conflicts before and after establishing a community garden.

What is **different** is the policy's purpose and the challenges related to opening a space. In *Berlin*, the program aims to "secure existing gardens and promote new gardens."[121] The community gardens are seen through the lens of social, educational, and environmental contributions. Given this, the food availability is regarding the freedom of self-production. *Rio de Janeiro* aims to offer the "service of technical assistance and promotion of urban agriculture initiatives in the city."[122] Their gardens are a source of food to sell (income generation) and to eat (nutrition) by food gifting to gardeners and neighbors or complementing meals at the school kitchen. Given that, further than the freedom of choice to self-produce food, there is an important contribution to food availability in the sense of supplementing dietary needs and food distribution.

The possible **explanation** for the difference is that *Berlin*'s gardens have "irrelevant" production. In contrast, *Germany* has low food insecurity and high city development, and the interviewees did not mention difficulties finding food in the supermarkets. In *Rio de Janeiro,* there is a large amount of food production but also high demand in unequal city development, and it is situated in a country with intermediate food insecurity. Moreover, segregation on food *availability* and *access* is a serious problem widely identified in the empirical data collected.

Regarding food availability, the **literature** proposes using unoccupied land as a strategic method, primarily *not focused* on food-related objectives but rather on converting or averting the formation of wastelands and dumping sites[123] and on social justice and environmental sustainability.[124] In *Rio de Janeiro*, these are combined motivations when discussing the suppression of drug-related operations, encompassing sales, acquisitions, consumption, and illegal house constructions in green areas.[125]

The results regarding *Berlin* and many cases in *Rio de Janeiro* presented **coincident lines to the literature, except** for the part where the findings about *Rio de Janeiro* pointed out that community gardens *focus* on food-related goals. A possible **motivation** for the variant result is that most of the places investigated in *Rio de Janeiro* are part of Hortas Cariocas, where food security is a central pillar, and gardens unrelated to the city hall share the same goal. Nonetheless, it is important to exercise **caution** in drawing broad conclusions, as these findings may not necessarily apply to a wider array of community gardens in *Rio de Janeiro* due to the limitations in gathering empirical data within this study.

---

[121] Giseke, Reis, Mees.

[122] Rio de Janeiro.

[123] Magalhães, op. cit., Véron, op. cit.

[124] Rekow (2015), op. cit., Rekow (2016), op. cit.

[125] Magalhães, op. cit.

In summary, this research underscores the multifaceted role of community gardens in urban environments and the contextual variations in their goals and impacts. The **implications** highlight the significance of recognizing and supporting community gardens to address food accessibility and other urban challenges while also acknowledging the uniqueness of each city's circumstances and policy objectives.

b. The **similar** community gardens' urban food sharing activities related to **food accessibility** in *Berlin* and *Rio de Janeiro* are (a) eating self-produced food, sharing foodstuff for free, buying foodstuff for a symbolic price, or acquiring foodstuff by swapping, and (b) income generation opportunities by gardening, and administrative work, and vegetable sales.

The interesting **contrast** among cities is that economic savings in *Berlin* were just mentioned by a few interviewees, and when it happened, it was related to inexpressive savings. In *Rio de Janeiro*, the savings were also mentioned as symbolic. Still, some interviewees expressed that it was relevant for the household income of unemployed people and those living in food insecurity. The **justification** could have the same socioeconomic ground already mentioned regarding food availability. The additional scenario is the COVID-19 pandemic. The crisis brought more social inequalities and vulnerability to *Brazil*,[126] including *Rio de Janeiro*,[127] affecting many people's purchasing power and low-income communities' lives.[128] Consequently, food insecurity levels in *Rio de Janeiro* rose,[129] and *Brazil* reappeared on the FAO hunger map (2022). At the same time, most of the interviewees in *Berlin* said that the pandemic affected only their social life, and one of the city hall program's concerns is to activate community gardens as a strategy to access shared areas, allowing freedom, "especially in times of crisis like the COVID-19 pandemic."[130]

On income generation, the **dissimilarity** is that in *Berlin*, the work payment was related to undertaking administrative tasks typically filled by *experts*. Conversely, in *Rio de Janeiro*, the registered income generation options were selling vegetables and receiving financial support for gardening activities in Hortas Cariocas, primarily occupied by *gardeners*. *Gardeners* in *Berlin* were usually volunteers without any financial subside, and *experts* in *Rio de Janeiro* were not paid for their work in gardening but for other roles, such as being university professors, city hall employees, or technical assistants at non-governmental organizations. This discrepancy's **elucidation** can be attributed to most interviewed *gardeners* in *Rio de Janeiro* who were part of Hortas Cariocas, a program dedicated to providing remunerative opportunities for individuals facing social vulnerability (lacking formal employment ties) in a city.[131]

The **previous studies** on physical and economic food accessibility indicated that in *Berlin*, the gardens serve as a symbolic addition to people's daily food intake over time

---

[126] Silveira (2022).

[127] Regueira, op. cit.

[128] Agência Brasil (2020).

[129] Oliveira, Galdo, op. cit.

[130] Giseke, Reis, Mees.

[131] Rio de Janeiro.

by subsistence gardening.[132] On the other hand, in *Rio de Janeiro*, the literature[133] examines the role of community gardens in mitigating, though not eliminating, food insecurity challenges arising from the absence of markets and street fairs, as well as due to the economic hardships, especially experienced by Black communities (referred to as food apartheid).[134] This research **contradicts** only the part regarding the "subsistence character" of agriculture in *Berlin*. The argument is grounded on the information that all questionnaire's participants in this city revealed to **buy food** from supermarkets, and they are not dependent on the garden for daily nutritional needs.

Furthermore, this study **adds value to the current body of literature** through a comprehensive investigation of food accessibility due to the potential income-generating opportunities within community gardens of *both cities*. Nevertheless, it is essential to consider the potential for **bias** resulting from the relatively limited sample size, which could restrict the broader applicability of the results. This limitation arises from funding constraints in both cities, where gardens exclusively rely on voluntary efforts.

In conclusion, this research provides valuable **insights** into the role of community gardens in addressing food accessibility and income generation, highlighting their significance in urban environments. The **implications** emphasize the need for supportive policies and tailored approaches that consider local conditions and challenges to maximize the positive impact of community gardening initiatives.

c. The **similar** community gardens' urban food sharing activities related to **food acceptability** in *Berlin* and *Rio de Janeiro* by (a) agroecological food production (regarding no use of artificial chemicals, fertilizers, pesticides, etc.) and (b) knowledge transfer about food culture. The most engaging aspect of the data is the ethnic background **distinction** in each city. This is relevant to understand what particular culture the food sharing is about. In *Berlin,* the general profile of *gardeners* and *experts* was composed of White people, while in *Rio de Janeiro,* there was a strong influence of Black people and some participation of Indigenous ethnicities, but almost exclusively among *gardeners.* Most *experts* in *Rio de Janeiro* declared themselves as White people. The dissimilarity between the countries can be **attributed** to their unique historical and ethnic compositions.

So far, very little has been found in the literature on the acceptability of food within community gardens. In *Berlin*, this connection primarily revolved around disseminating information and education about food culture, with a particular emphasis on imparting knowledge about food preparation and consumption, especially among children.[135] It also promoted the preservation of culinary traditions and enabled individuals to grow plants native to their countries or cities of origin.[136] In contrast,

---

[132] Halder, op. cit., Steuri and Vignola, op. cit.

[133] Beck (2018, pp. 9–383), Zanotto, op. cit., Lima, op. cit., Siniscalchi, op. cit.

[134] Zanotto, op. cit., Lima, op. cit., Siniscalchi, op. cit.

[135] Gobster et al., op. cit.

[136] Karge, op. cit.

Rio de Janeiro's cultural connection centered on the ancestral wisdom of medicinal plants.[137]

This study discovered **corroborative** evidence supporting the existing **literature** regarding the food acceptability by chemical pesticide disuse and the knowledge transfer about food culture. A remarkable discovery of this study was identifying elements from the literature of *Berlin* in *Rio de Janeiro* and vice versa. On the one hand, this included data's reference in *Berlin* to ancestral wisdom related to plants and cultivation techniques. On the other hand, there was evidence of food education programs for both children **and adults** in *Rio de Janeiro.* The research findings also **contributed to the broader literature** on ethnic backgrounds and migration, shedding light on significant factors that differentiate food cultures. Nevertheless, it is crucial to acknowledge the potential **biases** inherent in these responses due to limitations in our data collection methods. Notably, the absence of ethnic identification in the *Berlin* questionnaires is a significant constraint. *Berlin* hosts community gardens promoting the integration of migrants, such as Intercultural Gardens, which were not included in this doctoral study. Additionally, in the case of *Rio de Janeiro,* the empirical investigation primarily had access to community gardens within areas predominantly inhabited by Black communities (Favelas and Urban Communities).

To sum up, the research sheds light on the complex interplay of cultural factors within the context of community gardens and their impact on urban food sharing activities. It **indicates** the significance of understanding the role of ethnicity and cultural backgrounds in shaping food practices and highlights the importance of robust data collection and interdisciplinary research perspectives.

d. The **similar** community gardens' urban food sharing activities concerning **food sustainability** in *Berlin* and *Rio de Janeiro* are (a) sharing of the excess foodstuff, (b) gifting or swapping foodstuff; and (c) provision of (public) spaces for growing by the transformation of vacant land.

The most important result was social, economic, and environmental sustainability perspectives of providing (public) spaces for growing by transforming vacant land. During this process, in *both cities,* there is the *social* development of the belonging sense, community integration, and the **fight against commodification of resources and the city**. They also face problems in social relations with non-gardeners, such as vandalism and acceptance of the garden's importance from neighbors and politicians. The **difference** is that political disputes already resulted in gardens being forced to move to *Berlin*, while in *Rio de Janeiro,* the land tenure issue is related to peace infringement involving militia, drug dealers, and police. The possible **explanation** is the conflict of interest on the urban land with particularities in each city. On *economic* findings, in addition to the job creation, *Berlin*'s cases of community gardens in former or current cemeteries are unexpected data related to saving costs with the maintenance of vacant areas. *Rio de Janeiro* calls attention to the fact that the public funding for Hortas Cariocas depends on political decisions, and no specific law regulates the program. Regarding the environmental dimension data,

[137] Silva et al., op. cit.

both cities preserve or create green areas, develop environmental education, resource regeneration (compost for soil), and pay attention to waste (water).

As highlighted in the **literature**, both cities' community gardens exhibit characteristics of food sustainability. However, *Berlin*'s gardens emphasize the *social* and *environmental* dimensions of sustainability. In the case of *Berlin*, the sustainable maintenance of food cultivation sites has been jeopardized when the state, often acting as the landowner, shifts its interests towards alternative land use, frequently for recreational purposes. This shift results in imminent threats to the gardens and necessitates compulsory relocations.[138] Conversely, in *Rio de Janeiro*, prior research underscores the significance of multiple sustainability dimensions, including *social, economic, and environmental* aspects, as essential components of food security and a peaceful strategy for mitigating risks associated with criminality.[139]

This study yields **approximate** findings to **prior research** on food sustainability and goes a bit further. In the case of *Berlin*, the **contribution** is regarding the *economic* aspect of garden work. In *Rio de Janeiro*, the literature improvement concerns the social dimension of gender empowerment. Nevertheless, the restricted sample size makes it impossible to generalize these findings to all community gardens.

Closing this chapter, this research provides valuable **insights** into community gardens' role in promoting community integration, resistance against commodification, job positions (gardening as professional work), and alternative resource management (urban commons). These insights can inform policy development regarding the scenario in each city—and abroad—such as observed in the following chapter.

References

Agência Brasil (2020) Covid-19: 87% dos moradores de favelas conhecem alguém que adoeceu. https://agenciabrasil.ebc.com.br/geral/noticia/2020-09/na-favela-quase-todo-mundo-conhece-alguem-que-teve-covid-19. Accessed 09 Jun 2024

Allmende-Kontor (2023) Chronik. https://www.allmende-kontor.de/der-garten/allmende-kontor-chronik/. Accessed 29 May 2024

Allmende-Kontor. FAQS—Unser Garten—ABC. https://www.allmende-kontor.de/der-garten/faqs/. Accessed 18 Aug 2024

AS-PTA—Agricultura Familiar e Agroecologia. Site institucional. http://aspta.org.br/. Accessed 11 Jun 2024

Bauhütte Kreuzberg. Willkommen Bei Der Bauhütte Kreuzberg. https://bauhuette-kreuzberg.de/. Accessed 18 Aug 2024

Beck V (2018) Iniciativas urbano sustentáveis no Rio de Janeiro: a experiência da horta carioca do Jardim Anil. In: Direito da Regularização Fundiária Urbana Sustentável

Berarcurb (2016) Tempelhofer Feld. https://www.architektur-urbanistik.berlin/index.php?threads/tempelhofer-feld.245. Accessed 09 Oct 2024

Berlin. Government. Berliner Gemeinschaftsgarten Programm. https://www.berlin.de/gemeinschaftsgaertnern/_assets/programm/gemeinschaftsgarten-programm.pdf?ts=1677511936. Accessed 28 Aug 2024

[138] Davies et al. (2019), op. cit.

[139] Rekow (2015), op. cit. Rekow (2016), op. cit.

Braswell TH (2018) Fresh food, new faces: community gardening as ecological gentrification in St. Louis, Missouri. Agric Hum Values 35(4):809–822. https://www.webofscience.com/wos/woscc/full-record/WOS:000447701800005. Accessed 16 May 2024

Butterfield K (2021) Framing Food Access: do community gardens inadvertently reproduce inequality? Health Educ Behav 48(2):160–168. https://pubmed.ncbi.nlm.nih.gov/32806951/. Accessed 16 May 2024

Centro e Inteligência Em Orgânicos (2022) Brazil will have the largest urban garden in the world by 2024. https://ciorganicos.com.br/noticia/brasil-tera-o-maior-horta-urbana-do-mundo-ate-2024/. Accessed 26 Aug 2024

City Index. https://cdindex.net/. Accessed 18 Aug 2024

Colding J et al (2013) Urban green commons: insights on urban common property systems. Glob Environ Change. 23(5):1039–1051. https://www.sciencedirect.com/science/article/abs/pii/S0959378013000800?via%3Dihub. Accessed 16 May 2024

Correia AF (ed) Pesquisa, teoria e prática em torno da Lei Federal n. 13.465/2017. Editar, Juiz de Fora-MG, v 1, pp 9–383

Davies A et al (2019) Food sharing initiatives, and food democracy: practice and policy in three European cities. Polit Gov 7(4):8–20. https://www.cogitatiopress.com/politicsandgovernance/article/view/2090. Accessed 26 May 2024

Der Tagesspiegel Online (2019) Scharfe Kritik an Vorstoß der FDP: so reagiert die Berliner Politik auf die Idee eines neuen Tempelhof-Volksentscheids. https://www.tagesspiegel.de/berlin/so-reagiert-die-berliner-politik-auf-die-idee-eines-neuen-tempelhof-volksentscheids-4678597.html. Accessed 09 Oct 2024

FAO (2008) An introduction to the basic concepts of food security. Food security information for action practical guides. https://www.fao.org/3/al936e/al936e00.pdf. Accessed 05 July 2024

FAO (2010) The right to adequate food. Geneva, p 5. https://www.ohchr.org/sites/default/files/Documents/Publications/FactSheet34en.pdf. Accessed 05 July 2024

FAO (2022) Urban and peri-urban agriculture sourcebook. Rome, p 16. fao.org/3/cb9722en/cb9722en.pdf. Accessed 13 Sept 2024

Freundeskreis Videoclips. Aktion: Squat Tempelhof Airport/Tempelhofer Feld. https://www.youtube.com/watch?v=v-4SEp4X8cI. Accessed 09 Oct 2024

G1. Vídeo Horta Comunitária está sendo tomada pelo tráfico em Manguinhos. https://g1.globo.com/rj/rio-de-janeiro/rj1/video/horta-comunitaria-esta-sendo-tomada-pelo-trafico-em-manguinhos-10992135.ghtml. Accessed 16 Jun 2024

GCAP UCR (2020) Environmental justice: food deserts. https://www.gcapucr.com/environmental-justice-food-deserts. Accessed 20 Aug 2024

Giseke U, Reis L, Mees C. Berliner Gemeinschaftsgarten Programm. https://www.berlin.de/gemeinschaftsgaertnern/_assets/programm/gemeinschaftsgarten-programm.pdf?ts=1677511936. Accessed 28 Aug 2024

Global Alliance for Food Security. Global food and nutrition security dashboard. https://www.gafs.info/country-profiles/?state=Advice&country=BRA&indicator=IPCC. Accessed 18 Aug 2024

Gobster PH, Stewart SI, Bengston DN (2004) The social aspects of landscape change: protecting open space under the pressure of development. Landsc Urban Plan. 69(2):149–151. https://www.sciencedirect.com/journal/landscape-and-urban-planning/vol/69/issue/2. Accessed 23 May 2024

Gordillo G, Jerónimo OM (2013) Food security and sovereignty. Canada, p 4. https://www.fao.org/3/ax736e/ax736e.pdf. Accessed 02 July 2024

Halder S (2017) Gemeinsam die Hände dreckig machen: Aktionsforschungen im aktivistischen Kontext urbaner Gärten und kollektiver Kartierungen. Dissertation an der Freien Universität Berlin, p 169. https://katalog.dnb.de/EN/resource.html?hit=2&t=gemeinsam+Landwirtschaft+&fD=fmt.hss&key=all&sp=dnb&th=5&tk=F83EFEEC49340E77BD8177FD0B844C927AD17C35&pr=0&sortA=bez&sortD=-dat&v=plist. Accessed 23 May 2024

Harvey D (1980) Social justice and the city. Hucitec, São Paulo

Hora do Povo (2021) Disputa por ossos no Rio expõe drama da fome. https://horadopovo.com.br/disputa-por-ossos-no-rio-expoe-drama-da-fome-no-brasil-sob-bolsonaro/. Accessed 19 Aug 2024

Instituto Escolhas (2022) Políticas Públicas de Agricultura Urbana. São Paulo. https://100politicas.escolhas.org/estudo/programa-hortas-cariocas/. Accessed 18 Aug 2024

Jardim F et al (2023) How is a community urban garden program related to the law? Analysis of Hortas Cariocas (Rio de Janeiro, Brazil). St. Thomas J Law Public Policy 16(1). https://ir.stthomas.edu/ustjlpp/vol16/iss1/9/. Accessed 13 Sept 2024

Karge T (2015) Neue urbane Landwirtschaft: Eine theoretische Verortung und Akteursanalyse der Initiative Himmelbeet im Berliner Wedding. Universitätsverlag der TU Berlin, Berlin. https://d-nb.info/1156274923/34. Accessed 23 May 2024

Kiesel Von (2019) Langer Weg bis zum Referendum: Dritter Tempelhof-Volksentscheid geplant. https://www.tagesspiegel.de/berlin/dritter-tempelhof-volksentscheid-geplant-4131568.html. Accessed 09 Oct 2024

Kiesel Von (2020) Exklusiv FDP plant 12.000 Wohnungen: Initiative will neuen Volksentscheid zum Tempelhofer Feld Geht es nach dem Willen der FDP, soll erneut über eine Bebauung des Tempelhofer Feldes abgestimmt werden. Ein Antrag wurde an den Innensenator verschickt. https://www.tagesspiegel.de/berlin/initiative-will-neuen-volksentscheid-zum-tempelhofer-feld-5047498.html. Accessed 09 Oct 2024

Lichterbeck P (2021) Uma horta que muda vidas. https://www.dw.com/pt-br/uma-horta-que-muda-vidas/a-58194269. Accessed 26 May 2024

Lima C (2019) Agriculturas na cidade do Rio de Janeiro: dicotomias e as especificidades da agricultura urbana. Dissertação, Instituto de Ciências Sociais Aplicadas, Universidade Federal Rural do Rio de Janeiro, Seropédica, p 119 et seq. https://tede.ufrrj.br/jspui/bitstream/jspui/5596/2/2019%20-%20Caren%20Freitas%20de%20Lima.pdf. Accessed 23 May 2024

Lopes L, Brêtas P (2022) "Eu e meus filhos comemos comida que estava há um mês vencida": homem relata busca por sustento em caminhão de lixo. https://extra.globo.com/economia-e-financas/eu-meus-filhos-comemos-comida-que-estava-ha-um-mes-vencida-homem-relata-busca-por-sustento-em-caminhao-de-lixo-25553698.html. Accessed 28 Aug 2024

Magalhães MJ (2021) Hortas Comunitárias in the Favelas of Rio de Janeiro: how new ideas are adopted and spread across communities. In: Trapani F et al (eds) Advanced studies in efficient environmental design and city planning. Springer, Cham. https://link.springer.com/chapter/ https://doi.org/10.1007/978-3-030-65181-7_21. Accessed 20 May 2024

Maricato E (1997) Housing and city, 7th edn. Atual, São Paulo

Martinez-Alier J (2014) The environmentalism of the poor. Geoforum 54:239–241. https://www.sciencedirect.com/science/article/pii/S0016718513000912. Accessed 19 Aug 2024

Oliveira N, Galdo R (2022) No Rio, o número de pessoas que não têm o que comer aumentou 400% nos últimos quatro anos. https://oglobo.globo.com/rio/noticia/2022/06/no-rio-o-numero-de-pessoas-que-nao-tem-o-que-comer-aumentou-400percent-nos-ultimos-quatro-anos.ghtml. Accessed 18 July 2024

Prinzessinnengarten Kollektiv Berlin. https://prinzessinnengarten-kollektiv.net/ueber-uns/faq/. Accessed 19 Aug 2024

Prinzessinnengarten. Der Neue St. Jacobi Friedhof. https://prinzessinnengarten-kollektiv.net/ueber-uns/standort/. Accessed 16 May 2024

Prinzessinnengarten. Wolfundwaldkauz. Wolf und Waldkauz: Wilde Küche. https://prinzessinnengarten-kollektiv.net/wolf-und-waldkauz-wilde-kueche/. Accessed 22 Aug 2024

Rede Carioca de Agricultura Urbana. Rede CAU. http://ppad.org.br/coletivo/rede-cau-rede-carioca-de-agricultura-urbana. Accessed 13 Jun 2024

Regueira C (2021) Número de pobres no RJ aumenta em 745 mil durante a pandemia e atinge 10,5% da população, diz FGV. https://g1.globo.com/rj/rio-de-janeiro/noticia/2021/02/25/numero-de-pobres-no-rj-aumenta-em-745-mil-durante-pandemia-e-atinge-105percent-da-populacao-diz-fgv.ghtml. Accessed 20 Aug 2024

Rekow L (2015) Fighting insecurity: experiments in urban agriculture in the favelas of Rio de Janeiro. Field Actions Science Reports, vol 8. https://journals.openedition.org/factsreports/pdf/4009. Accessed 16 May 2024

Rio de Janeiro (2020) Prefeitura. Prefeitura do Rio doa mil tilápias para a comunidade de Urucânia, em Paciência. https://coronavirus.rio/noticias/prefeitura-do-rio-doa-mil-tilapias-para-a-comunidade-de-urucania-em-paciencia/. Accessed 28 Aug 2024

Rio de Janeiro. Programa de Hortas Cariocas. Prefeitura. https://100politicas.escolhas.org/estudo/programa-hortas-cariocas/. Accessed 27 Aug 2024

Silva SHC et al (2014) Plantas medicinais: tradições e saberes de mulheres de uma comunidade urbana do Rio de Janeiro, RJ, Brasil. https://www.arca.fiocruz.br/handle/icict/11037. Accessed 23 May 2024

Silveira D (2022) Extrema pobreza bate recorde no Brasil em dois anos de pandemia, diz IBGE https://g1.globo.com/economia/noticia/2022/12/02/extrema-pobreza-bate-recorde-no-brasil-em-s-anos-de-pandemia-diz-ibge.ghtml. Accessed 19 Jun 2024

Siniscalchi M (2020) Semeando o comum na metrópole contemporânea: as hortas urbanas comunitárias no Rio de Janeiro (RJ). Dissertação de Mestrado, Departamento de Geografia e Meio Ambiente, Pontifícia Universidade Católica do Rio de Janeiro, p 241 et seq. https://www.maxwell.vrac.puc-rio.br/49639/49639.PDF. Accessed 23 May 2024

Steuri B, Vignola G (2022) Towards productive and socio-natural urban landscapes: tapping urban agriculture's potential as a tool for sustainable development. Universitätsbibliothek der HafenCity Universität Hamburg (HCU), Hamburg, p 77. https://repos.hcu-hamburg.de/bitstream/hcu/650/2/2022-06-01_steuri-bettina_vignola-gionatan_masterarbeit.pdf. Accessed 23 May 2024

United Nations (2017) Statement to the media by the United Nations' Working Group of Experts on People of African Descent, on the conclusion of its official visit to Germany. https://www.ohchr.org/en/statements/2017/02/statement-media-united-nations-working-group-experts-people-african-descent. Accessed 16 May 2024

Véron O (2023) 'We're Just an ambulance at the bottom of the cliff': strategies and (a)politics of change in Berlin's community food spaces. Environ Plan A. https://journals.sagepub.com/https://doi.org/10.1177/0308518X231158101. Accessed 26 May 2024

Wikifavelas (2023) Teia de Solidariedade da Zona Oeste. https://wikifavelas.com.br/index.php/Teia_de_Solidariedade_da_Zona_Oeste. Accessed 10 Jun 2024

World Bank. Glossary. https://databank.worldbank.org/metadataglossary/gender-statistics/series/SI.POV.GINI#:~:text=Metadata%20Glossary&text=The%20Gini%20index%20measures%20the,of%20100%20implies%20perfect%20inequality/. Accessed 18 Aug 2024

Zanotto LC (2016) Semeando o almoço na laje: manual de implementação de hortas urbanas em comunidades de baixa renda, uma alternativa frente a problemas de desigualdade social. (Dissertação) Programa de Pós-Graduação em Práticas em Desenvolvimento Sustentável, Universidade Federal Rural do Rio de Janeiro. https://tede.ufrrj.br/handle/jspui/1397. Accessed 23 May 2024

Zenker A (2008) Negros são maioria nas favelas, segundo estudo do Ipea. https://memoria.ebc.com.br/agenciabrasil/noticia/2008-12-16/negros-sao-maioria-nas-favelas-segundo-estudo-do-ipea. Accessed 16 May 2024

Chapter 6
Conclusions and Policy Recommendations

6.1 The Answer to the Research Question

How do notions of the right to food connect to food sharing activities in *Berlin* and *Rio de Janeiro* community gardens, and, within and between cities, how do we explain these connections' similarities and differences? This study confirmed the research hypothesis that urban food-sharing activities in community gardens are closely linked to the right to food through dimensions of *availability, accessibility, acceptability, and sustainability*, while also reflecting the specific socioeconomic contexts and urban challenges of each city.

Multiple **similarities** were identified in the activities of *gardeners* and *experts* in both cities, highlighting their contributions to urban commons and food-related rights. This can be exemplified by transforming vacant land into (public) open spaces for growing on a not-for-profit basis, swapping seeds, and knowledge transfer about food culture. However, a few **variations** emerged within and between cities, such as the presence of garden cafés or differing approaches to income generation. These differences are influenced by factors like food insecurity, poverty, unemployment, and distinct urban dynamics, such as criminality, shaping the roles and goals of community gardens in each city.

The **only completely compatible** commoning activity (in other words, urban food sharing without any exception or dissimilarity) among all investigated gardens is the **agroecological food production** (regarding no use of artificial chemicals, fertilizers, pesticides, etc.). This implies that the perfect link of the right to food between *both cities* is (only) one activity related to *food acceptability*. This also means that the socioeconomic background and the city's particularities are *irrelevant* in this very specific situation.

What could explain this is the ordinary agroecological *action* in community gardens and the application of theoretical background *knowledge* of urban commons governance towards sustainability. Moreover, given that community gardens are an *empowerment* tool to change the worldwide conventional agrifood system, this result

F. Jardim, *Right to Food in Community Gardens*, LITES - Legal Issues in Transdisciplinary Environmental Studies 6,
https://doi.org/10.1007/978-3-032-19612-5_6

suggests that one **step towards the social-ecological transformation of food and land in the city has been consolidated since the beginning of this century**. It is almost like an *unwritten*[1] international and interpersonal agreement, a form of law based on collective trust among and between commoners, focusing on use-value of resources and fighting city commodification. Then, promoting community gardens and protecting them from public and private threats means the long-term maintenance of the steps already achieved and the solidification of a stage for the new ones.

Another **interesting discovery** was that transforming vacant land into spaces for growing food (*food availability*) was mostly based on public land, which demonstrates the importance of the governmental role. In addition, the result shows that in *Berlin*, the motivation for gardening among the interviewed commoners was focused on socialization and environmental issues, while in *Rio de Janeiro*, it was primarily about food security, followed by ecological themes and economic reasons.

In addition, an **unexpected result** is the role of work opportunities as *food accessibility* and the economic dimension of *food sustainability* in *Berlin*. Also, there were gardens in a former airport and a former cemetery. In *Rio de Janeiro*, remarkable outcomes are the case of a garden's use as a gender empowerment tool, and the link to the education of adults.

Nevertheless, the creation, organization, and maintenance of community gardens face significant hurdles. In view of that, policy recommendations can be made for the governments not only from the above cities to address or avoid multiple challenges.

6.2 Policy Recommendations to Protect and Promote Community Gardens

This section is organized in three subtopics. The first is related to issues faced by community gardens and the respective proposals to overcome or mitigate the problems. The second subtopic is regarding the expected outcomes if the policies are successful. Closing the book, the last subtopic warns about potential contradictions and trade-offs in the policy.

6.2.1 Issues and Proposals

The below problems are barriers to social, economic, and environmental benefits that community gardens can provide. Given that, discussing policies to protect and promote them is relevant to governments in view of their responsibility for legal frameworks and sustainability of urban dynamics.

---

[1] "Knowledge + Action = Power. The future is unwritten." Fairey (2018).

a. Legal and institutional constraints, sociocultural biases, and scepticism This includes social, legal, and political issues, such as no recognition of benefits, prohibition of agricultural activities in urban areas, gap of land possession security, low visibility on decision-makers agenda, as well territorial loss for real estate market, political interest, or criminal agents.[2] For these issues, the governments could:

- *Offer legal support* to enact legislation that recognizes community gardens as valuable urban commons. This could involve incorporating community gardening provisions into local zoning ordinances, land use plans, and development regulations. More than that, it could establish mechanisms for community input and participation in decision-making processes related to urban development, such as the ones related to the definition of public funds priorities. By recognizing food as social function of property and the urban areas of the city, the legal codes could induce the transformation of vacant land[3] such as by predicting tax benefits or punishments and forcing the transference of vacant property to public land banks. The law could develop a role presenting community gardening as a profession with labor and social security rights. Moreover, the law has the potential not only to establish agroecology as a milestone for community gardens, which is essential to the social-ecological transformation of urban land and food, but also to certify organic production. Additionally, the legal system could foresee long-term land tenure by collective forms of land possessing.
- *Prepare institutional organization* for urban agriculture/community gardens in public administration, such as creating a program and establishing a specialized office or department for policy development. They would be tasked with various responsibilities, including identifying and securing resources such as land, water, and technical support. Furthermore, the office or department should take on the responsibility of funding and identifying potential funding sources. Moreover, fostering collaboration among different stakeholders is paramount. This involves facilitating communication and coordination between government departments, community organizations, non-profits, educational institutions, food banks, community kitchens, and other relevant entities. Establishing regular meetings and communication channels will facilitate effective collaboration and information sharing among these diverse groups, including public security. In addition, the public administration could implement systems for monitoring and evaluating the impact of community gardens on various indicators such as food security, public health, environmental sustainability, and community well-being. Collecting data on garden participation, crop yields, and other relevant metrics

[2] Steuri and Vignola (2022, pp. 59–79, 121) and Jardim et al. (2023).

[3] This concept can be categorized into three types: *unused land*, which is not currently in full use and may be disused or in a state of disrepair; *underutilized land*, which still has potential for use but falls below parameters defined by laws such as the Master Plan or construction codes; and *unbuilt land*, which is completely unoccupied with no structures and can be classified as closed or abandoned based on its current status. They can be linked to many problems, including socio-spatial segregation and maintenance of socioeconomic inequalities. Jardim (2024).

are important to assess the effectiveness of policies and programs. The governmental channels should have easy and open access not only to this data, but also to updated information related to community gardens' location and how to get access to grow or collect food, or to visit, for example.

- *Foster public awareness and education campaigns* to raise attention about the benefits of community gardens and stimulate their widespread participation. This could involve media outreach, community events, and educational programs for children and adults.
- *Advocate for social inclusion and diversity* by actively engaging marginalized and underrepresented groups, including low-income individuals, women, LGBTQIA+, immigrants, seniors, people with disabilities, and people serving sentences or resocialization measures. Governments should support outreach efforts to ensure equitable access to community gardening opportunities and foster a sense of belonging and ownership among all participants.

b. Constrained access to resources, inputs, and financial means This embraces natural, political, bureaucratic, and economic conflicts, such as competition with other land uses and constrained access to water, and tools, in addition to problems related to financial maintenance and high amounts of money as a mandatory security deposit for land access.[4] Regarding these problems, the governments could:

- *Guarantee the resource allocation.* In the case of land, it should happen by transforming vacant land into public open spaces for growing on a not-for-profit basis, including the offer of acquiring food in exchange for labour. Furthermore, financial security deposit should not be a barrier for land access. Concerning water and electricity, the stakeholders could adopt the necessary measures to provide sustainable and continuous access. Regarding inputs, the policy could stimulate the exchange of seeds and the excess of plant seedlings, as well as promote composting.
- *Promote environmental protection and sustainable practices* within community gardens, including the use of organic gardening methods, water conservation techniques, and biodiversity conservation measures. Governments should provide support for the adoption of agroecological principles and sustainable land management practices to minimize environmental impacts and enhance ecosystem resilience.
- *Develop financial support and funding mechanisms* could be established to support the establishment and maintenance of community gardens, particularly in economically disadvantaged areas. This could include providing grants, subsidies, or low-interest loans to community garden initiatives from municipal funds and from environmental compensation fines, as well as incentivizing private sector investment in community gardening projects through tax incentives or public–private partnerships. For instance, multilateral organizations could support

[4] Steuri and Vignola (2022, pp. 59–79, 121) and Jardim et al. (2023).

"to design policies, strategies and programs, delivering assistance, or negotiating trade, finance and investment,"[5] such as the United Nations World Food Program (WFP), Office of the United Nations High Commissioner for Refugees (UNHCR), United Nations Children's Fund (UNICEF), United Nations Food and Agriculture Organization (FAO), United Nations Development Assistance Framework (UNDAF), United Nations International Fund for Agricultural Development (IFAD), International Monetary Fund (IMF), World Bank, and regional development banks. Furthermore, to generate income, the gardens could establish a restaurant or café and selling points, which depends on administrative permissions, construction materials, and human resources. The funding could be destined for buying tools, seeds, constructing toilets, hiring professionals etc.

c. Special risks of cultivating in the city This counts social and natural limitations, for instance, pollution, vandalism, and driving gentrification.[6] Given them, the governments could:

- *Establish guidelines* encompassing safety measures, quality control standards, and best practices of gardening, such as monitoring and managing water quality for irrigation, determining protocols for regular testing to detect pollutants and ensure safe practices. Additionally, the policy could conduct soil testing to assess contamination levels and develop strategies for remediation. Safety could also propose measures related to pest control and waste management, including recycling and composting organic materials to minimize environmental contamination risks. The instructions should not only promote agroecological practices and exclude the use of harmful chemicals to minimize soil contamination risks, but also provide education on proper handling, storage, and processing techniques to prevent contamination and ensure safe food production. The guidelines should be regularly reviewed and updated based on feedback and experiences.
- *Stimulate research, innovation and information sharing* aiming low-cost and low-tech mitigating measures to enhance safety and quality control.

d. Organizational constraints, considering human resources difficulties For example, lack of networking, know-how on gardening or management, and data. Consequently, sometimes community gardens have temporary uses and structures that later will be removed.[7] To face that, the governments could:

- *Organize the capacity building and training programs* to equip community gardeners with the knowledge and skills necessary for successful garden management. This could involve providing technical assistance, workshops, and educational resources on organic gardening practices, soil management, water conservation, and community organizing. The information sharing among different community gardens and gardeners could represent a relevant step.

---

[5] FAO (2007).

[6] Steuri and Vignola (2022, pp. 59–79, 121) and Jardim et al. (2023).

[7] Steuri and Vignola (2022, pp. 59–79, 121) and Jardim et al. (2023).

- *Invest on monetary subsidies* to attract more gardeners, especially in low-income areas. The amount could variate according to the responsibilities, such as (i) gardener; (ii) gardner-leader, at least one representative person per garden to communicate with the integrator and other stakeholders, as well guiding the team; (iii) community integrator, seeking solutions to gardening, administrative, and social problems of multiple gardens; and (iv) technical assistant (Jardim et al. 2023).
- *Integrate the participation* among food banks, community kitchens and other urban food sharing activities that advocate for food security.

6.2.2 Expected Outcomes

If the proposed recommendations are adopted by decision-makers, several scenarios could unfold, embracing recognition and protection of community gardens as valuable urban commons, allowing them to operate within zoning ordinances and development regulations. This recognition could foster community involvement, granting participants a sense of ownership and empowering them in decision-making processes and promoting the right to the city. Legal codes promoting agroecology and certifying organic production could align community gardens with sustainability goals, ensuring stability through long-term land tenure. The implementation of measures could result in vacant land transformed into public gardening spaces, guaranteeing access to land while promoting environmental protection through sustainable practices. Funding mechanisms such as grants and subsidies could support community gardens, particularly in economically disadvantaged areas, potentially attracting more gardeners and enhancing their impact. The measures also may mitigate risks associated with urban agriculture and encourage research and innovation to develop cost-effective solutions for safety and quality control within community gardens. Efforts to address human resource difficulties could result in capacity building through training programs and technical assistance, equipping community gardeners with the necessary skills for successful garden management.

In addition, another expected outcome is the **food security**[8] for gardens' members, or for society.[9] Regarding the **benefits to human right to adequate food**, recent studies have focused on the potential of community gardens serving as transformative spaces within urban landscapes, reclaiming vacant land (underutilized, unused, or unbuilt area) for the benefit of individuals and communities, such as addressing the lack of *food availability* in food deserts in low-income and Black neighbourhoods.[10] Consequently, the benefits are also related to the Right to the City, and environmental justice.

Furthermore, research has explicit results demonstrating that community gardens can enhance physical and economic *access* to fresh products, essential to combat

[8] Magalhães (2021) and Rekow (2015).

[9] Ferris et al. (2001), Beilin and Hunter (2011), Rosol (2011), and Jardim et al. (2023).

[10] Gripper (2014), Krajewski (2021), Drake (2014), and Beam (2021).

food insecurity among various vulnerable social groups, including students and older adults.[11]

Studies also have indirectly highlighted the importance of community gardens in promoting food *acceptability* by providing opportunities for education and cultural exchange,[12] including learning and practicing nutrition, how to co-produce food, identifying places where gleaning or foraging might occur, seed swapping, and knowledge transfer. Also, the agroecological food production (regarding no use of artificial chemicals, fertilizers, pesticides, etc.) is part of *acceptability*.

Moreover, precise evidence or results can be interpreted as the contribution of community gardens to food *sustainability* in three dimensions. Firstly, they can have positive impacts on biodiversity by supporting local ecosystems.[13] They also offer a practical solution to various challenges within the agri-food system, including production, distribution, and waste management. By promoting local food production and consumption, they contribute to reducing reliance on long-distance transportation and mitigating environmental impacts associated with food distribution. Secondly, they can contribute to supplying local markets[14] and income generation opportunities by gardening, social, administrative work, and vegetable sales. This can represent the reduction of socioeconomic disparities. Thirdly, community gardens can enhance social equity and justice[15] by providing equal access to nutritious food for marginalized communities, and by fostering inclusive and participatory approaches to sustainable development.

6.2.3 *Potential Contradictions and Trade-Offs*

Overall, these measures can lead to the establishment and maintenance of sustainable community gardens, fostering social inclusion, environmental sustainability, and food security within urban areas. However, there are also potential contradictions and trade-offs that may arise concerning:

- *Contradict of land use priorities*, given that community gardens may compete with other urban development projects, such as affordable housing or commercial developments, raising questions about the allocation of limited urban space.
- *Conflict of funds priorities*, in view that allocating resources to community gardens may divert funds from other pressing social needs, creating a trade-off between promoting equity in access to food production and addressing other societal challenges.

---

[11] Tims et al. (2021) and Thorman and Dhillon (2021).

[12] Heerink et al. (2021) and Lloyd et al. (2022).

[13] Chan et al. (2016) and Felderhoff et al. (2023).

[14] Chow et al. (2020).

[15] Burt (2021) and Barron (2017).

- *Financial unsustainability* when observed heavily on public funds may strain government budgets, while relying on private investment may prioritize profit-making over community well-being.
- *Controversial social inclusion* caused, for instance, by lack of mobility inside or to access the garden. Another example is that language barriers could exclude community members or perpetuate power imbalances within garden governance structures.
- *Regulatory burden*, having in mind that establishing excessive regulations and bureaucratic processes may deter participation in community gardening initiatives, particularly for grassroots organizations with limited resources.
- *Questions about labour and participation* may surge considering the nature of participation in community gardens. Trade-offs may arise between incentivizing labour and volunteerism, potentially undermining the social cohesion and community-building aspects of gardening initiatives. Furthermore, labour and social security rights must be protected when gardening is related to a professional work.

In navigating these contradictions and trade-offs, governments must engage in inclusive and participatory decision-making processes, considering diverse perspectives and balancing competing interests to ensure the sustainable and equitable creation, organization, and maintenance of community gardens.

References

Barron J (2017) Community gardening: cultivating subjectivities, space, and justice. Loc Environ 22(9). https://www.tandfonline.com/doi/abs/10.1080/13549839.2016.1169518. Accessed 13 May 2024

Beam DR (2021) Vacant lot to community garden conversion and crime in Milwaukee: a difference-in-differences analysis. Inj Prev 27(5):403–408. https://pubmed.ncbi.nlm.nih.gov/32912967/. Accessed 13 May 2024

Beilin R, Hunter A (2011) Co-constructing the sustainable city: how indicators help us "grow" more than just food in community gardens. Loc Environ 16(6):523–538. https://www.tandfonline.com/doi/abs/10.1080/13549839.2011.555393. Accessed 16 May 2024

Burt K (2021) A systematic, mixed studies review of the outcomes of community garden participation related to food justice. Loc Environ 26(1). https://www.tandfonline.com/doi/abs/10.1080/13549839.2020.1861589. Accessed 13 May 2024

Chan J et al (2016) Social-ecological refuges: reconnecting in community gardens in Lincoln, Nebraska. J Ethnobiol 16(4):842–860. https://bioone.org/journals/Journal-of-Ethnobiology/volume-36/issue-4/0278-0771-36.4.842/Social-Ecological-Refuges--Reconnecting-In-Community-Gardens-In-Lincoln/10.2993/0278-0771-36.4.842.short. Accessed 13 May 2024

Chow E et al (2020) The socioeconomic and health impacts of community gardens. Pacific Northwest Medical Student Research Journal. https://pnwmsrj.org/meta-analysis/2020/10/the-socioeconomic-and-health-impacts-of-community-gardens/. Accessed 13 May 2024

Drake L (2014) Validating verdancy or vacancy? The relationship of community gardens and vacant lands in the US. Cities 40:133–142. https://www.sciencedirect.com/science/article/abs/pii/S0264275113001042. Accessed 13 May 2024

FAO (2007) What is the right to food? https://www.fao.org/3/i0094e/i0094e.pdf. Accessed 02 July 2023
FAO (2020) COVID-19 and the role of local food production in building more resilient local food systems. p 7. https://www.fao.org/3/cb1020en/CB1020EN.pdf. Accessed 04 Oct 2023
FAO (2023) Food and Agriculture Organization of the United Nations. The State of Food Security and Nutrition in the World. Urbanization, agrifood systems transformation and healthy diets across the rural–urban continuum, p 250. Rome. https://www.fao.org/3/cc3017en/cc3017en.pdf. Accessed 01 Sept 2023
Fairey S (2018) Knowledge + Action. https://obeygiant.com/prints/knowledge-action/. Accessed 20 Aug 2024
Felderhoff J et al (2023) Vegetation complexity and nesting resource availability predict bee diversity and functional traits in community gardens. Ecolog Appl 33(2). https://esajournals.onlinelibrary.wiley.com/doi/10.1002/eap.2759. Accessed 13 May 2024
Ferris J et al (2001) People, land and sustainability: community gardens and the social dimension of sustainable development. Soc Pol 35(5):559–568. https://onlinelibrary.wiley.com/doi/10.1111/1467-9515.t01-1-00253. Accessed 16 May 2024
Foster SR, Iaione C. Urban commons. https://www.oxfordbibliographies.com/display/document/obo-9780190922481/obo-9780190922481-0015.xml. Accessed 28 Aug 2024
Gripper A (2014) Practices of care and relationship-building: a qualitative analysis of urban agriculture's impacts on Black People's agency and wellbeing in Philadelphia. Int J Environ Res Public Health 20(6). https://www.mdpi.com/1660-4601/20/6/4831. Accessed 13 May 2024
Heerink S et al (2021) Expanding field education: hope trust community garden. Aotearoa New Zealand Soc Work 33(1):112–115. https://anzswjournal.nz/anzsw/article/view/829. Accessed 13 May 2024
Jardim F (2024) The relation of community gardens and human right to food: a case study in Berlin and Rio de Janeiro, p 244. Doctoral thesis (Doctorate in Law). Law Faculty, State University of Rio de Janeiro, Rio de Janeiro; Doctorate in Sociology—Faculty of Social and Behavioural Sciences, Friedrich-Schiller University Jena, Jena
Jardim F, Santos A, Eversberg D, Moura E (2023) How is a community urban garden program related to the law? Analysis of Hortas Cariocas (Rio de Janeiro, Brazil), St. Thomas J L Pub Pol 16(1). https://ir.stthomas.edu/ustjlpp/vol16/iss1/9/. Accessed 13 Sep 2024
Krajewski M (2021) Reflections on the North Central community gardens branch out project. J Agri Food Syst Commun Dev 10(4):51–54. https://www.foodsystemsjournal.org/index.php/fsj/article/view/1015. Accessed 13 May 2024
Lloyd D et al (2022) Learning science locally: community gardens and our future. Front Educ 7. https://www.frontiersin.org/articles/10.3389/feduc.2022.850016/full#:~:text=The%20wholistic%20nature%20of%20gardening,%E2%80%94knowing%2C%20feeling%2C%20connecting. Accessed 13 May 2024
Magalhães MJ (2021) Hortas comunitárias in the favelas of Rio de Janeiro: how new ideas are adopted and spread across communities. In: Trapani F et al (ed) Advanced studies in efficient environmental design and city planning. Springer International Publishing, Cham. https://link.springer.com/chapter/10.1007/978-3-030-65181-7_21. Accessed 20 May 2024
Rekow L (2015) Fighting insecurity: experiments in urban agriculture in the favelas of Rio de Janeiro. Field Act Sci Rep 8. https://journals.openedition.org/factsreports/pdf/4009. Accessed 16 May 2024
Rosol M (2011) Community gardens in Berlin: A new form of citizen participation. In: Endlicher W (ed) Perspectives in urban ecology: Studies of ecosystems and interactions between humans and nature in the metropolis of Berlin. Springer, Berlin, pp 263–270
Steuri B, Vignola G (2022) Towards productive and socio-natural urban landscapes: tapping urban agriculture's potential as a tool for sustainable development. Universitätsbibliothek der HafenCity Universität Hamburg (HCU), Hamburg, pp 52–79, 121. https://repos.hcu-hamburg.de/bitstream/hcu/650/2/2022-06-01_steuri-bettina_vignola-gionatan_masterarbeit.pdf. Accessed 04 Oct 2024

Thorman A, Dhillon H (2021) No food for thought: documenting the prevalence of food insecurity among medical students at One Western University. J Hunger Environ Nut 16(5):643–649. https://www.tandfonline.com/doi/abs/10.1080/19320248.2021.1873885. Accessed 13 May 2024

Tims K et al (2021) Gardening for change: community giving gardens and senior food insecurity. J Agri Food Syst Commun Dev 10(4):85–101. https://www.foodsystemsjournal.org/index.php/fsj/article/view/1018#:~:text=Community%20giving%20gardens%2C%20like%20the,while%20building%20local%20food%20economies. Accessed 13 May 2024

Westley FR et al (2013) A theory of transformative agency in linked social-ecological systems. Ecol Soc 18(3):27. https://doi.org/10.5751/ES-05072-180327. Accessed 04 Oct 2024

World Charter for the Right to the City (2001) Right to the city. Porto Alegre. https://www.right2city.org/document/world-charter-for-the-right-to-the-city/. Accessed 19 Aug 2024

GPSR Compliance

The European Union's (EU) General Product Safety Regulation (GPSR) is a set of rules that requires consumer products to be safe and our obligations to ensure this.

If you have any concerns about our products, you can contact us on ProductSafety@springernature.com

In case Publisher is established outside the EU, the EU authorized representative is:

Springer Nature Customer Service Center GmbH
Europaplatz 3
69115 Heidelberg, Germany

Batch number: 10837251

Printed by Printforce, the Netherlands